Private Lives, Public Histories

Private Lives, Public Histories

An Ethnohistory of the Intimate Past

Edited by
Rachel Corr
and Jacqueline H. Fewkes

LEXINGTON BOOKS
Lanham • Boulder • New York • London

Published by Lexington Books
An imprint of The Rowman & Littlefield Publishing Group, Inc.
4501 Forbes Boulevard, Suite 200, Lanham, Maryland 20706
www.rowman.com

6 Tinworth Street, London SE11 5AL, United Kingdom

British Library Cataloguing in Publication Information Available

Library of Congress Cataloging-in-Publication Data

Names: Fewkes, Jacqueline, 1973- editor. | Corr, Rachel, editor.
Title: Private lives, public histories : an ethnohistory of the intimate
    past / edited by Jacqueline Fewkes and Rachel Corr.
Description: Lanham : Lexington Books, [2020] | Includes bibliographical
    references and index. | Summary: "Private Lives, Public Histories
    explores conceptions of public and private spaces, activities,
    discourse, and social interactions. Contributors to this edited
    collection draw on ethnohistorical and material sources to depict
    history as a lived experience"— Provided by publisher.
Identifiers: LCCN 2020009492 (print) | LCCN 2020009493 (ebook) | ISBN
    9781793604286 (cloth) | ISBN 9781793604293 (epub)
    ISBN 9781793604309 (pbk)
Subjects: LCSH: Ethnohistory—Methodology. | Social history—Methodology. |
    Public sphere—Research—Methodology. | Colonies—Research—Methodology.
    | Anthropology and history.
Classification: LCC GN345.2 .P75 2020 (print) | LCC GN345.2 (ebook) | DDC
    305—dc23
LC record available at https://lccn.loc.gov/2020009492

LC ebook record available at https://lccn.loc.gov/2020009493

Contents

Acknowledgments

As the editors we would first like to thank all of the contributors to this volume whose wonderful work, cooperation, and dedication made the book possible. Kasey Beduhn from Lexington Books deserves special thanks for first inspiring us to transform our conference discussion into a book format, and then supporting us along the publishing journey for successful completion of this work.

For their support over the years, Rachel Corr would like to thank Norman E. Whitten Jr., the late Dorothea (Sibby) Scott Whitten, and Karen Vieira Powers, with whom she has had intellectual exchanges that have enriched her understanding of the interconnections of culture and history. She also thanks Juan Gonzalez and her family for their encouragement in pursuing this project.

Jacqueline H. Fewkes is thankful for the support of all her peers/colleagues from Johns Hopkins University, the University of Pennsylvania, and Florida Atlantic University (particularly Jeff Buller, Rachel Corr, Praveena Gullapalli, William O'Brien, Uzma Rizvi, Christopher Strain, Miguel Ángel Vázquez, and Laura Vernon for help on specific points, and mentors Brian Spooner, the late Sidney Mintz, and the late Michel-Rolph Trouillot. To all of her family members in the USA and India she would like to say "thank you" for the continuing years of support in her work, especially to Nasir, Amina, and Zayd.

Preface

This volume is the result of a panel organized by the editors (in alphabetical order, Rachel Corr and Jacqueline H. Fewkes) for the one hundred seventeenth American Anthropological Association (AAA) meetings held in San Jose, California, in 2018. The panel's inspiration was our shared interest in ethnohistory and ongoing conversations about the complexity of applying anthropological research methods (particularly for those trained in ethnography) to historical contexts given that information about private lives is often hidden from public, historical records.

When we sent out the initial general call for papers, we invited potential participants to share insights into how they applied analytical methods from anthropology when reading ethnohistorical sources and archaeological evidence to understand people's conceptions of public and private spaces, activities, discourse, and social interactions. Following a brief summary of such ideas, we shared a list of questions to consider to our potential contributors. Can we tease out private acts of resistance from ethnohistorical sources, or are we confined to analyzing the public transcripts? How have public spaces been historically constructed and contested? What happens when the private is inserted into the public discourse/space/activity? What is the role of private space in allowing people to adapt to or resist dominant cultural narratives? The response to this call was enthusiastic, and we were gratified to find a group of anthropologists interested in discussing these issues whose work spanned geographic areas and crossed subdisciplinary divides. Our developing panel promised to provide stimulating conversation with diverse perspectives.

The ensuing AAA meetings took place in an almost surreal atmosphere, as in November 2018 smoke from the Camp Fire fires in Butte County, California, covered much of the greater San Francisco Bay area. Participants in the conference walked through the hazy streets of San Jose with N95 respirator masks or scarves covering their mouths to protect from inhaling what was declared "very unhealthy" by the U.S. Environmental Protection Agency. Despite this almost postapocalyptic setting, our panel, "Rethinking Public/ Private Dichotomies: Spaces of Resistance, Resilience, and Adaptation in Ethnohistorical Contexts," met successfully and began a fascinating conversation. Participants brought together their experience with varied research methods from the subfields of archaeology and cultural anthropology, enabling us to glean fascinating information on private lives from the historical record, and in relation to how people experience historical sites. Many of the contributors to this volume were the original participants in that panel, while still others were members of the audience that joined our conversation. This organic growth of the conversation led to the resulting volume, with its broad geographic diversity as pictured in figure 0.1.

From this start we have brought together a collection of seven chapters that encourage readers to explore the concept of public/private dichotomies critically, challenging a strict concept of that divide through careful examination of topics such as the public significance of private sentiments, the links between individual bodies and community histories, hidden relationships or intimate connections, and gendered interactions. In doing so this book highlights entanglements between private lives and public settings that have allowed people to continue to exist within, adapt to, and/or resist dominant cultural scripts about the past. The works in this book are meant to highlight the significance of these connections for understanding the past holistically (as a lived experience) and reveal the roles of the most intimate aspects of human experience—in terms of interior lives and/or interpersonal relationships—in constructing imagined public identities and notions of the public sphere.

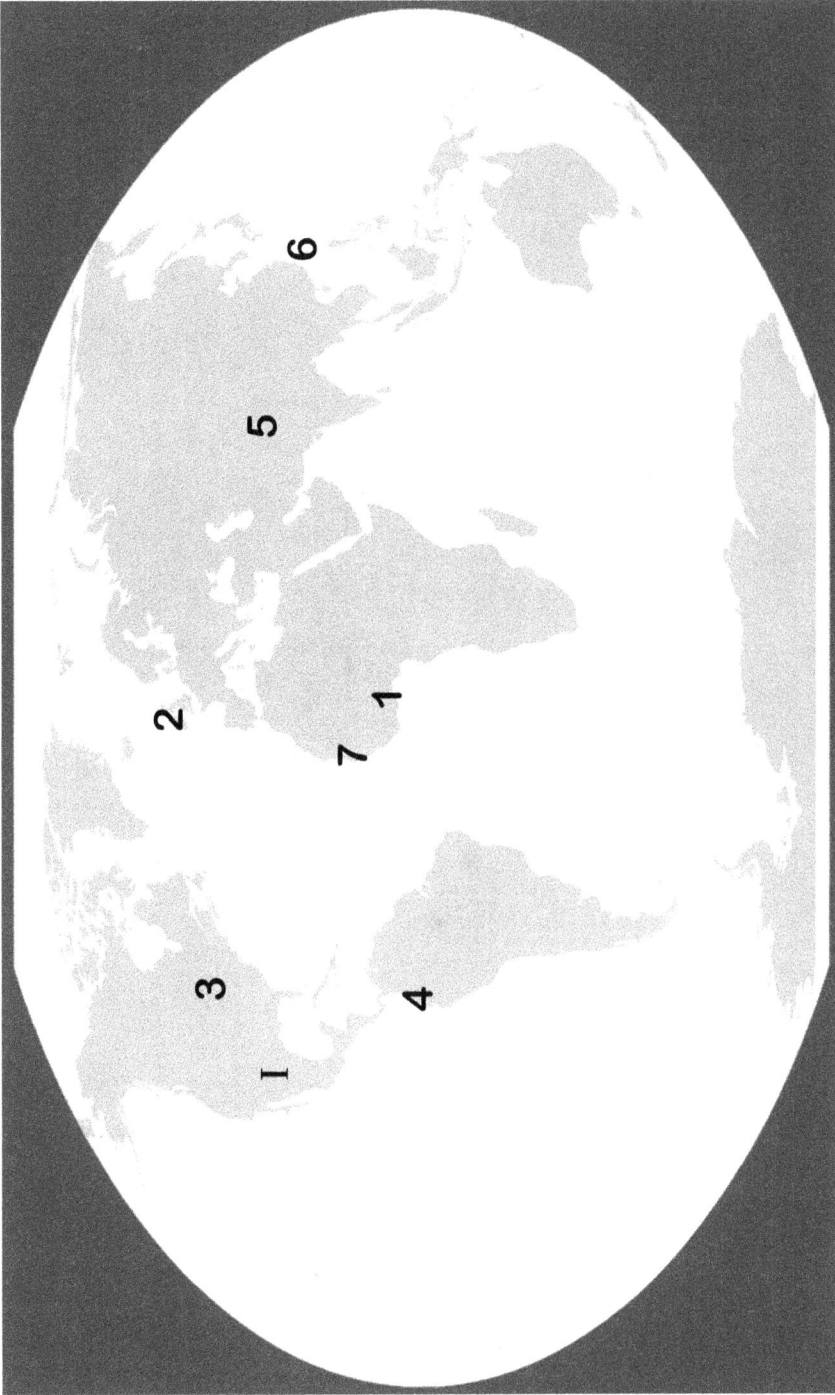

Figure 0.1. Map of main areas discussed in book. Each letter/number corresponds to a chapter in the volume with "I" standing for the Introduction. This map was developed using a public domain version of a blank Winkel-Tripel projection world map as the base layer.

Jacqueline H. Fewkes, 2020.

Introduction

Intimate Interdependencies

Colonization, Capitalism, and Impositions of Public and Private

Minette C. Church

In classic economic models of history and globalism, scholars often take dichotomous concepts of private and public for granted as an analytical tool. An important question raised by the works in this book, either implicitly or explicitly, is whether such a dichotomy even existed outside of contexts of colonization and capitalism, and their associated surveillance cultures. If such categories did exist, how did existing indigenous or subaltern categories get upended by overweening colonizing construal of private behaviors and the public square? And perhaps more intriguing, how did such groups challenge the new status quo in different times and places?

As Niklas Hultin notes in this volume, Habermas's description of the public sphere was laden with European assumptions (Habermas 2012 [1964]). Scholars also commonly assume that the urban (urbane) core is the most cosmopolitan (public) place, and rural areas, indigenous villages, or other "peripheries" are least so; we conflate the metropole with the cosmopolitan. In her chapter, Melissa Brown notes that this is a markedly un-anthropological definition of cosmopolitanism. Cosmopolitanism in its non-elitist sense is sited locally, within scales of household and village, and is intertwined with gender and kinship. Brown takes a diachronic view of the ebb and flow of cosmopolitanism in different historical moments, and the effects of violence, with a nice sorting of what variables, indigenous and colonial, gendered, external and internal, seem to be at play or in the ascendant during which periods. What is it about matrilineality, work, and space that encourage cosmopolitanism, blurring of private and public, in some historical moments and not in others? The authors in this book examine particular historical moments to which we as ethnohistorians, historical anthropologists, and archaeologists have unique access. Doing so, we collectively find that

1

the more cosmopolitan the space, the more fraught and fuzzier the distinction of public and private spaces, social action, and social power becomes. Often, colonized places are where, as Rachel Corr and Anna Agbe-Davies show, the personal becomes political. Brown notes further that the "veiled" becomes "visible" and "visibility matters, because women's public presence and contributions have to be visible—and accurately socially credited—in order for women to win power and social status, whether within households or in the political arena." All of the authors in this volume, to one degree or another, challenge or otherwise complicate and destabilize the public/private dichotomy which is so often also gendered, class-driven, colonial, capitalist, and, I would argue, often carries a research bias that is WEIRD—Western, Educated, Industrialized, Rich, Democratic (Bennis and Medin 2010).

Working as an archaeologist in classically colonial settings in and around British Honduras, as well as the international borderlands of southern Colorado (where the U.S. border with Mexico was until 1848), it is ever clearer to me that colonial projects often begin with imposition of a private/public dichotomy where there had been very different existing categories of social action. President Polk's policy of "Manifest Destiny" carried explicitly governmentalized, racialized, militarized, and fundamentally protestant religious values to the western Plains and Southwest in acts of U.S. imperialism modeled in many ways, I would argue, on models of British colonial expansion. In British Honduras the colonizers were British. In such contexts, colonial "information policy" (Hultin, this volume), settlement policy (Horning, this volume), commercial practices (Fewkes, this volume), and/or gender norms (Brown, this volume) were all tools to (re)categorize the indigenous, female, or subaltern as "private" while imposing white, male, privileged, governmentalized values and practices as "public." Small wonder that indigenous and other disenfranchised groups resisted and persisted through leveraging personal or private behaviors, over which they had some power, into public political action, and in Jean Rahier's case study, fostering a transnational identity (see Agbe-Davies, Corr, Rahier, this volume). Much of Hultin's chapter in this volume dissects the tug of war for control of information between various sectors of rural and urban elite Gambians, and the British colonial imposition of a "facsimile of a public sphere." It seems from his description that either the British information officers seek to divert the Gambian public's attention from their own local version of "public" affairs (which were "of no great interest to Europeans"), or alternatively to create a sector of "public affairs" as a discursive category where none had existed before. I see this imposition of colonial and capitalist power repeating itself in other cases as well.

SUGAR WITH YOUR TEA?
COLONIALISM AND CAPITALISM

Recent archaeology in British Yucatan[1] and Yucatan more broadly engages with the production of sugar (e.g., Gust 2016) in a colonial resource frontier, illuminating the living conditions engendered by exploitive labor practices on *haciendas* and sugar mills (Alexander 2004; Álvarez 2014, 2017; Meyers 2012). In this book, Brown's work at a certain point fronts gender and the production of tea in colonial Taiwan, but in an endnote notes that the production of sugar and tea are interconnected: "[i]n 1868, sugar was about 60 percent of Taiwan's exports and tea was only 9 percent, by 1876 sugar and tea were both about 46 percent, and by 1881 tea was 60 percent of exports" (Brown endnote 9). In British Honduras, British colonial tastes and market demands in some ways parallel the Chinese demands for colonial production in Taiwan. In his book on the Caribbean, *Sweetness and Power* (1986), Sidney Mintz links sugar (and tea) to colonialism, industrialism, modernity, and capitalism, asking, "How do we get from one child's sweet tooth to the history of slavery, of war, and of corporate lobbying in the Congress? And how do we retrace our steps backward, this time to the significance of that child's sweet tooth?"[2]

Sugar accompanied the rise of the global market in coffee, chocolate, and above all tea because it was most affordable and, Mintz hypothesizes, even weak tea tastes good with sugar, whereas weak coffee or chocolate is not so good, however much sugar one adds (1986, 112). "Sugar as sweetener came to the fore in connection with three other exotic imports—tea, coffee, and chocolate—of which one, tea, became and has since remained the most important nonalcoholic beverage in the United Kingdom" (1986, 108). Tea played an important British Colonial role in the entanglement of the private, the public, the political, and the personal and could be a tool of rebellion as well as subjugation and class consciousness. A North American example plays out in Laurel Thatcher Ulrich's work, *A Midwife's Tale: The Life of Martha Ballard, Based on Her Diary, 1785–1812* (1990), about the life of a late eighteenth-century New England midwife. It is a commonplace interpretation in U.S. history textbooks that tea was a particularly politicized commodity for both the loyalist Tories and the rebel Whigs. Dumping tea in Boston Harbor (public) or drinking tea (private) were both political (public?) acts in defiance of political forces. During pre–Revolutionary War boycotts, according to Ulrich, including one on tea, Stephen Barton was on a committee to see that no one purchased it in his Massachusetts town. Yet he "was wont to put on his hat and go without while his sympathetic wife and her sister, Martha Moore Ballard, made a cup of tea in the cellar for some sick mother in the neighborhood whose sufferings patriotism and loyalty failed to heal" (Ulrich 1990,11). Thus the political and public valence of tea consumption was in this case trumped by kinship and transgressive "private," gendered behaviors by women in control of the food/medicine continuum. Furthermore, in Brown's chapter, it is the gendering of tea production rather than consumption that is at issue. It is a commodity processed literally in the public square by Taiwanese women in a display of public work and sociality directly counter to colonial Chinese, Confucian gender ideology.

Charles Cheek's archaeological work on Garinagu villages in nineteenth-century south coastal Belize (British Honduras) also focuses on the social ritual and public signaling function of drinking tea. He found evidence that villagers were purchasing matched ceramic tea sets whereas all other ceramics reflected non-British foodways and eclectic, decorated, mismatched table wares. Pairing this information with documents, he noted how the British perceived these villagers differently than their progenitors on Jamaica and Haiti who engaged in violent revolutionary revolt, which activities caused the Caribbean British settlers no little anxiety. Some Garinagu villages, Creek argues, adopted the colonial British social ritual drinking of tea with its particular compliment of ceramic accoutrements, and thus behaved in a manner, in the eyes of the British, both familiar and civilized. By dint of this perhaps strategic change in behavior (which can be constituted as public or private depending on context), the Garifuna speakers of these villages advertised themselves as cultivated and eminently hirable for wage labor in British logging banks (Cheek 1997). Answering Mintz's question above, about the significance to global economies of personal tastes, we often see food and taste (sweetness and tea) as inherently personal and domestic, yet in these case studies, tea and sugar consumption are part of discursive and public practices in dialogue between colonized and colonizing peoples, constituting resistance in some cases and hegemonic dominance in others.

WHEN DOMESTIC IS PUBLIC:
PRIVATE CONSUMPTION AS PUBLIC MESSAGING

While women's consumption in particular is often glossed as domestic and private (and white and middle class), Agbe-Davies examines messaging aimed at black women of all walks of life, in the early twentieth-century pages of the newspaper *The Defender,* as relevant to her archaeological exploration of the Phyllis Wheatley Home for Girls on the southside of Chicago. In *The Defender*, material culture at scales ranging from body and dress to "world" were depicted in advertisements and advice columns as public messaging (Agbe-Davies, this volume). Domestic objects (private?) around hostessing (public?) and foodways could be deliberately selected and purchased in an explicit and reflexive practice of "meaning-making" (see also Mullins 2006; Wilkie 2012). We often hear these contemporary arguments for "racial uplift" or rights work expressed in men's voices (for example Du Bois 1903; Garvey 2012; Randolph 1919; Washington 1901). In Agbe-Davies's chapter we hear that women like Nannie Burroughs advocated particularly class-conscious materialities of consumption as visible, strategic, and engaged in messaging beyond the domestic and into the public sphere. Such advice is set in explicit contrast to the invisible, intimate, and exploitative labor of so many black women in white households. Agbe-Davies cites organizations "who sought to train young women 'for service, not servants.'" In a similar vein, Corr (this volume) cites bell hooks, describing "African American home-making activities as political acts in which women created an intimate, private world that countered the dehumanizing racism of the dominant white society." This work is both political, and therefore public by definition, and simultaneously intimate. In asserting that "the 'private' realm of morality and cultivation was an essential component of a woman's public persona," Agbe-Davies intentionally fronts the work of women like Burroughs in this kind of "rights work" rather than other more familiar, but gender-exclusive turn-of-the-twentieth-century public discourses. Traditionally invisible domestic practice is reframed visibly as leverage for political power.

In Corr's study women also bring that which we often consider to be private (foodways) into public testimony, where indigenous men and women described to Spanish authorities the delivery of support in the form of food to male relatives doing forced labor in Andean textile mills. Foodways are often not only considered domestic and therefore private (by post-enlightenment western standards) but also conservative in terms of change, precisely because usually they are considered not part of public identity signaling. Yet at one British plantation site in Ulster, Audrey Horning (this volume) notes ceramic diversity that speaks to changing foodways, including a mix of "(Irish) locally made, hand-built cookpots and imported English wheel-thrown wares," where O'Cahan-Phillips's illegally mixed group of Irish and English tenants were housed. Similarly, at the plantation site of Movanagher, in Mrs. Browne's unlicensed alehouse, "prior to the arrival of the attackers, the Brownes and John Williams were sitting together *with* their Irish neighbors and enjoying drink and food." These archival and archaeologically data-driven histories define "public intimacies" that were forbidden by Protestant English authorities.

In these cases, foodways are neither conservative in the sense of "tradition," nor private. As an archaeologist, I must note that foodways are a universal human behavior that we have the richest evidence for when we triangulate documentary or oral narratives with archaeological data, which is no doubt why archaeologists so often focus on ceramics (Horning, this volume). Ceramic vessels tell us about distinct and sometimes longstanding cooking techniques, but also hybridity, ethnogenesis, social class, and hospitality; there is an extensive literature in historical archaeology circles about Colonowares, which are ceramic wares made by subaltern enslaved and indigenous groups found primarily in the U.S. south and Caribbean, that use familiar techniques and clays to make new forms that are inherently colonial and creolized (Crane 1993; Ferguson 1992; Singleton and Bograd 2000). Such vessels used in the purportedly "private" sphere or household are quintessentially socialized material forms.

ARCHITECTURE: ACCESS AND SURVEILLANCE

Just as ceramics and foodways fail to fall neatly into public and private realms, interior and exterior architectural spaces also do not align plainly with western private and public norms, particularly in the tropics and global south. As Bonnie Clark notes for southern Colorado and New Mexico, the Laws of the Indies under Phillip II of Spain established ordinances in 1573, as explicit colonial means to "pacify the New World, both its landscape and its inhabitants" (Clark 2011, 91). "The public square" is an explicit directive in these laws, in the form of the Latin American "plaza." Cynthia Robin and Nan Rothschild (2002) collected works in a thematic issue of the *Journal of Social Archaeology* titled "Archaeological Ethnographies: Social Dynamics of Outdoor Space," emphasizing "social and historical analyses of space as actually lived" (2002, 159), thereby following Wendy Ashmore's call to "socialize spatial archaeology" in a distinguished lecture to the American Anthropological Association (2002). While not explicitly engaging concepts of private and public, these works do call attention to the overweening attention archaeologists often pay to architectural remains and enclosures rather than the open, socialized spaces between them. Throughout Latin America, including the U.S.-Mexico borderlands, the distinction between private and public architecturally demarcated spaces in settlements organized around plazas are fluid at best, and generally unclear. Most of the rooms around plazas were primarily for sleeping or storage and were more multi-purpose in winter months. However, sleeping and cooling often took place outside in communal spaces on warm nights. In these regions, Spanish colonizers were a diverse group ranging in origins from North Africa to the Pyrenees, and the colonized were an assortment of all these groups mixed with diverse Native American nations ranging from New Mexico to South America. Indeed, among North

American native groups who built multi-family dwellings with multiple hearths, privacy was maintained more as a matter of etiquette, refraining from observing another family's hearth area, than by any sort of physical barrier to sight or sound (Roberts and Gregor 2017). The same was no doubt the case in multi-ethnic plazas.

The schematic plaza spaces called for by officials in town planning changed through time and across the geography of New Spain, ranging from loosely enclosed and urban to dispersed and fortified, depending on the geopolitical context. As was true elsewhere in Latin America, in southern Colorado the plaza space itself was publicly held within a community, and *hornos* or beehive ovens were common features where households did their cooking of meats and baked goods. Archival documents and informants mention aromas bringing children from all over the community to these public spaces to ask for a bit of whatever is in the oven (e.g., Clark 2011, 96). Plaza spaces also feature in primary accounts as sites of *fandangos* (parties with music), feasting, and diplomacy with potentially hostile visitors (LeCompte 1978; Sunseri 2018). The foodstuffs themselves can be communal: Elfido Lopez, who lived along the Purgatoire River in southern Colorado, describes in memoirs the early days of settlement of his family's plaza:

> The poor men that went with wagons would get 2 or 3 sacks of dried [buffalo] meat and bring bone from the hind leg. They would take the bone home to season the food. This bone was called *El Gueso Gisandero* and the woman of the family would cook a pot of beans with the bone in it, and then lend it to another woman who did not have a bone for her beans. The next day it would go to another woman and so on. Maybe it would be 8 or 10 days before it would get back to the owner. Then it would make the rounds again. My mother said she knew of one bone that went around the neighborhood for two years. So I guess you could call that sure enough hard times but mother said she never did know of anyone to starve to death. (Louden 1998, 25)

El Gueso Gisandero confounds concepts of public and private property, to say the least.

Further south, in Yucatan as colonized first by Spain, then Mexico and British Honduras, more hierarchical planned settlements on *haciendas* or plantations were constructed in such a way that both the living and the workspaces of colonized and indigenous people could be surveilled by colonizers (Alexander 2004; Álvarez 2014, 2017; Meyers 2012). Maya and mestizo peoples fled these haciendas and their attendant debt peonage and settled farflung areas of southern Yucatan and the Peten region, in widely dispersed villages connected by elaborate systems of complicated and narrow footpaths, which rendered entire villages of several hundred people essentially private.

They could not be found by outsiders, such as census takers, or if they were found, there was time to abandon them and sojourn deeper into the forest (Gann 1997 [1925]; Thompson 1963).

In fact, from pre-colonial times through the nineteenth century, leaving settlements, temporarily or permanently, to live in smaller hamlets invisible to colonial officials was a form of mobility and resistance afforded by systems of swidden agriculture with field houses away from village cores. From the Terminal Classic onward, Maya farmers responded to onerous state impositions such as taxes, combined with weak state control in border regions, using their traditional ecological knowledge to make their households harder to find. They could disperse into forested areas while increasing their balance of hunting and forest farming against settled slash-and-burn or terraced farming techniques. At a time when British colonial capitalism in the form of logging companies used wage labor as a way to keep Creole and Maya workers dependent and indebted, charging food supplies against wages, the ability of these villagers to feed themselves became a form of overt political action; Lt Governor Austin responded with legislation forbidding indigenous people from owning land and forcing them to pay rent (Boland 1977), a policy not always easy to enforce when villagers could move back and forth at will across vast forested territories weakly claimed by Guatemala and Mexico.

HERITAGE SITES AND STRONG EMOTIONS: PERSONAL RESPONSES AND GLOBAL IDENTITIES

The architecture of such mobile village sites is difficult to find archaeologically, and certainly does not feature as a draw for heritage tourism and public history the way ancient Maya cities and grand, colonial haciendas do. The emotional impact of grand architectural spaces and engineered landscapes on people, whether surveilled labor or modern visitors, is both publicly experienced and elicited by design (Leone 1984). The rise of both heritage and ecotourism has ensured that documentary and archaeological research on such visible and imposing architectural sites, with an eye to architectural stabilization and reconstruction, is generally well funded. But what of the emotional impact of such glorified tourist destinations on descendants of workers who toiled and often died there, in deplorable conditions, just a generation or two ago? Intimate familial histories including the trauma of being confined to such sites can leave descendants ambivalent at best about preserving the sites of their labor (e.g., Saitta 2007; Shackel 2006). This initial ambivalence can break two ways, as a desire to have the story made public, or as a wish to erase such monuments to personal and painful family histories.

In the case of visitors to Elmina and the Cape Coast Castles whose responses are analyzed by Rahier (this volume), these sites memorialize individual traumas experienced in exposed and public architectural spaces by people of various African nationalities who were destined to be sold into bondage. Rahier observes a full range of visitor reactions as related in interviews with tour guides and observed in entries in visitors' books. We generally think of strong emotion, particularly intense sadness, as something experienced privately, but in the visitors' books Rahier notes that emotional responses forge a public bond between people of various backgrounds, with personal or private emotions eliciting globalized pan-African identities for political purposes including fighting systemic, global white supremacy. Affect, and the debate about where emotions "reside" in terms of individuals and what emotions do in terms of "alignment" to "larger collectives," completely confound any superficial dichotomizing of private and public behavior in this context. The specific emotional states that tours of these architectural spaces elicit vary from wanting revenge or wanting to ban white people from visiting these architectural spaces altogether, to a sense of pride in the public memorialization of survival and strength of ancestors. However, the evocation of a "horizontal" and "transnational" racial identity across all these individual responses, as well as across individual nationalities and heritage histories, publicly expressed for all to read in the visitors' books, is striking.

Architectural heritage tourism in Yucatan has taken a very different course, far less aligned with any sense of personal or familial pilgrimage, yet the spaces are similarly fraught in memory. At Hacienda Tabí, archaeologist Allen Meyers (2012) noted that

> hacienda tourism is becoming an increasingly important part of Yucatán's service economy. Many grand plantation houses, restored to varying degrees, now serve as luxury hotels, fine restaurants, and banquet halls. To a much lesser extent, they operate as heritage museums. To my knowledge, only two estates, Yaxcopoil and Sotuta de Peón, are open regularly to the public as plantation museums with guided tours. (2012, 169)

An additional note of interest, if not surprise: no sugar mills in the Yucatan appear to have been restored or converted into either a heritage museum or other manner of tourist destination, to date. According to Meyers, architectural historians at University of Yucatán have been asking, "How has the rural experience of forced labor been remembered at plantation museums? And who does and does not benefit from the selling of hacienda heritage?" (Meyers 2012, 169). The grand and romantic architecture of the haciendas themselves have been more or less lovingly or accurately restored, yet aside from the attention of the occasional archaeologist (Alexander 2004; Alvarez 2014, 2017; Meyers

2012), the workers' quarters in the villages so carefully platted by nineteenth-century hacienda owners which lie "outside the hacienda walls" are left over-grown by forest. Meyers notes the impact of these decisions about architectural restoration on individuals' emotions and their political identities: "what is feel-good history to some invariably becomes feel-bad history to others. No matter the stated economic benefits to local Maya speakers who are employed at plantation museums . . . the deliberate forgetting of the more painful side of the Porfirian past alienates the hacienda's historical related population, who in both cases still live in the shadow of the plantation smokestacks" (Meyers 2012, 171). The history of debt peonage, hard labor, and disease is neither a popular museum investment nor a prospective tourist draw.

Corr, in her work on forced indigenous labor in colonial textile mills, learned that Pelileo "was more diverse in the seventeenth century than it is today." I am struck by how often that is the case in our various research areas. The history of enslaved and indebted labor is inherently diverse, or even cosmopolitan in Brown's non-elite, anthropological sense of "citizens of the world" versus kin group and community. This cosmopolitanism, past and present, is also at the heart of Rahier's strong rebuttal of Bruner's argument that "blackness means profoundly different things for African Americans and Ghanaians" (Bruner 1996, cited in Rahier, this volume). At heritage tourism sites, diversity of stakeholder and descendant populations in the present reflects like diversity in the past. We often fall into the trap of thinking that an "indigenous" village was inherently less cosmopolitan than the colonizing settler source, but despite that unexamined perception—that the past is simpler, that village life is simpler than urban life, socially, politically, and economically—it is so very often not the case.

If we think about Rahier's Elmina and Cape Coast Castles, if we think about African diaspora beginning as people who were ripped from their village lives and coerced through those public architectural spaces, people harking from so many regions across the second largest continent on the planet, we are confronted with (among other things) how many mutually unintelligible languages must have been spoken in these spaces of public confinement. On the streets of eighteenth-century Charleston, South Carolina, the ultimate destination for just a fraction of these people, over fifty European, African, and American Indian languages were spoken within and between households (Ferguson 1992; Rudes 2004). One can imagine how that must have impacted both public discourse or intimate conversations during the sixteenth and seventeenth centuries. These historical moments in the U.S. south were followed by the white slaveowner project of de-emphasizing African American diversity and expertise during the more immediately antebellum period of the nineteenth century; paternalism and concomitant infantilization of enslaved or otherwise coerced labor is common to nineteenth-century hacienda and planta-tion sites. Systematically denying or dismissing African American cosmopoli-tanism was a necessary precondition to defending the system of slavery during the Civil War. Likewise, naturalizing the dependencies of indigenous labor on the hacienda system makes the diversity and ugly history of that labor easier to elide in public discourses at heritage museums and luxury hotels today.

GENDERED DIMENSIONS
OF PUBLIC COMMERCE

Jacqueline Fewkes's chapter in this volume addresses a different elision of historically disenfranchised, cosmopolitan peoples, this time in the public and purportedly male economic domain of trade. Fewkes's work (this volume) resonates particularly well with interpretive results from history and archae-ology along the Santa Fé Trail, another trade route. Fewkes notes that "mar-riages represented alliances between local and foreign trading networks." She goes on: "while historical South Asian colonial and economic power is often framed in terms of public—and frequently male—interactions, consideration of the private in the form of kindship relations and domestic spheres in elite families can help develop alternative perspectives on the topic that demon-strate the porosity of public/private spheres in this historical context." It is worth noting that the nineteenth-century settings for both North Indian trade and the Santa Fé Trade in the southwest United States are situated at historic high points of both sexist and racialized gender ideologies in colonizing set-tler societies and liberalized economies. In British holdings and the United States, this is the "gilded age" of "gilded cages" and cloistered female do-mesticity. However, neither strictly bimodal Victorian nor Edwardian gender systems nor strict dichotomies of public and private pertained in many Native American groups trading along the southwestern United States borderlands.

As in North India, historical narratives about the nineteenth-century Santa Fé trade have generally omitted women. Several other scholars and I have argued that the Santa Fé Trail and the larger southwest trading sphere of the *Camino Real* between the United States and Mexico was a domain where indigenous and Latina women and Anglo, French, and Mexican men created intimate marriage bonds which structured and fundamentally made possible international networks of trade between Osage, Ute, Apache, Arapaho, Co-manche, Navajo, Pueblo, Mexican nationals, emancipated African American, French, and other U.S. traders (Barr 2009; Brooks 2011; Church 2018; Clark 2011; Frank 2000; Hyde 2011). Fewkes points out a trope that scholars fall prey to in colonial settings, describing the "international man" married to a "local woman" with the implication that "local" means parochial or "not cosmopolitan." Particularly in colonial trade entrepôts, local women married to foreign or colonizing men are often the polyglot cultural brokers who safely traverse fraught public social and geographical terrain, whether through marrying across regional and ethnic lines, or even engaging directly in travel, trade, and diplomacy themselves. Historian Julianna Barr's evocatively titled *Peace Came in the Form of a Woman* recounts how in fact Native American women could cross contested indigenous territories in Spanish Texas to trade with sometimes enemy groups where men, who were traders but also warriors, could not without provoking open conflict. Over and over, captive native women allowed foreign colonizers to successfully explore, settle into, or expand existing trade networks. La Malinche to Cortez, or Sacagawea for Lewis and Clark, reflect millions of "local," indigenous, and cosmopolitan women across such historical transnational settings and moments.

As Fewkes points out for North India, intermarriage creates ties not only privately between individual traders, but between entire kin networks and communities. These couples had children who confronted heavily gendered realities growing up and making their way in the emerging *laissez-faire* economic systems their parents helped to create. Historian Anne Hyde (2011) has looked at inter-ethnic families-cum-trading companies created in various trade entrepôts in nineteenth-century North America and Canada, with specific regard to how the visibility, freedoms, and access/affordances of mixed-heritage women and men changed across generations. In Fewkes's work on kinship, the blurring of family intimacies and domestic partnerships with public merchant capitalism results in intensification and spread of cosmopolitanism within and between British and Indian networks of kin through time. In contrast, Anne Hyde's work *Empires, Nations, and Families: A History of the North American West, 1800–1860* shows that marriages and family alliances between more-or-less Victorian white men and Native American women intensify cosmopolitanism for a generation or two. However, racialized attitudes shift with Manifest Destiny and the Plains Indian Wars. As Brown states (this volume), such conflict is inimical to any truly cosmopolitan social relations. After that, "mixed heritage" daughters continue to marry white partners. In contrast, "mixed heritage" sons find more and more options, both marital and economic, closed to them, often despite being sent "back east" or abroad to Europe for apprenticeship or formal Edwardian education by their white fathers. Within two generations, across all these North American trade networks and families, different descendant portions of the same family are racialized as "Indian" or "White," and the former are blocked from public trade and access to resources.

Fewkes makes an important point about doing research on the colonial and nascent capitalist past in service of explaining broad and persistent patterns leading to the present. The blurring of intimate familial and entrepreneurial business relationships that she describes in northern India, and that Anne Hyde (2011) describes across North America, pertain to similar circumstances in late nineteenth- and twentieth-century settings in the United States. There is a reason we know the laissez-faire business enterprises of the robber barons by their family names—Vanderbilt, Mellon, Carnegie, Rockefeller—and we still recognize these family names as figures of public philanthropy today. Even at the apex of nineteenth-century gender dichotomies of private/public, family/business that was the 1890s, the distinction between the privacy of marriage and family and the public sphere seems to have been more ideological gloss than lived reality, and that is true for all social classes. Brown argues convincingly that despite all the historical ebbs and flows, the way that current gendered cosmopolitanism manifests in Taiwan, distinct from neighboring parts of the Sinosphere, is only understandable in the context of history. The linkages created in the everyday language of the letters Fewkes analyzes, the prosaic inquiries about the wives and children of British or Indian trading partners in various cities, are ways the intimate is intertwined with the public and economic even in the setting of business letters.

CONCLUSION

I find myself concluding this introduction with an even stronger skepticism about the existence of public/private dichotomies, not only in past indigenous and non-western settings, but even as a lived reality in colonizing western societies. And I am even more convinced of the epistemological dangers of imposing this dichotomy in our analysis. Fewkes asks an important question: "how can we observe the relationship between the intimate spaces of the home and public forms of colonial power?" Here I hark back to Sidney Mintz speaking of the Caribbean:

> One is led to ask in just what ways beyond the obvious ones the outer world and the European world became interconnected, interlocked even; what forces beyond the nakedly military and economic ones maintained this intimate interdependence; and how benefits flowed, relative to the ways power was exercised. (1986, xiv)

His phrase "intimate interdependence" is striking here. Other superficially contradictory phrases the authors in this book have used or brought to mind include "public intimacies," and even "public confinement." In these chapters, are "domestic economies" and "political economies" ever really discrete domains? Again, "How do we get from one child's sweet tooth to the history of slavery, of war, and of corporate lobbying in the Congress?" Or are these domains already so intertwined as to resist the prevailing dichotomy altogether?

I also find myself grappling with the gendered and racialized nature of these inquiries in the academy. Fewkes critically references the unfortunate linking of kinship studies with the Victorian and Edwardian evolutionary anthropology of Lewis Henry Moran and his ilk. Regardless of our backgrounds we are trained in western intellectual traditions, often in western, primarily English-speaking traditions, steeped in a sense of public/private gendered ideas about spaces and activities within spaces. Whether we fight to deconstruct those dichotomies, or question them, or even disregard them, we are still working with them as a premise. We work in a field, anthropology, with origins in a Victorian nineteenth-century progressivism that grew out of the very colonial settings that we are all engaged in the project of examining.

It is striking and somewhat dismaying, if unsurprising, that in 2020 it is still primarily women and scholars of color at the forefront of deconstructing these dichotomies. I am reminded of the likes of Carrie Nation taking the elite Edwardian women's role of "Angel of the House," the wielder of moral authority in the home, and transforming it by taking that authority (along with a baseball bat) out to the corrupt taverns and brothels as a driver of the temperance movement and (if anachronistically) "First Wave" feminism. Women of the progressive movement, temperance movement, "racial uplift" or rights work, and suffragists were turning the private/public dichotomy on its head at the height of its patriarchal power to suppress their public voices. As I mentioned above, in 2002 I contributed to Cynthia Robin and Nan Rothschild's thematic journal issue, which was in turn influenced by Wendy Ashmore's AAA Distinguished Lecture of 2002. In this work, we as archaeologists were deconstructing private/public dichotomies as part of site/landscape ones, albeit implicitly, and analyzing the implications for power relationships and colonization, among other things. I am left with the impression that it is women and people of color who are still primarily doing this work: questioning the relationship between dichotomies, colonialism, capitalism, and patriarchy, and pointing out the visible and the "veiled," as Brown put it. So I'll end by asking: what does it say about our own cultural cosmology, disciplinary and intellectual history around public and private, personal and political, that the work around these questions is still so heavily weighted by gender, race, and class in the academy? I am deeply grateful to the authors in this volume for taking this important work, undaunted, into the Roaring 2020s.

NOTES

1. Throughout this chapter I will refer to Yucatan and Peten without diacritics to refer to the Yucatan Peninsula and Peten Basin as geographic regions and to distinguish them from the political entities Yucatán and Petén, which refer to the Mexican State and Guatemalan department.

2. Quote as summarized at sydneymintz.net/sugar.php.

REFERENCES

Alexander, Rani T. 2004. *Yaxcabá and the Caste War of Yucatan: An Archaeological Perspective*. Albuquerque: University of New Mexico Press.

Álvarez, Héctor Hernández. 2014. "Corrales, Chozas y Solares: Estructura de Sitio Residencial de la Hacienda San Pedro Cholul, Yucatán." *Temas Antropológicos. Revista Científica de Investigaciones Regionales 36*(2): 129–52.

———. 2017. "Childhood and Material Culture at Hacienda San Pedro Cholul During Yucatán's Gilded Age." *Childhood in the Past 10*(2): 122–41.

Ashmore, Wendy. 2002. "'Decisions and Dispositions': Socializing Spatial Archaeology." *American Anthropologist 104*(4): 1172–83.

Barr, Julianna. 2009. *Peace Came in the Form of a Woman: Indians and Spaniards in the Texas Borderlands*. Chapel Hill: University of North Carolina Press.

Bennis, Will M., and Douglas L. Medin. 2010. "Weirdness Is in the Eye of the Beholder." *Behavioral and Brain Sciences 33*(2–3): 85–86.

Boland, Nigel O. 1977. "The Maya and the Colonization of Belize." In *Anthropology and History in Yucatán*, edited by Grant D. Jones, 69–99. Austin: University of Texas Press.

Brooks, James F. 2011. *Captives and Cousins: Slavery, Kinship, and Community in the Southwest Borderlands*. Chapel Hill: University of North Carolina Press.

Bruner, Edward. 1996. "Tourism in Ghana: The Prepresentation of Slavery and the Return of the Black Diaspora." *American Anthropologist 98*(2): 290–304.

Cheek, Charles. 1997. "Setting an English Table: Black Carib Archaeology on the Caribbean Coast of Honduras." In *Approaches to the Historical Archaeology of Mexico, Central & South America* (Vol. 38), edited by Janine Gasco, Greg C. Smith, and Patricia Fournier–García, 101–9. Monograph 38, UCLA Institute of Archaeology, Los Angeles.

Church, Minette C. 2018. "'La Luz de Aciete es Triste': Nighttime, Community, and Memory along the Santa Fé Trail." *Archaeology of the Night: Life after Dark in the Ancient World*, edited by Nancy Gonlin and April Nowell, 78–95. Louisville: University Press of Colorado.

Clark, Bonnie J. 2011. *On the Edge of Purgatory: An Archaeology of Place in Hispanic Colorado*. Lincoln: University of Nebraska Press.

Crane, Brian D. 1993. *Colono Ware and Criollo Ware Pottery from Charleston, South Carolina and San Juan, Puerto Rico in Comparative Perspective.* Doctoral dissertation, University of Pennsylvania.

Du Bois, W. E. B. 1903. *The Souls of Black Folk.* Chicago: A. C. McClurg & Co.

Ferguson, Leland 1992. *Uncommon Ground: Archaeology and Early African America, 1650–1800.* Washington, D.C.: Smithsonian Institution Press.

Frank, Ross. 2000. *From Settler to Citizen: New Mexican Economic Development and the Creation of Vecino Society, 1750–1820.* Berkeley: University of California Press.

Gann, Thomas. 1997. *Mystery Cities of the Maya.* Reprint, Kempton, IL: Adventures Unlimited Press. First published 1925.

Garvey, Marcus. 2012. *Selected Writings and Speeches of Marcus Garvey*, edited by Bob Blaisdell. New York: Dover Publications.

Gust, John. 2016. *Bittersweet: Porfirian Sugar and Rum Production in Northeastern Yucatán.* Doctoral dissertation, University of California, Riverside.

Habermas, Jürgen. 2012 (1964). "The Public Sphere: An Encyclopedia Article." In *Media and Cultural Studies: Keyworks*, edited by Gigi Meenakshi Durham and Douglas M. Kellner, 75–78. New York: John Wiley & Sons.

Hyde, Anne F. 2011. *Empires, Nations, and Families: A History of the North American West, 1800–1860.* Lincoln: University of Nebraska Press.

LeCompte, Janet 1978. *Pueblo, Hardscrabble, Greenhorn: The Upper Arkansas, 1832–1856.* Norman: University of Oklahoma Press.

Leone, Mark P. 1984. "Interpreting Ideology in Historical Archaeology: Using the Rules of Perspective in the William Paca Garden in Annapolis, Maryland." *Ideology, Power, and Prehistory 25*(3): 5.

Louden, Richard 1998. "'Some Memories from My Life,' as Written by Elfido Lopez, Sr., Edited and With an Introduction by Richard Louden." In *La Gente: Hispano History and Life in Colorado* (No. 2), edited by Vincent C. de Baca, 21–44 . Colorado Historical Society.

Meyers, Allen. 2012. *Outside the Hacienda Walls: The Archaeology of Plantation Peonage in Nineteenth-Century Yucatán.* Tucson: University of Arizona Press.

Mintz, Sidney W. 1986. *Sweetness and Power: The Place of Sugar in Modern History.* New York: Penguin Books.

Mullins, Paul R. 2006. *Race and Affluence: An Archaeology of African America and Consumer Culture.* New York: Springer Science & Business Media.

Randolph, A. Philip. 1919. "A New Crowd—A New Negro." *Messenger,* May–June, Vol. 27.

Roberts, John M., and Thomas Gregor. 2017. "Privacy: A Cultural View." In *Privacy and Personality* edited by J. Roland Pennock and John W. Chapman, 199–225. London: Routledge.

Robin, Cynthia, and Nan A. Rothschild, eds. 2002. "Archaeological Ethnographies: Social Dynamics of Outdoor Space." *Journal of Social Archaeology 2*(2).

Rudes, Blair. 2004. "Multilingualism in the South: A Carolinas Case Study." In *Linguistic Diversity in the South: Changing Codes, Practices, and ideology*, Vol. 37, edited by Margaret Bender, 37–49. Athens: University of Georgia Press.

Saitta, Dean J. 2007. *The Archaeology of Collective Action.* Gainesville: University Press of Florida.

Shackel, Paul A. 2006. *Archaeology and Created Memory: Public History in a National Park.* New York: Springer Science & Business Media.

Singleton, Theresa A., and Mark S. Bograd. 2000. "Looking for the Colono in Colonoware." In *Lines that Divide: Historical, Archaeologies of Race, Class, and Gender,* edited by James A. Delle, Stephen A. Mrozowski, and Robert Paynter, 2–21. Knoxville: University of Tennessee Press.

Sunseri, Jun. 2018. *Situational Identities along the Raiding Frontier of Colonial New Mexico.* Lincoln: University of Nebraska Press.

Thompson, J. Eric S. 1963. *Maya Archaeologist.* Norman: University of Oklahoma Press.

Ulrich, Laurel Thatcher. 1990. *A Midwife's Tale: The Life of Martha Ballard, Based on Her Diary, 1785–1812.* New York: A. A. Knopf.

Washington, Booker T. 1901. *Up from Slavery: An Autobiography.* New York: Doubleday, Page and Co.

Wilkie, Laurie A. 2012. *The Archaeology of Mothering: An African-American Midwife's Tale.* London: Routledge.

Chapter One

Affect and the Memorialization of the Transatlantic Slave Trade

Spontaneous Expressions of Synchronic Global Black Consciousness in the Visitors' Books at Elmina and Cape Coast Castles-Dungeons, Ghana

Jean Muteba Rahier

Among the West African sites associated with the memorialization of the slave trade—most are in Senegal, the Gambia, Benin, and Ghana—the Ghanaian Elmina and Cape Coast Castles/Forts/Dungeons are certainly those that draw in the most visitors from Europe, North America, Australia, Latin America and the Caribbean, Asia, and the rest of Africa, all year 'round.[1] The visits to each of these castles-dungeons take place as poignant narratives about the mechanics of the enslavement of African bodies and the technologies used to control and transport them, making sure they remain in a subjugated state, are performed by (usually male) Ghanaian guides in different locations in the forts/dungeons. Groups of racially and nationally diverse tourists follow the guides throughout, listening most of the time soundless to his detailed descriptions of what is presented as anti-black horror. These narrative and emotionally painful descriptions of raw brutality against the enslaved exacerbate among visitors black versus white racial identifications, accelerating and intensifying their differences, the distance that separates them, while recalling some of the most violent aspects of global white supremacy's long history.

At Elmina castle-dungeon, the guide's narrative begins near the main entrance door, where he usually shares general information about the origin of the name Elmina for the town and the castle-dungeon; the foundation and construction of the castle by the Portuguese; the initial use of the castle's ground floor as a storage space for merchandise prior to export to Europe; and the barter of mirrors, beads, guns, and powder in exchange for gold, ivory, and later spices. The narrative transition from these commercial exchanges to the commerce in enslaved Africans is rather short and impacts the visitors suddenly:

> When the slave trade started, these same warehouses were converted into dungeons where the Africans were kept. This castle-dungeon could hold a total of 1,000 Africans at a time, usually 400 women and 600 men. (Tour led by Philip, guide at Elmina, June 10, 2017)

The guide goes on to explain that after the beginning of the slave trade, the Dutch took the castle from the Portuguese. Later on, the Dutch were forced to cede the castle to the British. When the British are evoked in the guide's otherwise pre-colonial and transatlantic slave trade focused narrative, it often happens that references to the colonial period are also nonetheless made, in passing, which bring another layer to the quintessential white versus black opposition that characterizes the narrative. While the tour and the guide's explanations begin in the usually very sunny entrance of the castle, as the tour moves on visitors are progressively brought in the dark dungeons, which augments even more the emotional impact of the violence the guide describes.

> This is where the women were kept, all 400 of them. They had to sleep on the floor. There were no toilet facilities here, so they gave them containers to go to the toilet. The slaves that were brought here did not come from Ghana alone. They were also brought from Burkina Faso, Mali, Benin, Togo, Côte d'Ivoire, Nigeria, and so on. . . .
>
> When women had their menstruations, they had no access to proper hygienic care, and when one of them died, they were not buried, they were thrown in the sea for the fish to feed. (Tour led by Philip, guide at Elmina, June 10, 2017)

As the tour progresses, the descriptions of white violence against African bodies continue unabashed, like the never-ending rhythmic sound of a bell announcing a midnight mass:

> When the governor of the castle stood at his balcony, he could see the female slaves they brought in the small patio to wash. He then chose the one he liked and had sex with her in his quarters. She could eventually have died if she resisted. If she acquiesced, she could see an improvement in her living conditions. She could even hope to remain on African soil longer. If he didn't like her, he could take another one of his choice. (Tour led by Philip, guide at Elmina, June 10, 2017).

By the end of the tour, visitors are emotionally drained after about an hour of exposure to the narrative details of what comes through as white brutal and racist management of black bodies, while walking in the rooms where it all happened.

As I argue below, the physical experience of these visits of the dungeons as the guide's descriptions of white racial commandment unfolds, intensifies the circulation among black visitors from any origin, of strong identity-making and identity-sharing emotions. The racialization processes illustrated and described in the guide's narrative from the tour's beginning through its culmination at the "door of no return" (see figure 1.1) in each one of the two castles-dungeons are easily understandable as the visitors can simply relate the guide's descriptions to the varied known *répertoire* of still ongoing global white supremacy. Accessing the affective dimensions of the social interactions that make the entire visit, and especially the separate emotional economies in which black and non-black visitors eventually participate, helps one to understand the state in which "guests" are when—at the very end—they are invited to share whatever comment or feelings they might have in books placed near the exit doors. Some visitors definitely take the time to write individual comments, many do not and prefer to quietly keep to themselves.

This essay is grounded on a work of systematic examination of the visitors' books (see figure 1.2) covering the years between 1990 and 2016 in both Elmina and Cape Coast Castles-Dungeons in Ghana. It is also grounded on interviews with visitors and guides, and on participation in many guided visits in both locations in June and July 2017. I photographed about 1,500

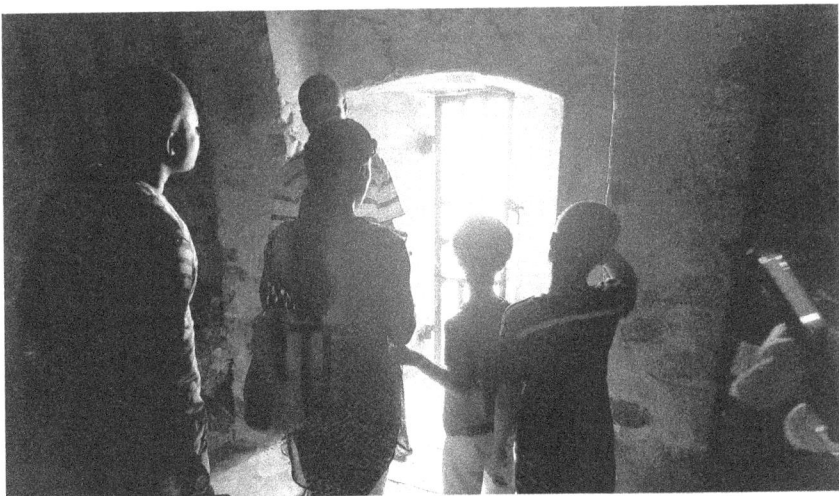

Figure 1.1.   African and African diaspora tourists at the Elmina dungeon's "door of no return."
Photograph by Jean Muteba Rahier, 2017.

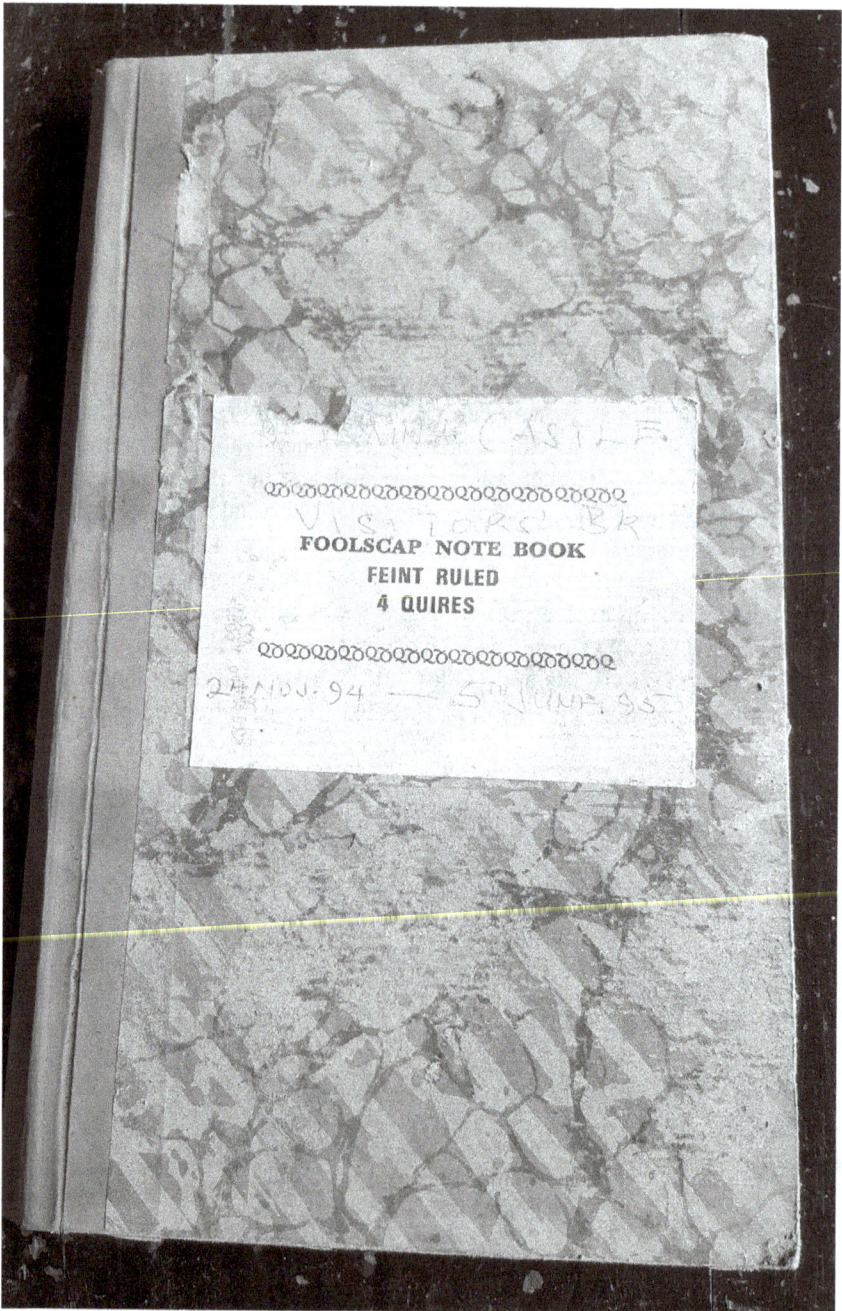

Figure 1.2. Cover of the Elmina book of comments from November 24, 1994, to June 5, 1995.

Photograph by Jean Muteba Rahier, 2017.

double pages of these books in each Castle (for a total of about 3,000 double pages), which has allowed for a careful reading and processing in an office setting back home in Miami. Each entry identifies the first and last names of its author, the date of the visit, along with the author's country of origin and even sometimes his or her e-mail address. In this essay, I keep the authors' identities anonymous and pay special attention to the comments left by black visitors,[2] without ignoring the others.

AFFECT AND SYNCHRONIC THEORIZING OF THE AFRICAN DIASPORA

In an essay soon to be published (Rahier, forthcoming), I have suggested that when facing the myriad theorizings of "the African diaspora," one can see two major orientations emerge: 1) the theorizings that are diachronically focused, which I call the vertical, diachronic, often monocultural and nationalist analytics and politics of the African diaspora, and 2) the theorizings that are more synchronically inspired and that result in conceptualizing the African diaspora as synchronic, horizontal, transcultural, and transnational networks of blackness. The theorizings I regroup under the label "diachronic" are all exclusively centered on a narrative of origin that elaborates on a vertical, time/space displacement from "homeland" to "hostland." This displacement, which can be the Middle Passage, the trans-Saharan voyage and the crossing of the Mediterranean to reach Europe, or the flight from war zones in Eastern Africa to the Global North, became a *sine qua non* identity foundation for specific African diaspora communities, along with their national and cultural origins (when these can be determined).

On the other hand, the synchronic orientation regroups the various theorizings that lead to conceptualizing the African diaspora in terms of manifold synchronic and horizontal transcultural or inter-ethnic, translocal and transnational networks of blackness that can potentially begin, pass through, and end anywhere. Here, the spatial displacement at the center of diachronic approaches is taken for granted, as is the position of continental Africa as primordial source and origin. The theoretical focus is not on the production of a vertical "narrative of origin." Instead, it is focused on what Michelle Wright calls the phenomenology of the "here and now" (2015). Horizontal synchronic analytics of "the African diaspora" are preoccupied with making sense of the complex ways nationally, socially, culturally, sexually (and the list is long) diverse black individuals and communities who live in a given location (let's say Miami, Santiago de Cuba, New York, Los Angeles, London, Paris, Montreal, Accra, Dakar, Johannesburg, Buenos Aires, or Salvador da

Bahia [Brazil]) interact with each other and with African diasporic individuals and communities based anywhere else in the world through both "frictions" and "conviviality." While "conviviality" evokes the congeniality and friendliness of particular encounters in recognition, "frictions"—as theorized by Anna Tsing (2005)—account for the diverse and often conflicting social interactions that make up the contemporary world and that produce new meanings and interpretations of the things in focus. Synchronic politics of the African diaspora conceive these inter-community interactions as involving a convivial acceptance of respective cultural particularities, projecting a mutual recognition that denotes nothing but the affirmation of a "transcultural Pan-African sibling-hood." Such politics come with the acknowledgment of the existence of multiple historical and individual trajectories of blackness, which must join for the coordination of political actions against anti-black racism and global white supremacy.

Synchronic theorizings of the African diaspora are associated with politics and analytics of transcultural racial solidarity sometimes referred to as "Pan-Africanism," with a capital "P."[3] Indeed, where European states and European-dominated settler colonial states, in their objective to reproduce white authority, have mis-recognized black subjects in accordance with transnational ideological distortion and its related processes of black abjection, exclusion, and erasure, synchronic politics of "diaspora" have opened up spaces of emotionally charged black universal collective recognition against the global hegemony of black misrecognition. Synchronic theorizing of the African diaspora made it possible to emphasize the horizontally unifying experiences of African and Afrodescendant peoples displaced and dispersed, directly or indirectly, and always affected directly by global white supremacy (see Hintzen and Rahier 2010).

My argument in this essay consists in showing that many, if not most, comments written by black visitors in the visitors' books at Elmina and Cape Coast Castles provide ideal illustrations—as shown in the quotations that follow—of what I call a celebration of synchronic theorizing of the African diaspora, of horizontal and transcultural global black consciousness and solidarity.

Misrecognition is at the core of black individual and social existence, of black emotional landscapes. Misrecognition is part and parcel of black people's lives. It erupts in our lives relatively early on as we grow up, anywhere in the world. Indeed, while a white person could care less of what a black person thinks of her, a black person cannot escape from the power of the white gaze's sentiment and evaluation. This is W. E. B. Du Bois's point with his coining the concept of "double consciousness": the imperative and existential predicament black people are in to always have to look at ourselves through a consciousness produced by the ideology of a racial statist pedagogy. In *The Souls of Black Folk*, Du Bois wrote words that could be generalized—with qualifications—to all black folks, above and beyond African Americans:

the Negro is a sort of seventh son, born with a veil, and gifted with second-sight in this American world—a world which yields him no true self-consciousness, but only lets him see himself through the revelation of the other world. It is a peculiar sensation, this double-consciousness, this sense of always looking at one's self through the eyes of others, of measuring one's soul by the tape of a world that looks on in amused contempt and pity. One ever feels his two-ness— an American, a Negro; two souls, two thoughts, two unreconciled strivings; two warring ideals in one dark body, whose dogged strength alone keeps it from being torn asunder. (Du Bois [1903] 1989, xxii–xxiii)

Franz Fanon (1967), mostly inspired by French Caribbean and North African colonial realities, has notoriously discussed the nature of colonialism and racism and their devastating psychological and emotional impact on both black and brown colonized people and also on their white colonizers.

As I show below, some scholars working on the memorialization of the slave trade in West Africa have adopted a research approach that is oblivious to the existence of emotions in the social world, and even more so of the workings of a black emotional economy with a global circuitry. Contrastingly, I contend that being black entails the sharing of experiences of double consciousness–making processes that any black person, anywhere in the world, has been burdened with in one or another of global white supremacy's many formations. Those shared experiences provide the ground for the making of global, synchronic, horizontal, transcultural, and transnational networks of blackness.

The consultation of the visitors' books of comments provide a privileged access to private and even intimate feelings and emotions that are otherwise not easily available, at the exception perhaps of the fragments from memoirs or other texts by writers who visited such sites (e.g., Angelou 1986; Wright 1954; Richards 2005). They open up a door onto the emotional and rather private impact of these visits and allow for the comprehension of the emotional fields they produce. This essay is particularly concerned with the emotional field of anti-global white supremacy and global black solidarity these visits create or provoke as revealed in Elmina and Cape Coast Castles' visitors' books of comments.

AFFECT, RACIALIZATION, AND THE MEMORIALIZATION OF THE TRANSATLANTIC SLAVE TRADE: BLACK VISITORS' COMMENTS

Many African and African diaspora visitors' comments adopt a humanist perspective that goes above and beyond racial identifications to lament the practice of slavery and call (sometimes to an un-specified universal divine authority) for it to "never happen again," eventually underlining the spiritual dimension of the visit for them, without delving into the issue of anti-black racism.

> Very informative, yet emotional tour. It was like I was here centuries ago. I could feel it in the waves at the sea and in the emptiness of the castle. Many thanks for the spiritual journey. Mama Africa lives! (Male visitor of Cape Coast from Trinidad, 2013)

> May God receive the souls of our ancestors who have passed through these premises before being brought to the Americas and the Caribbean. May their memories be forever engraved in us, their descendants in our struggle for a more united and fraternal world. (Female visitor of Cape Coast from Burkina Faso, 2013)

> The tour was very detailed. I enjoyed every bit of it. It was at times emotionally sad. I join in the resolve to end slavery wherever I find it, even in modern times. I will be back again. Thanks. (Male visitor of Cape Coast from Nigeria, 2012)

> Man is a monster and the proof of his monstrosity is here in this castle. Thank you for this lesson of memory. (Male visitor of Cape Coast from Senegal, 2011)

However, other African and African diaspora visitors' comments are written in an idiom of black resistance that posits more straightforwardly the existence of a global, transnational, and transcultural black "we" that is unambiguously united against anti-black racism and global white supremacy. Those statements' celebrations of a synchronic, horizontal, transcultural, and transnational black consciousness and networks of solidarity are based on emotionally charged politics of mutual recognition, above and beyond national, religious, linguistic, and sociocultural differences. As white supremacy spread globally along with the mis-recognition of black bodies, global and transnational black solidarity and mutual recognition have continued to expand (see Hintzen and Rahier, 2010). Other comments say:

> Wonderful history. It should teach us a lesson, as Africans to UNITE [*sic*] and gain economic independence from the whites. (Male visitor of Cape Coast from Ghana, 2013)

> The whites should be made to pay for their atrocities against tortured human beings. May they NOT rest in PEACE. (Male visitor of Elmina from Nigeria, 2013)

> Sankofa! This partially expresses my feelings. As an African American, my heart is full of the memory of the suffering and endurance of my ancestors. I am

truly humbled and grateful for their sacrifice. As a daughter of the dust, I have come back through "the door of return" and my journey is almost complete. (Visitor from New York, USA, 2006)

The tour was worthwhile, though painful and nauseating. So much for the white man's religious beliefs. (Female visitor of Cape Coast from Nigeria, 2011)

Let's enslave Europeans! (Male visitor of Cape Coast from Nigeria, 2011)

Great tour and experience. It brought tears to my eyes to see what my great grandparents went through. May God comfort all black people's hearts and forgive the white oppressors. (Female visitor of Cape Coast from Jamaica/ Canada, 2014)

So ugly, so shameful. Better to die than to be treated so badly. Europeans should hang their heads in shame. (Male visitor of Cape Coast from Australia/Ghana, 2011)

You people should sack all white people who come here, they don't deserve to be here. They are wicked and continue to be wicked. I hate them. (Male visitor of Elmina from the United States, 2012)

What a very heart touching experience throughout the rooms. The black race deserves a sincere apology including reparations from the white world. Irrespective of whether their great great grandfather, or their great grandfather, or their grandfather, or their father or themselves committed the atrocities against us. (Male visitor of Elmina from Ghana, 2013)

Scholarship on affect and racialization (Athanasiou, Hantzaroula, and Yannakopoulos 2009; Lutz and White 1986; Skoggard and Waterston 2015) is useful to make sense of the contents of the black visitors' comments that proclaim and acclaim global black consciousness and solidarity. The question Sara Ahmed asked—"How do emotions work to align some subjects with some others and against other others?" (Ahmed 2004, 117)—has great relevance for the examination of the spontaneous comments from many black visitors in focus here. The actual visit of each castle-dungeon consists in experiencing while walking through the built environment a narrative in which black and white racial categories are intensified, made sublime and otherwise reified as mutually and definitely exclusive and antagonistic. That narrative took shape progressively as the castles-dungeons became tourist attractions about enslaved Africans' forced departures for the transatlantic transplantations in the Americas.[4] Many scholars have discussed how much the narratives the guides provide to tourists in both castles-dungeons are inspired by a (U.S.) African American perspective on the transatlantic slave trade as opposed to a "Ghanaian one"

(Bruner 1996; Hartman 2002; Hasty 2002; Hosley 2013). Writing about these narratives performed by guides in Elmina Castle-Dungeon, but also about similar narratives that can be heard elsewhere,[5] Edward Bruner commented upon, in passing, how their reifications of racial identities immediately impact black visitors of different national backgrounds, often giving them anti-white revengeful sentiments (1996, 296). For Bruner, whose research only considers the actual situation of roots-heritage tourism in the space of the castles-dungeons of the Ghanaian coast, the perspectives on the transatlantic slave trade of African American tourists and of Ghanaians in general are definitely separated and completely different. He wrote:

> In interviews and focus groups, many Ghanaians noted that African Americans become very emotional during visits to the castle and dungeons. From a Ghanaian perspective, they become almost "too emotional," which suggests that the Ghanaians do not understand the feelings of diaspora blacks. Obviously, Ghanaians have not shared the diaspora experience, and they may not have read works by such writers as Maya Angelou, Richard Wright, or Eddy L. Harris. In black diaspora literature, there is an almost mythic image of Africa as a Garden of Eden. (1996, 293)

Brunner refers to African Americans' affective emotions in the face of the recalling of the inhumane treatments enslaved Africans endured[6] as if such emotions were completely different and separate from Ghanaians' emotions when dealing with the same material. He asserts:

> Most Ghanaians . . . are not particularly concerned with slavery. Although there was domestic slavery in Africa, that experience was different from the one undergone by those who were transported to the New-World and suffered the indignities of the black diaspora. For Ghanaians, Elmina Castle represents a part of Ghanaian history, from the Portuguese who built Elmina in 1482 primarily to facilitate trade on the Gold Coast, to the Dutch who captured the castle in 1637, to the British who gained control of Elmina in 1872, through to Ghanaian independence in 1957. (Bruner 1996, 292)

For Bruner, the separation of African Americans from Ghanaians and Africans in general is not limited to the consideration of the slave trade. "Blackness"—as he affirms—also means profoundly different things for African Americans and Ghanaians:

> Ghanaians . . . do not share an essentialist view of blackness, for although they are very aware of the similarity in skin color, it is not for them the single overriding classificatory criterion for the sorting of human beings, for they see the returning African Americans primarily as foreigners, as Americans, as wealthy, and as tourists. In my view, not to "see" African Americans as black provides a

liberating corrective for an American society beset with racial problems, where race, defined solely by skin color, is widely perceived as a "natural" and biologically given categorization. (Bruner 1996, 301–2)

As already revealed by the argument I develop in this essay, and following the contents of the visitors' books at both castles-dungeons, I could not disagree more with Bruner. Indeed, I contend that for all individuals who consciously self-identify as "black"—wherever they are from, or wherever they were born—the narrative evocations of the histories of enslavement of Africans in West Africa and of their forced voyage to the Americas, of the African genocides that came with European colonialisms and imperialisms in continental Africa, and of so many other stories of racialization and anti-black brutality in Africa or elsewhere do not only deeply resonate with our own experiences as racialized subjects. They are lived as our own stories and provoke strong emotions that are

profoundly felt, experiential, and [that carry] actively embodied conceptions of a social reality and historical reference. Being a racial subject is thus a highly historically conscious way of existing at multiple scales—as an individual, as part of a community, as part of a nation, and transnationally. (Berg and Ramos-Zayas 2015, 663)

Bruner's mistake has certainly been to only conceive of continental Africans and members of the transatlantic slave trade–based African diaspora as existing in completely separate realities, as if the history of European imperialist expansion had not contributed to the establishment of a system of global white supremacy that has for centuries racialized both continental Africans and members of the African diaspora in comparable and related ways.

Sara Ahmed (2004) showed how crucial emotions are for racial and national identifications, and for the alignment of individuals and their bodies to larger collectivities. For Ahmed, emotions do not reside in individuals, instead they "circulate and are distributed across a social as well as a psychic field" (2004, 120) in affective economies. I would suggest that Bruner's rigid and empiricist construction of the distance between Ghanaians and African Americans is at best partial or incomplete, as it comes from a perspective that seems to suffer from a lack of direct access to, or a failure to actually consider the existence of these very concrete emotions that circulate among those racialized and consciously self-identified as blacks, globally.

To use Achille Mbembe's terminology, we could see the Cape Coast and Elmina Castles guides' narratives as detailing the practice of a "Western consciousness of blackness" that structures the world around its own identity posited as a highest and grounding principle, thereby providing the rationale with which to exclude and subordinate alterity. For most black visitors, being exposed to the violence described in the guides' narratives triggers a "black consciousness of blackness" that potentially allows for individual self-liberation and a declaration of identity (Mbembe 2017, 28–30).

All racial orderings implicate the engagement of, and impacts on, affects. Ulla Berg and Ana Ramos-Zayas (2015, 662) theorized "racialized affect" and distinguished between black and brown people's "liable affect" and white people's "empowering affect," as they refer to blacks' and whites' positionings vis-à-vis race, racialization, and the racial ordering of peoples and things anywhere in the world:

> "Liable affect" [refers to] the affective practices that serve to racialize, contain, and sustain conditions of vulnerability and a constitutive element of subject formation for poor, migrant, and socially marginalized populations. . . .
>
> "[E]mpowering affect" [points to] the affect associated with privilege and always-already perceived as complex, nuanced, and beyond essentialism. While a conception of "liable affect" results in a simplified and essentialized "inner world" that undermines the complexity and subjectivity of populations racialized as Other, a conception of "empowering affect" perpetuates the privileged and nuanced subjectivity frequently reserved for [whites] and . . . self-styled whitened elites. . . .
>
> "Liable affects" and "empowering affect" . . . operate in multiple, shifting, and complex configurations. . . . There is a relational and mutually constitutive aspect to these affective modes. (2015, 662–63)

When considering the guides' narratives, it is indeed because of their empowering affect vis-à-vis the slave trade that white Europeans—in smaller numbers than the enslaved Africans routinely under their control—were able to run the castles-dungeons and the many enchained Africans. They were not only convinced of their own greatness. For them, the inferiority of the enslaved was also "undeniable." The enslaved Africans, for their part, were very much aware of their place within the newly established racial order. However, the use of a "black race" category (and any other vocabulary used to express that idea) to regroup peoples indigenous to continental Africa, and construct them as inferior to European slave traders, and later colonizers, also opened up a field of potential, political, rallying solidarity from where to project black resistance against anti-black racism. As Judith Butler put it: "[p]ower that at first appears as external, pressed upon the subject, pressing the subject into subordination, assumes a psychic form that constitutes the subject's self-identity" (1997, 3).

For black visitors, such tours about white supremacy-inspired anti-black violence are profoundly affective and emotional experiences and eventually produce difficult self-reflections, and the reopening of affective wounds initially inflicted during past experiences with anti-black racism somewhere else in the world. We identify with the enslaved and feel the weight of our own experiences when considering the imposition upon us of a racialized liable affect. Black visitors are so emotionally invested in the visits that we experience very strong feelings toward the sites (see Richards 2005), unbeknownst to other non-black visitors, perhaps. Black visitors'—including Ghanaians and other Africans—feelings of political identification with the victims of anti-black racist acts perpetrated centuries ago are grounded on our recognition of the fact that we share with them the experience of generally similar, or at the very least comparable, processes of racialization. The guides' narratives unfold referring to nameless Africans caught up in the slave trade and who became commodities to be used and abused at will by white slaveowners. But black visitors' in-flesh memories of anti-black racism allow them to recognize—and feel—white supremacy and the racialized empowering affect exerted by the white personnel of the forts as uncovered in the guides' narratives, bringing about the issue of the many intimate/private receptions or impacts of public narratives.

Not considering the importance of affect in black visitors' experiences at Cape Coast and Elmina Castles-Dungeons can only lead to an unfinished or incomplete understanding of what these sites actually represent. Often, visitors from the Middle Passage–based African diaspora in the Americas get upset. Many cry, overwhelmed with the imagination of what their ancestors went through, and with the consideration of their personal, family connections to this excruciating history; Ghanaians, other Africans, and other members of the African diaspora often join to shed tears.

> This is my third visit, each time I am emotionally moved to tears at the suffering and death of our ancestors. Never again!!! (Female visitor of Cape Coast from the United States, 2011).

> The tour is very educative. I could see that white people are wicked and should not be tolerated . . . but this type of place should carry the flags of all African nations as it affects them all. (Male visitor of Cape Coast from Nigeria, 2009)

> Very, very sad today, because of what the whites did to our precious great grandparents. I pray that their souls rest in perfect peace. We will forever be grateful for their precious blood. (Male visitor of Cape Coast from Ghana, 2011)

On July 10, 2017, I interviewed Mr. Ato Ashun, the Officer-in-Charge of Elmina Castle. Our conversation mostly focused on different visitors' emotions at the end of the tour. He confirmed that every group of tourists comes with their own ways of expressing emotions. His comments illustrate, in passing, the assuming on his part of that transnational, transcultural, synchronic, horizontal black "we" I mentioned earlier:

> African Americans often cry. Jamaicans are angry, they want to fight. On tours, my staff and I avoid putting people from the African diaspora (particularly Jamaicans) with other foreigners [that is to say "whites"], in the same group. They can provoke the white tourists, asking questions like: "How do you feel coming here? Do you see what your ancestors did to us?" White tourists in such a group would then leave the visit because of the anger and animosity. With the Americans, if they come in one group with blacks and whites, they often decide to take the tour separately because blacks are often offended by the silly questions some whites can ask.

Ashun summarized white visitors' reactions as follows:

> White Europeans and white Americans could be placed in three groups when considering the emotions the visit provokes in them. There are those who cry and feel ashamed to be Dutch or British; there are those who blame us, Africans, for having sold our brothers and sisters into slavery, which frees them from culpability; and there are those who don't really care, who are not even interested in the narrative and prefer instead to take pictures of the Castle's structure.

Ashun confided that sometimes he cries with black visitors, that he tells them to take inspiration in the strength the enslaved demonstrated having as opposed to dwelling on what must have been their unbearable pains.

My examination of the visitors' books at both castles illustrates well Ashun's characterization of the emotional reactions of the visitors. On July 12, 2013, three different visitors of Cape Coast Castle left comments in the visitors' book, one after the other. The first one, from Germany, could not have expressed better the distance between him and the history of African enslavement he just listened to. He wrote: "Thank you very much for this nice information, here in Cape Coast Castle. Thanks also for very nice holidays here in Ghana, staying with our family. God bless all people." Right below, an African American woman contrastingly shared her engagement with the fort-dungeon's slave trade–focused history. She wrote: "To God be the Glory. I made it back home to honor the memory of that African whose blood runs through my veins. God bless him for his strength!" A male Ghanaian visitor wrote: "We Africans must be proud of our colors and . . . never again allow the white people to rule us anymore."

It is both African and African diaspora visitors' recognition of the enslaved Africans' pains that bring some who write in the visitors' book to shout their feelings of hurt, sorrow, and profound solidarity with all black people across the globe, against white supremacy. When doing so, not only African diaspora people but also those born in Africa conceive of the enslaved who lived centuries ago as their ancestors:

> It was painful to see what many of our ancestors suffered in the hands of European slave traders. Europe must pay reparation for it. (Male visitor of Cape Coast from Nigeria, 2012)

> It was written, those who were taken away shall be returned by the power of the Almighty. Repatriation is a must. (Male visitor of Cape Coast from Jamaica, 2013)

> Ancestors rise up and fight for vengeance *cos* Africans are still enslaved. (Visitor of Cape Coast who self-identified as "African" instead of entering nationality, 2012)

> Tour guide was excellent. Matilda was wonderful. I am angry. I hope my Christian love will fill my heart to forgive the atrocities done to my ancestors. All should know of man's inhumanity. (Female visitor of Cape Coast from the United States, 2011)

THE MULTIPLICITY OF BLACK SUBJECTIVITIES AND PERSPECTIVES ON THE TRANSATLANTIC SLAVE TRADE

Bruner is not the only author to posit that Ghanaians and African Americans have different perspectives on the slave trade. Previously published scholarship on tourists' visits to Cape Coast and Elmina Castles-Dungeons and other West African sites associated with the transatlantic slave trade has emphasized those differences as well. At first glance, such work might appear as going in the opposite direction than the one I adopt in this essay to make sense of the expressions of shared global black solidarity in Cape Coast's and Elmina's books of visitors' comments. The thing we must keep in mind is that Africans and people from the African diaspora do have multi-dimensional relationships to the issues raised by the transatlantic slave trade, and what I write in this essay should not be seen necessarily in opposition to the argument developed by these other scholars but instead as targeting one particular dimension of the complex realities of black peoples' affective engagements with the transatlantic slave trade, which many of these scholars have left on the side.

Jennifer Hasty's argument (2002) about "heritage tourism" in Ghana sees the state as wanting to be the ultimate arbiter for all comings in and goings out of the country. In an attempt to consolidate its power and revenues, the Ghanaian state wants to take advantage of African American needs for spiritual and cultural identification with Africa in a "trans-Africanist" logic that posits a cultural and racial unity between the African diaspora and continental Africans (2002). This logic is based, writes Hasty, on "political agendas predicated on essentialist antinomies" that have no value in the local realities of everyday Ghanaians. This brings about a picture where people of the black diaspora do not do anything but connect very superficially with Ghana, and Africa at large. At the end of the day, for Hasty, African American presence and "pilgrimages" are not seen as beneficial for Ghanaians; on the contrary, they threaten "to destabilize the routine production of national locality, predicated on historical, regional, ethnic, and political hierarchies" (2002, 63).

In that regard, Saidiyi Hartman (2002) followed Hasty and Bruner when she wrote that slavery memorials produce a particular African diaspora identity, a black diaspora identity, in terms of "a collective memory of the past" that is edified on "loss" and "grief" (2002, 758). This has brought about an "ideological construction" of slavery by diasporic blacks that emerges out of their political interests for the themes of "racial subjection, incarceration, and impoverishment" (2002, 765–66). Hartman is particularly concerned with debunking the racial and cultural essentialism behind African Americans' search for origins. She represents Ghanaian locals as cynical in front of African American preoccupations.

Sandra Richards, an African American theater studies scholar, has written about Elmina and Cape Coast Castles-Dungeons as "contact zones" where various dissimilar interpretations are performed and where perspectives meet or collide. She makes references to African Americans' feelings when visiting these sites, including the initiatives some have taken to stage and perform acts of on-site memorialization. In an article she wrote (Richards 2005), which is filled with considerations of the circulating emotions Ahmed wrote about, Richards assumes her perspective as an "African American heritage tourist" while she progresses through the various stages of the visit to Elmina, sharing the emotions she felt:

> But, on site, as I descend from the officers' balcony to the women's pens and courtyard below, and as additional senses come under attack, it is hard to preserve an emotional distance. Dark, with mold and mildew plainly visible on the wall, some of the dungeons receive their only air source from what was once a magazine storage for armaments, meaning that overcrowded female captives would have inhaled Sulphur in addition to the odors of bodily fluids and fear. Surprisingly, a stench that momentarily catches and stops the breath remains. It activates the imagination, destroying temporal distinctions and flattening historical and individual subjectivities into one force-field of pain. (2005, 624)

In her book *The Predicament of Blackness: Postcolonial Ghana and the Politics of Race* (2013), Jemima Pierre seems to have as a target Bruner and his claim that the perspectives on the transatlantic slave trade of African American tourists and of Ghanaians in general are definitely separated and completely different, and that Ghanaians do not share an essentialist view of blackness. She rejects what she characterizes as the simplistic and erroneous assumption that race is of no use to make sense of contemporary continental African realities, which is found in Bruner's work, and instead argues that postcolonial African societies have been structured through and by global white supremacy. For her, African societies should be approached within current discussions of race and blackness. This is exactly what she does when she revisits Ghana's racial colonial history, Ghana's position in the slave trade, its continuing prominence in African diaspora politics, and its more locally initiated racialization processes, which she calls "racecraft," which all reveal how much the country has been immersed in race-based global circulations. She revisits the installation of British colonial rule on the Gold Coast in light of a careful examination of its racialist and racist foundations, colonial imaginations/constructions of ethnic groupings ("nativization"), and native spatial separation/segregation away from white Europeans. She zeroes in on the ways the colonial racial hierarchy continued operating despite the unfolding of the processes that led to independence, and uncovers the processes by which racial hierarchy also determined the global relations of economic and political power that began during the colonial period and that continue to operate in myriad ways in the postcolony to limit options available to the new independent countries' leaders. Pierre proclaims that decolonization went hand in hand with unrelenting racialization, unabashed even in the contemporary postcolonial moment.

Although she also rightfully asserts the existence of very concrete differences in African American and Ghanaian perspectives on the slave trade, Bayo Hosley (2013) presents a complex picture of the situation in and around the Ghanaian castles-dungeons, which takes distance from Bruner's suggestion of the existence of a complete separation between Ghanaians and African American and other African diaspora visitors. In an article that takes as a departure point the 2009 visit of Ghana by then U.S. president Barack Obama and his family, she makes reference to Ghana's Afro-cosmopolitanism, as it has been developing over many decades, particularly through the high global visibility of African American musicians and celebrities. She interprets the Obamas' visit within the preexisting discourse about blackness that has so much characterized Ghana's history and showed that by identifying with them, many Ghanaians were actually constructing a notion of community that goes beyond:

national borders and embrace a broader conception of a black cultural citizenship. In this context, black cultural citizenship refers to a notion of belonging and community determined not by legal status but instead through other forms of recognition. These forms might include the recognition of shared histories, cultures and tastes, or political commitments. (Hosley 2013, 505)

For Hosley, the Obamas' popularity in Ghana at the time of their visit had to do with the fact that some Ghanaians imagined a transnational community based on certain understandings of black style (2013, 506). She argues that many Ghanaians disassociate themselves from the history of the slave trade because those who were traded usually came from the northern region of the country, which continues to be looked down upon, in the Ghanaian ethnoracial-spatial order, as rural backwaters when compared to coastal urban Ghana, where the forts-dungeons are located. Embracing slavery would only create a major obstacle for the participation in urban-based Afro-cosmopolitanism. She notes that most urban youth self-identify using a notion of cultural citizenship that connects them to modernity and the African diaspora without being mediated by the history of the slave trade. Hosley sees the distancing from slavery and the state embrace of slave ancestry through the support and development of the sites of memorialization of the slave trade to attract tourists as the two sides of the same coin: "as differing ways of grappling with an intimate and painful relationship to the history of Atlantic slavery, they both represent modes of black Atlantic identification in the modern world" (2013, 506).

Notwithstanding the assessments of, and discussions about, the differences in perspectives on the slave trade, between white and black visitors, or between Ghanaian and African American and other African diaspora visitors, I contend that by reaching the end of the visit, and the relatively long experience (about an hour long) of a narrative about the dungeons' history under European slavers' management, black visitors find themselves in an emotional situation that triggers or is propitious for the manifestation of a synchronic, horizontal, transcultural, and transnational black consciousness, in a spontaneous move of resistance against global white supremacy.

Some black visitors express that consciousness while also complaining about the different admission rates for Ghanaians as opposed to the rate paid by all foreigners, including other Africans and African diasporans:

Considering the history of the place, there should be a special rate for Africans. How can we pay the same as our oppressors? (Female visitor of Cape Coast from Kenya, 2011)

The castle is a historical masterpiece. I am glad the government has been able to maintain the site. On the contrary, I am not happy about your charges for non-Ghanaians. I think all blacks should be given the same charge as Ghanaians. Instead, the high fees should be passed to the whites due to the loss they made our generations suffer. Up Black Star!!! (Male visitor of Elmina from Nigeria, 2010)

I enjoyed the tour, and the guide leader was very nice. As an African American coming back home-roots [*sic*], it was sad learning of the history of the slave post. Also, it saddens me that we as African Americans have to pay to come back to our roots. We were sold and betrayed. And also, why should we pay more than local Ghanaian brothers? We are all the same. What a shame. Please, change these rules, please welcome us home in a better way. Thank you! *Medaase* ["Thank you" in Akan]. (Male visitor of Cape Coast from New Jersey, in the United States, 2011)

Other visitors seem to feel guilty of the freedom they are enjoying while learning details about what their ancestors went through.

This was a very educational experience, one I will never forget. I would like to say I am sorry to my ancestors for the pains they endured for my freedom in this world. THANK YOU! THANK YOU! THANK YOU! Rest in peace! (Female Visitor of Elmina from the United States, 2010)

CONCLUSIONS

The systematic examination of the visitors' books of both Elmina and Cape Coast Castles-Dungeons over a relatively long period of time (1990–2016), and my declared objective to especially pay attention to black visitors' comments from both continental Africa and numerous communities of the African diaspora, has allowed me to directly engage with the work of Edward Bruner and reveal it for what it does not do: it is completely deprived of any consideration for the strong emotions black people share in those places. Indeed—and perhaps as a testimony that positivism continues to influence the way social science research is conducted and conceptualized—Bruner is completely oblivious to the centrality of emotions in his approach to the castles-dungeons' visits and to the way these emotions simultaneously trigger an affective network in which all people self-identified as black find themselves entangled because of their having shared, wherever they are from, similar processes of racialization as "blacks." The positivist and empiricist traditions in the social sciences have eschewed the serious consideration of emotions, our own as researchers, and those from the people with whom we interact. And when dealing with black peoples and our global networks of political and affective solidarity when faced with expressions of global white supremacy, there is only one way to go: the consideration of affect as inseparably articulated with racialization processes. A focus on affect

gives us a vocabulary to talk about intersubjectivity in a way that does not ne-
gate, but in fact necessarily evokes, a series of broader material conditions and
historical trajectories of which populations of color are highly conscious. (Berg
and Ramos-Zayas 2015, 654)

The many comments left by African as well as African diaspora visitors
show how mistaken Bruner's statements—according to which Africans and
African Americans relate to slavery completely differently—are. The way
we identify is very much multi-dimensional and situational. And while there
certainly are situations in which religious, linguistic, or generally cultural
distinctions among black people are made prevalent, there is no doubt that
on the other hand, there are situations in which on the contrary transcultural,
transnational, horizontal, and syncretic black consciousness and solidarity arc
actualized and made extremely relevant and unavoidable. My argument in
this piece is that visits to Elmina and Cape Coast Castles-Dungeons provide
such situations that are privileged opportunities for the emulation of such
synchronic and horizontal theorizing (analytics and politics) of the African
diaspora against white supremacy. This is not different from the way anti-
black police violence against a Haitian or African immigrant in New York
or Miami provokes an easily unified reaction from the various local black
populations (Haitian American, Jamaican American, African American, and
African immigrant communities) and their respective organizations, while in
other situations, the same communities and their organizations might have
been more preoccupied to assert cultural, national, and/or historical particularities. Identities and identifications should not be approached as if they were
monolithic and set once and for all.

The most politically engaged comments of black visitors in focus here
reveal synchronic politics of the African diaspora that conceive inter
community interactions as involving a convivial acceptance of respective
cultural particularities, and as projecting a mutual recognition in support of
the affirmation of a "transcultural Pan-African sibling-hood." Such politics
come with the acknowledgment of the existence of multiple historical and
individual trajectories of blackness, which must join for the coordination of
political actions against anti-black racism.

In its synchronic and horizontal understanding, "diaspora" provides a
space of mutual recognition, of a solidary consciousness shared across frag-
mented geographies. As consciousness it is constitutive of the conditions for
collective self-recognition made possible through entanglements across social, cultural, political, economic, psychological, national, and material fields
of engagement. Someone is "black" not on the basis of being West Indian, or
Jamaican, or African American, or African, or Black British but by virtue of
a black consciousness embedded in the materialities of the social, political,

and cultural geography produced out of the universality of hegemonic ruling ideas of supremacy inscribed through the violence of white commandment (Hintzen and Rahier 2010).

I feel that I must end with the words of Maya Angelou, as she explains how she felt when arriving in Cape Coast in the early 1960s:

> I allowed the shapes to come to my imagination: children passed tied together by ropes and chains, tears abashed, stumbling in dull exhaustion, then women, hair uncombed, bodies gritted with sand, and sagging in defeat. Men, muscles without memory, minds dimmed, plodding, leaving bloodied footprints in the dirt. The quiet was awful. None of them cried, or yelled, or bellowed. No moans came from them. They lived in a mute territory, dead to feeling and protest. These were the legions, sold by sisters, stolen by brothers, bought by strangers, enslaved by the greedy and betrayed by history. (Angelou 1986, 98)

NOTES

1. The research this chapter is grounded on could not have taken place without the support of a 2017 Carnegie African Diaspora Fellowship, and of the University of Cape Coast, Ghana's Department of Religion and Department of History.

2. The comments' authors' countries of origin and/or the actual comments' contents undoubtedly reveal authors' blackness.

3. A distinction is usually made between "Pan-Africanism" with a capital "P" and "pan-Africanism" with a small "p": "Pan-Africanism" with a capital "P" indicates the history of the transnational movement of the same name within the specific timeframe of the Pan-African Congress from 1900 on, while "pan-Africanism" with a small letter is not about one clearly recognizable movement such as the one led by W. E. B. Du Bois, but instead about a group of movements, which are often very ephemeral (church organizations, academic conferences and associations, lobbying and radical pressure groups) (Shepperson 1962).

4. As opposed to focus on other periods in the history of the castles, before and after the transatlantic slave trade. Bruner writes (1996, 293–94): "Which story shall be told? Vested interests and strong feelings are involved. Dutch tourists are interested in the two centuries of Dutch rule in Elmina Castle, the Dutch cemetery in the town, and the old Dutch colonial buildings. British tourists want to hear about colonial rule in the Gold Coast. Many Ashanti people have a special interest in the rooms where the Asantehene, their king Prempeh I, was imprisoned in Elmina Castle in 1896, after the defeat of the Ashanti forces by the British army. The king was later exiled to the Seychelles Islands and only returned to Ghana in 1924. He is important to all Ghanaians as a representation of resistance to British colonialism."

5. The narratives given to tourists at Cape Coast, Ghana, or at Williamsburg, Virginia, in the United States, for example, as Bruner suggests.

6. He also refers to texts by African American writers who visited Cape Coast and/ or Elmina Castle(s)-Dungeon(s) (Angelou 1986; Harris 1992; Wright 1954).

REFERENCES

Ahmed, Sara. 2004. "Affective Economies." *Social Text, 79*. 22(2): 117–139.
Angelou, Maya. 1986. *All God's Children Need Traveling Shoes*. New York: Vintage Books.
Athanasiou, A., P. Hantzaroula, and K. Yannakopoulos. 2009. "Towards a New Epistemology: The 'Affective Turn.'" *Historein 8*, 5–16. doi:http://dx.doi.org/10.12681/historein.33.
Berg, Ulla D., and Ana Y. Ramos-Zayas. 2015. "Racializing Affect: A Theoretical Proposition." *Current Anthropology* 56(5): 654–77.
Bruner, Edward. 1996. "Tourism in Ghana: The Representation of Slavery and the Return of the Black Diaspora." *American Anthropologist 98*(2): 290–304.
Butler, Judith. 1997. *The Psychic Life of Power: Theories in Subjection*. Stanford: Stanford University Press.
Du Bois, W. E. B. [1903] 1989. *The Souls of Black Folks*. New York: Bantam Books.
Fanon, Franz. 1967. *Black Skin, White Masks*. New York: Grove Press.
Harris, Eddy L. 1992. *Native Stranger: A Black American's Journey into the Heart of Africa*. New York: Vintage Books.
Hartman, Saidiya. 2002. "The Time of Slavery." *South Atlantic Quarterly 101*(4): 757–77.
Hasty, Jennifer. 2002. "Rites of Passage, Routes of Redemption: Emancipation Tourism and the Wealth of Culture." *Africa Today 49*(3): 47–76.
Hintzen, Percy C. and Jean Muteba Rahier. 2010. "Introduction. Theorizing the African Diaspora: Metaphor, Miscognition, and Self-Recognition. In *Global Circuits of Blackness: Interrogating the African Diaspora*, edited by J. M. Rahier, P. C. Hintzen, and F. Smith, xi–xxvi Urbana-Champaign. The University of Illinois Press.
Hosley, Bayo. 2013. "Black Atlantic Visions: History, Race, and Transnationalism in Ghana." *Cultural Anthropology 28*(3): 504–18.
Lutz, Catherine and Geoffrey White. 1986. "The Anthropology of Emotions." *Annual Review of Anthropology 15*: 405–36.
Mbembe, Achille. 2017. *Critique of Black Reason*. Durham: Duke University Press.
Pierre, Jemima. 2013. *The Predicament of Blackness: Postcolonial Ghana and the Politics of Race*. Chicago: The University of Chicago Press.
Rahier, Jean Muteba. Forthcoming. "The Actual Transnationalization of Black Studies/African Diaspora Studies: Diachronic and Synchronic Perspectives." In *Black Studies in Europe: Questioning the Politics of Knowledge*, edited by Sarah Fila-Bakabadio, Nicole Grégoire, and Jacinthe Mazzocchetti. Evanston: Northwestern University Press.
Richards, Sandra. 2005. "What Is to be Remembered?: Tourism to Ghana's Slave Castle-Dungeons." *Theatre Journal 57*(4): 617–37.

Shepperson, George. 1962. "Pan-Africanism and 'pan-Africanism': Some Historical Notes." *Phylon* 23(Winter): 346–58.

Skoggard, Ian, and Alisse Waterston. 2015. "Introduction: Toward an Anthropology of Affect and Evocative Ethnography." *Anthropology of Consciousness* 26(2): 109–20.

Tsing, Anna L. 2005. *Friction: An Ethnography of Global Connection*. Princeton: Princeton University Press.

Wright, Michelle. 2015. *Physics of Blackness: Beyond the Middle Passage Epistemology*. Minneapolis: University of Minnesota Press.

Wright, Richard. 1954. *Black Power: A Record of Reactions in a Land of Pathos*. New York: Harper and Brothers.

Chapter Two

Behind Closed Doors

*Rethinking Public and Private
in the Ulster Plantation*

Audrey Horning

INTRODUCTION

In the early seventeenth century, Britain sought to exert control over the north of Ireland through the mechanism of plantation: planting settlements of loyal, principally Protestant, settlers and displacing the Gaelic, principally Catholic population.[1] As a Crown-sanctioned colonial venture, the Ulster Plantation, launched in 1609, was planned out in detail and continually assessed. On paper, this public scheme to subdue the province of Ulster was all-encompassing and in memory successful in defeating Gaelic Ireland. Incoming planters were forbidden from engaging with the Irish while the numerically dominant Irish were banned from residency in plantation towns. The most strictly regulated effort within the Ulster Plantation was that focused upon the newly created County Londonderry, which relied upon a clever fiscal model of requiring the London Companies (wealthy merchant guilds) to underwrite the venture in exchange for land. The twelve premier London Companies were each allocated individual "proportions" of land within what had been the Gaelic O'Cahan Lordship and instructed to remove all Irish and to build villages and houses according to the latest English designs (Blades 1986). Furthermore, the Companies were to finance the establishment of two principal defended towns, Londonderry and Coleraine, in a process to be administered by a joint stock company, the Irish Society, consisting of representatives drawn from the fifty-five participating Companies (Curl 1986; Hill 1970 [1877]; Moody 1939a). Notwithstanding the fact that the Companies had minimal interest in participating in this Crown-sanctioned venture, they had little choice in the face of the command of King James.

Yet peering past the colonial rhetoric and into the households and private spaces of the new plantation settlements provides a very different view on the

process and practices of plantation, one with potential for reassessing historical memories in the present. Alternative readings of the evidence reveal a very
different, private side to this public scheme. Archaeological, documentary,
and cartographic sources indicate that far from the total displacement of the
Irish decreed by official regulations, co-residence was not uncommon. Maps
of plantation villages and towns allude to this reality through representations
of Irish vernacular dwellings and Gaelic routeways, field boundaries, and
place names in places where they were not supposed to be present (O'Keeffe
2008), and by extension not meant to be documented. Material culture from
Ulster Plantation sites adds further complexity by reflecting daily realities,
with incoming English and Scots adopting Irish buildings and Irish-made
ceramics (Horning 2013a, 220, 233–34; Horning 2018; Tracey and Horning 2019), just as Gaelic households incorporated newly imported goods
and practices (Gillespie 2009; Flavin 2014). Elite planters emulated Gaelic
lordly culture as evidenced in household assemblages relating to hospitality
practices and in the re-use and construction of seemingly archaic Gaelic-style
tower houses, while Gaelic leaders routinely code-switched in their efforts to
subvert the new order (Horning 2018; Logue 2018). Even religious practices
and identities were subject to negotiation, with some outwardly Protestant
planters tolerating and even encouraging Catholic practices (Horning 2018;
Lennon 2019; Tracey and Horning 2019). The case of the Ulster Plantation
raises fundamental questions about the role of the public/private dichotomy in
shaping historical memories, while showcasing the transformative potential
of a re-evaluation of the "past private" for the present and the future.

METHODS AND SOURCES

The evidence brought to bear in this consideration of private life in the
Ulster Plantation includes a range of documentary, cartographic, and material sources. As a Crown-sponsored venture, the Ulster Plantation was
extensively documented. Justifications for the scheme were written down,
rules for its oversight codified, lists of requirements drafted, and, eventually,
deeds for grants of land drawn up and duly recorded. Maps were made of
new territories, often shading the truth in order to appeal to investors. For
the Londonderry Plantation, each of the twelve premier Companies recorded
their discussions in their official minutes, and some retained correspondence
with their agents and envoys. Court documents as well as port records un-
derscore the ways in which the plantation process unfolded. But arguably,
the most useful sources on the Londonderry Plantation were compiled at the
instigation of Sir Thomas Phillips, an English planter and servitor (former

military man) who became the greatest critic of the Londoners. Phillips penned a range of complaints about the failings of the Companies to follow the precepts of plantation, including their inability to remove all Irish as they had been directed, and he commissioned the cartographer Thomas Raven to produce maps of all of the Company settlements in 1622, in order to expose their failings. Phillips's survey of the Londonderry Plantation, coupled with Raven's maps, serves as a rich (if obviously biased) source of evidence for what was and was not present on the lands. His findings so clearly contradicted the more positive claims of the Companies that they were subject to a Star Chamber trial in 1635 which found them in breach of regulations and owing a massive fine of £70,000 (Curl 2000, 140).

Alongside these documentary and cartographic sources, we have archaeological remains which include standing buildings from the plantation, as well as extant village and town layouts, and excavated materials. Excavations have taken place in a number of Company villages as well as in the urban centers of the period, uncovering material culture that speaks as much to the expanding global connections of the early modern world as to the complicated cultural entanglements that characterized daily life. In addition to the built environment, other key sources for studying the plantation period include a range of Gaelic literary sources, from bardic poetry, to historical annals, to the placenames that not only survive in contemporary Ulster, but often can be traced back at least to the early medieval period. Interrogating all of these sources, while not straightforward, provides for a much more nuanced understanding of the complexities of identity negotiation in the early modern period than that provided by traditional narratives of conflict, displacement, and transformation.

BEHIND THE DOORS: CIVIC IDEOLOGY AND LIVED EXPERIENCE

Newtown Limavady, 1622. A planned town designed and overseen by Sir Thomas Phillips, an English soldier, servitor, and plantation undertaker (Moody 1939b) originally responsible for formulating the idea for the Londonderry Plantation, Newtown Limavady appears for all intents and purposes as a successful, even quintessential plantation town as portrayed in a picture map by the cartographer Thomas Raven.[2] As favorably described in a 1611 survey, "Sir Thomas Phillips, Knight, hath erected a water-mill at Lemavady . . . he hath put in good forwardness an Inn builded English fashion, for the relief of passengers passing that way, containing in length 46 foot, and in breadth 17 foot, two stories high" (Brewer and Bullen 1867–1873, 572). Phillips's town, complete with its inn, was a model of what planters were supposed to do, with regular cross streets, timber-framed dwellings, and a central market place boasting stocks as a symbol of civic authority (Boyle 1911; Horning 2013b).

Yet a court case from 1615 provides a tantalizing hint of the very different dynamics occurring inside one of the overtly English-style timber-frame houses that lined the regular street plan of the settlement. In recounting a surprise visitation from an Irish woman, Newtown Limavady resident Anthony Mahue recounted on 24 April 1615 "that this present day Honora ny Gilligan . . . came to this examinate's house in Newtown Lymavaddy, and there desired to have some conference in secret with him; whereupon he called a maidservant of his who well speaks and understands the Irish, and willed her to tell him what the said Honora said" (Mahue 1615 in Russell and Prendergast 1880, 48). Mahue was compelled to rely on his Irish maid to accurately translate the details of the conversation, a conversation that in fact pertained to a seemingly outlandish plot to overthrow English rule and, as a crowning achievement, behead the servitor Sir Thomas Phillips. As this particular plot had been hatched in a pub (discussed below), it was unsurprisingly doomed to failure. But the surviving testimony provides a crucial glimpse into the reality of life in even the most outwardly planned and regulated English settlement. While we know nothing more about Mahue in terms of his own background and origins, it is clear that Honora ny Gilligan knew him, or at least knew of him, in so urgently seeking to speak with him. Further, Mahue's home included at least one Irish servant, an unnamed maid who nonetheless clearly wielded cultural power through her role as a translator. While English may have been common on the streets of Newtown Limavady, the dominant language of the country remained Irish Gaelic. Incoming English who were unable or unwilling to learn any Irish faced an uneasy dependency on Irish interpreters, who, in the words of Patricia Palmer (2003, 267), were of necessity hybrid figures "inhabiting and moving through two linguistic worlds."

To understand the significance of what was occurring behind closed doors in Newtown Limavady, it is worth reflecting on the central role of town building and civic ideology in early modern colonialism (Horning 2013a, 47–48, 242–45). Towns, to the seventeenth-century English mind, conveyed certain ideas and performed particular functions. Key for new towns in Ireland were the requirements to accommodate trade, defense, order, and civility. From a material perspective, towns were also meant to include public spaces. Public spaces were critical for presenting and underpinning civic ideology, for surveillance, and to facilitate emerging capitalistic market economies by providing space for trade and commerce. In keeping with civic ideology, each newly designed Ulster Plantation town was to include a church, a market, and a jail.

From the outside, Newtown Limavady looked to be upholding those principles of civility. Within the town, and inside its homes, the reality was apparently rather different. The dynamics in Mahue's home reflect the demographics throughout the Ulster Plantation, where numbers of incoming settlers were far lower than required by the ambitious plans. While we have as yet no archaeological evidence from the early years of Newtown Limavady, the documentary record is revealing. As late as 1659, and even following years of conflict at mid-century, the population of Newtown Limavady still included significant numbers of Irish. Of 116 individuals deemed to be taxable (male heads of households), 46 were identified as Irish, and 70 as English or Scottish (Pender 1939, 129). While the town thus had a majority of planters, the numbers of Irish residents are far from inconsequential. Interaction between the two groups would have been daily and routine, yet punctuated by episodes of linguistic and cultural incomprehension that undoubtedly heightened anxieties amongst all those present.

Sir Thomas Phillips personally must have embodied those colonial anxieties, as he concomitantly relied on the Irish while vocally condemning their culture and presence (Chart 1928). While his concept for the Londonderry Plantation required the Companies to remove all Irish, Phillips sagely requested and received permission to retain Irish on his own lands (Horning 2013a; Moody 1939b). Years on the ground had given him strategic insight into the actual challenges facing aspirational planters. In addition to founding his own plantation town at Newtown Limavady, Phillips also acquired and redeveloped an existing Gaelic stronghold; the fifteenth-century tower house of the O'Cahan lord, Sir Donal Ballagh O'Cahan, situated in the townland of Gortneyhanemagh. Archaeological excavation of a one-by-two meter trench at the tower house site in 2009 (Horning 2013b) unearthed occupation debris, traces of one wall, and evidence that the castle was demolished early in the eighteenth century. An 1835 description (Day and McWilliams 1991, 57) of the castle noted the periodic recovery of fragments of ornamental ceiling from the ruins of the building, and recent tree falls have displaced finely molded decorative plasterwork similar to that excavated at Dungiven, where another O'Cahan tower house was adapted by Phillips's brother-in-law Sir Edward Doddington, serving as agent for the Skinners' Company (Abraham 1986; Brannon and Blades 1980; Horning 2013a, b). Both men seemed to have been eager to demonstrate their elite positions in the new plantation society, and one can imagine some competitive posturing within their respective holdings, extending to hiring the same itinerant plasterer. Both men rehabilitated Gaelic tower houses, yet also built new manor houses according to English fashion, both with slated roofs, chimneys and ornate glazed windows. The message conveyed by the English-style manor houses seems clear in the context of plantation ideology. But why rehabilitate archaic Gaelic tower houses, and what happened inside, behind closed doors?

Use of the familiar tower house may have normalized the standing of Phillips and Doddington in the eyes of their largely Irish tenantry, previously accustomed to the rule of the O'Cahans as physically expressed in the same buildings. Inside, these English men may have endeavored to enact a version of the same hospitality rituals employed by the Gaelic elite to reify and codify sociopolitical standing (O'Sullivan 2004; Simms 1978), rituals that bore enough of a resemblance to late medieval aristocratic English modes of expression to permit their adoption. Were different visitors received in different buildings? Such was certainly the practice of the Gaelic lord Hugh O'Neill. As interpreted by Paul Logue (2018), O'Neill strategically deployed his own masonry castle at Dungannon, built to a fashion common in the English Pale around Dublin, and his nearby Gaelic *crannóg* (lake dwelling) in Ballysaggart Lough depending upon the identity of his guests, how he wished to self-present, and the nature of his strategic aims. A quintessential code-switcher, O'Neill had been raised in the English Pale but succeeded to the title of The O'Neill, chief of the most powerful Gaelic clan in Ulster. Such code-switching was clearly intended to facilitate particular political outcomes. Given how self-aware O'Neill appears to have been, one can imagine that the material culture employed in each building might also have been overtly chosen in terms of culturally appropriate messaging. Proving this suggestion, however, requires archaeological investigation. No work has taken place to date at the Ballysaggart *crannóg*, while excavations in the vicinity of O'Neill's Dungannon castle focused on architectural traces rather than domestic deposits (Donnelly, Murray, and Logue 2007). While those at the lower end of the social economic spectrum may have had fewer opportunities to selectively manipulate buildings and portable material culture after the fashion of the English as well as Irish elite, archaeological evidence does suggest processes of material exchange and accommodation. For example, the 2009 excavations in the vicinity of the O'Cahan-Phillips castle uncovered intact early seventeenth-century deposits in the same locale where Raven's 1622 picture map indicates the presence of tenant houses and/or ancillary buildings. Tellingly, these deposits included sherds of both locally made, hand-built cookpots and imported English wheel-thrown wares (Horning 2013b). The juxtaposition of these ceramics speaks to changing practices within the household, given the different foodways and cooking techniques implied by the divergent forms.

Forasmuch as Phillips was pragmatic in retaining Irish tenants, no one could accuse him of not promoting the ideals of plantation in his relentless pursuit of the London Companies for failing to uphold the precepts of plantation. In his estimation, the Companies "everywhere break through the terms of these agreements, and only avoid punishment because they are rich enough to purchase valuable friends in England" (Mahaffy 1900, 357). All evidence suggests that Phillips was correct in highlighting mismanagement on the London Company lands, whatever the veracity of his claims about bribery in England. Company agents, charged with following company policy and upholding plantation regulations, more often broke the rules in pursuit of personal gain. Examples abound. At Movanagher, the principal village of the Mercers' Company, the company agent Robert Vernon failed to collect rents, pocketed Company funds, built a gristmill that reportedly ruined grain and "let three townlands under value to some of his friends to be resigned again to his own use." Even more egregiously, Vernon converted the Company's castle (protected by a thick masonry bawn wall) into "a tap-house to sell aqua vitae."[3] Unlike Newtown Limavady, the Company village at Movanagher (as depicted by Thomas Raven in 1622) lacked any coherent street plan and consisted of a mishmash of English as well as Irish-style buildings dotted in and around a forested landscape. Excavations in 1998 in the location of the village, which was abandoned in the mid-seventeenth century, unearthed traces of one of these Irish houses: a subrectangular earthen dwelling with an open hearth rather than the mandated enclosed chimneys (Horning 2001). This structure lay close to the surviving bawn (figure 2.1).

Figure 2.1.   Surviving bawn wall and circular flanker (under tree) at Movanagher.
Photograph by Audrey Horning, 2014.

Associated artifacts include both locally made Irish wares and imported North Devon coarse earthenware. In terms of private lives, then, the English settlers at Movanagher appear to have resided within a clearly Irish-style dwelling with an open fire in the middle of the single room, with an earthen floor that appears to have been regularly swept. As in the Irish tenant houses at Limavady, cooking may have been done in an earthen pot nestled into the coals of the fire, rather than (or in addition to) the more familiar English mode of utilizing a suspended or tri-footed cast iron pot. The surrounding forest spoke of the potential riches to be made from the timber trade (Movanagher possessed a sawmill), but equally provoked fears of attack.

A particular vivid image of the precarity of the Movanagher settlement and the disconnect between public intention and private reality is painted in a 1615 report by the Ironmongers' agent George Canning of an incident that took place in a household about four miles from Movanagher. According to Canning,

> John Browne and his wife and one John Williams . . . and three and one Irishmen their neighbours were sitting by the fire (the wife of the house had beare, wyne, and ale for sale) and as they were sitting together, in came the rebels, some nine of them And fell down upon the Englishmen and bound them, after they bound the three Irishmen that were with, and gagged them with great sticks in their mouths, that they should not crye, they tarried all that day, drinking and making merry with such victuals as they found in the house.[4]

At the end of the day, the rebels killed two of the company and wounded several others. This incident is revealing in many ways. The violence perpetrated by the woodkerne,[5] or rebels, underscored the aforementioned precarity of planters. Yet it should not be forgotten that prior to the arrival of the attackers, the Brownes and John Williams were sitting together *with* their Irish neighbors, enjoying drink and food in Mrs. Browne's illicit alehouse. Such spaces were liminal in all senses—attracting the violence that was meted out by the rebel band, while also providing opportunities for individuals to ameliorate their hardships through the temporary relief provided by alcohol and tobacco. Unlicensed alehouses also are spaces that transcend the public/private divide. The intimate circumstances of the three English people sitting by the fire with their Irish neighbors speaks of familiarity and friendship, destroyed by the unwelcome intrusion of the rebels. But what if the nine had also just been seeking a drink too, and been refused?

When it comes to improper conduct as regards unlicensed drinking places, Mrs. Browne and Agent Robert Vernon were hardly the worst offenders in the Londonderry Plantation. That honor must go to the Drapers' Company agent, Robert Russell, appointed to oversee progress in the building of their principal village, Moneymore. In another Raven map of 1622, Moneymore looks much more functional than Movanagher, as like Newtown Limavady it boasts a gridded street plan, timber-framed houses, a central market, and an imposing castle at the top of the high street. The only questionable elements on the map are eight small Irish-style houses situated on the margins of the orderly settlement. Yet as detailed in a 1618 complaint to the Company, Russell had "built a great and very large and unnecessary brewhouse both to the hindrance and great disturbance of the whole towne," precipitating "drunkenness and profanity," and putting the "whole town in danger."[6] Russell's unnecessary enterprise sucked up all the water from the town's piped supply, while his products were sold in five houses that had been converted into alehouses. The principal consumers of Russell's beverages were inevitably the local Irish, who vastly outnumbered the incoming settlers. What conversations took place in these spaces? Whatever they were, they were most likely conducted in the Irish language, a tongue not understood by the Company's English tenants, who justifiably worried about the dangers to their town. Small wonder that another complaint of Phillips focused on the prevalence of unlicensed facilities throughout the plantation.

Phillips was right to be concerned, because the aforementioned plot in which his beheading was to feature had been concocted by eleven malcontents drinking in yet another unlicensed establishment in the Londonderry Plantation; this time, it was the home of Nicholas Gill on the outskirts of the principal town of Coleraine (Gillespie 1987). Led by Rory Oge O'Cahan, eldest son of the disenfranchised Donal Ballach O'Cahan, and Highlander Alexander MacDonnell (then on the outs with his own family), they hatched a plot designed to return the O'Cahan lands to Rory and to gain MacDonnell prestige and restore his own property rights. As described in the court testimony of co-conspirator Teage O'Lennan

> they should go upon Coleraine, and that Rorie Oge (with some others he would procure) would be drinking there all the day, and that he by a friend could command the guard to betray the town, as by letting them in, and that then, being in, they would burn the town and only take Mr. Beresford and Mr. Rowley prisoners, and to burn and kill all the rest, and to take the spoil of the town. (Russell and Prendergast 1877, 71)

While unsuccessful, it is notable that the centerpiece of their plan involved going unnoticed while drinking all day in a pub in Coleraine, suggesting that their custom was certainly routine, if not wholly welcome. The plotters had plenty of choices for drinking dens in that town, as the Irish Society had decreed in 1612 that Coleraine should only host three taverns and no more than ten alehouses. Insofar as the population of the town even by 1622 in-

cluded only 145 households (Chart 1928), that number of hostelries clearly
was intended to draw custom in from the countryside—including Irish and
Scottish rebels.

PUBLIC AND PRIVATE IN URBAN CONTEXTS

What else might be gleaned in terms of the dichotomy between public and
private in Coleraine town? While Londonderry (discussed below) could legitimately claim to be a relatively well-defended, sustainable English urban
settlement, Coleraine was a different story. The town was built up around the
ruins of a Dominican friary that Sir Thomas Phillips had once converted into
his own manor house, a manor house he was forced to surrender in favor of
the Londoners. A few traces of his manor house have been uncovered, accompanied by some domestic deposits. Imported North Devon pottery sat
on his table alongside expensive Venetian table glass, a tantalizing hint of
the material accoutrements of the entertaining that facilitated his diplomatic
engagements (Brannon 1985b, 1988). Intended to serve as a key entrepôt,
Coleraine was sited near the mouth of the River Bann. The Bann was crucial
for the supply of other Company settlements, while also serving as the chief
conduit for the raw goods being extracted from the Irish countryside—most
notably timber and the salmon and eels of the river itself. Yet Coleraine's
harbor was unapproachable for much of the year and the settlement itself
failed to attract sufficient numbers of investors and inhabitants. Brid McGrath
(2019) has recently highlighted how Coleraine's ruling class (as represented
by councilors) were also not the elite envisioned by plantation theorists, as
they were primarily drawn from the trades and included a significant percent-
age of individuals who were illiterate. Such men would have been reliant
upon scribes for the English language as well as upon those liminal Irish
interpreters previously mentioned. As she notes (McGrath 2019, 48), "the
councilors' limited literacy and consequent poor capacity led to problems
in Coleraine's management and to the exclusion of merchants and Scots. . .
in a naked abuse of power which damaged the town's commercial growth."
While the lower status of the town's councilors is clearly indicative of its
struggles, some of its more "respected" leaders seemed to have set even lower
standards for personal conduct. Tristram Beresford, Coleraine's first mayor,
notoriously embezzled funds and illegally exported the timber products of
the forests of Loughinsholin to England's greatest enemy, Spain (Curl 1986;
Moody 1939a; McGrath 2019).

Far from the highly ordered and well-defended port town depicted by
Thomas Raven in his map of 1622, Coleraine was poorly run by self-

serving individuals who focused on excluding anyone—English and Scots-who might prove to be economic rivals. Tellingly, however, they did not exclude the Irish who could perform labor and serve as a key source and market for local merchandise. Plainly, defense against the Irish was not viewed as a priority for the town, insofar as its defenses consisted of only poorly maintained earthen ramparts (still visible in one corner of Coleraine today). But what of the houses and households in early seventeenth-century Coleraine? According to a 1613 survey, Coleraine consisted of sixty-three houses (out of an intended 116) described as "pretty fine houses for there, but many of them slight and weak for that bleak place, and the reparations of manye of them have been and are verie chargeable to the citie."[7] The earliest houses were erected in linear rows of prefabricated timber framework, on stone sills, with brick chimneys and slate roofs. Excavations in the 1980s (Brannon 1985b; Robinson and Brannon 1982) found well-preserved traces of an early seventeenth-century sill beneath an extant stone house dating to 1674. Unfortunately, the nature of this construction style and the disruption caused by later building and demolition efforts mean that we as yet do not have any significant artifact assemblages in association with these early row buildings to reflect in more depth upon the material character of private life.

Somewhat more evidence exists for the new town of Londonderry, built at the behest of the Irish Society atop the medieval ecclesiastical center of Derry. Unlike Coleraine, Londonderry was well defended, enclosed by imposing schist walls 20 to 26 feet in height and up to 30 feet in width, with eight bastions and four defended gateways (Ó Baoill 2013, 103–5; Thomas 1995). While the new town of Londonderry also suffered from the same forms of corruption and graft that characterized Coleraine, by 1622 Sir Thomas Phillips was able to (grudgingly) report that 109 families were resident within newly built stone dwellings. Two adjoining masonry structures, which may be the remains of a pair of the "lyme and stone" houses recorded by Phillips, were uncovered during rescue excavations in 1980, providing the best evidence we have to date for the actual household spaces in either of the two principal towns. One of the houses measured 18 by 29 feet, the other (only partially uncovered) was 18.6 feet wide and likely of a similar length. The buildings had two-foot-thick stone walls, with flagstone floors, impressive in-built brick ovens, plastered walls, and pantiled roofs (Lacy 1981). These were no temporary or haphazard homes such as were found in the Company villages, but rather well-built urban dwellings whose thick walls and ovens speak to domestic comfort. The artifacts recovered from these buildings have not yet been analyzed[8] but include a range of utilitarian English ceramics as well as continental tablewares.

Evidence from extant port books from Londonderry for the years 1613 to 1615 give a general flavor of imports to the city, and the types of goods that would have been employed in homes like the two on Linenhall Street. The lists are dominated by building materials, foodstuffs, clothing and fashion items, and wine and spirits. One illustrative example is the cargo of the ship the *Bride* that, on October 23, 1614, brought a cargo consisting of coal, salt, aquavitae, hops, green glasses, lanterns, and a range of clothing items and fabric including broadcloth, frieze, cotton, and Genoa fustian. A few weeks later, the ship *Margaret* of Barnstaple brought a more varied cargo, including Spanish and English iron, French vinegar, sugar, salt, fabrics again, cinnamon, prunes, ceramics ("earthen pots," likely North Devon products), twenty-four iron shovels, locks saws, and Newfoundland salted fish (Hunter 2012, 18–19). Such documentary evidence is significantly augmented by finds from the town ditch that encircled the exterior of the walls of Londonderry. A section of this town ditch at Fountain Street was excavated in 1978. Vast quantities of artifacts that had been dumped into the ditch, likely in the aftermath of a fire that swept through the city in 1668, were recovered. Again, this assemblage has not been fully analyzed, but a cursory look at the materials highlights both global connections in the presence of Chinese porcelain cups, French Saintonge tableware, Rhenish stoneware jugs, and Mediterranean storage vessels. The rare recovery of a small wooden wine cask from this feature materializes the alcohol trade and evokes similar images of hospitality and tavern life as referenced above.

Notable as well are the stories hinted at by several surviving pieces of shoe leather found in the ditch which exhibit both Irish and English cobbling techniques. Late medieval/early post-medieval Irish shoemaking techniques relied upon leather thongs to join together the component parts (Lucas 1956), whereas English cobbling practice employed woolen and/or linen thread to stitch together the elements (Grew and deNeergaard 1988). Similar hybrid shoes have been identified in a mid-seventeenth century-context at the Salters Company village of Salterstown (Miller 1991), and in association with the so-called Dungiven costume, a set of clothing (including shoes) found in a bog in 1956 that appears to date to the very late sixteenth or early seventeenth century (Henshall et al. 1961/1962; Horning 2014). Like the transformation in cooking practices implied by the finds of Irish cookware in English plantation villages, the shift in cobbling technology exhibited by the shoes from the town ditch speaks to a process of technology transfer at the level of the individual craftsperson. Someone watched another cobbler and sought to replicate and learn new techniques. This was not a one-way street. The Dungiven shoes were first made in an English manner, and then repaired in an Irish style. It is difficult to ascertain the identities of the cobblers, and indeed of the wearers, but it is possible to consider the time and proximity involved in facilitating shifts in production as well as use. This was an era when people really did believe that clothing, and footwear by extension, had the capacity to transform a person's identity in more than a superficial manner.

RITUAL AND RELIGION

Plantation was supposed to be about identity transformation, but only the uni-directional sort, with the Irish becoming "civilized" through adopting and internalizing English ways of being. Central to this notion of civilizing the Irish was religious conversion. Historical memory teaches us that the religious divide in plantation-period Ulster was absolute, and it is undeniable that the plan for plantation was founded on the importation of loyal Protestants, and the expectation that Catholics would convert, through persuasion or compulsion. Once again, however, what happened in private, and even not so private, undermined the rhetoric. Some prominent planters were in fact practicing Catholics, such as the Hamilton earls of Abercorn, who opened their homes in and around the plantation town of Strabane for Catholic worship. Their actions went uncircumscribed, insofar as they were the wealthiest settlers in the region. Nor were they particularly clandestine in their activities, given that it was obvious that they were attracting principally Catholic Scottish settlers to their lands (Lennon 2019, 165).

In 1629, the Bishop of Derry, George Downham, sent a somewhat equivocal letter of protest to Claud Hamilton:

> I hear that, though your father was given land in Strabane in order to maintain the reformed religion, the place is become the sink into which all the corrupt humours purged out of Scotland are run. Idolatrous Popish masses are daily celebrated. As your Church is heretical and your Pope an anti-Christ, I think it my duty to oppose you, but, before appealing to higher authorities, I write to ask you to come and see me in order that I may convince you that you are in the wrong. (Mahaffy 1900, 511)

Clearly the Bishop was not pleased with what was happening behind closed doors in Strabane, but at the same time, his letter exposes his personal inability to directly impose any change or to mete out any punishment. The letter reads more as an exhortation to talk about the issue in private with the likeliest intended outcome merely to encourage Hamilton to be less overt about his activities, and in fact that is precisely what he exhorted Hamilton to do: "if he would not embrace the reformed religion, that he should keep his own religion to himself and not to seek by himself and such as he entertaineth to pervert others" (Mahaffey 1900). As argued by Robert Hunter (2011, 44), the Catholicism of the Hamiltons had only become an issue in 1629 because of the Anglo-Spanish War (Hunter 2011, 44).

Undoubtedly to the Bishop's chagrin, the Hamiltons were not the only members of Strabane society opening their homes for Catholic worship. James Ferrell, a merchant, also welcomed priests into his home and facilitated Mass for dozens (Lennon 2019, 162). While the Strabane masshouses were intended primarily for incoming Scottish Catholic planters, elsewhere it is clear that English and Scottish Catholics also welcomed Irish Catholics. For example, the English Catholic Brownlow family of Armagh brought Catholic Irish tenants to their lands, and pursued what can only be described as a well thought through strategy of intermarriage with Gaelic elites to facilitate and cement their land claims (Clendenning 2004). The Brownlows had come to Ulster from Nottinghamshire, where they (ostensibly) were practicing Anglicans. They seem to have viewed their arrival in Ulster as an opportunity to practice more openly as Catholics—certainly not the intention of plantation planners and theorists. Yet they were certainly not alone in leveraging their capital to outweigh concerns over their religious beliefs. Randal Arranagh MacDonnell, a Highland Scot, remains the best example of an individual savvy enough to deploy both his political nous and his economic assets to benefit from plantation while remaining resolutely Catholic. MacDonnell, who had once fought against the English on the side of the Irish, curried sufficient favor with James I to not only retain lands in north Antrim on the eve of plantation, but to significantly augment them with further grants of land. Projecting himself as a dutiful servitor, MacDonnell constructed a Protestant house of worship for his settlers near his principal castle at Dunluce. Yet he maintained a private chapel for Catholic worship within this home, actively funneled monies to the Franciscans, and ensured that the nearby friary of Bonamargy was re-edified and updated for open Catholic worship (Breen 2012).

But the Hamiltons, Brownlows, and MacDonnell were operating as planters under a different set of rules than the London Companies were in the Londonderry Plantation. Clearly villages like Moneymore and towns like Coleraine and Londonderry would not be places where evidence of Catholic practices would be found. Or would they? In 1632, Phillips complained that "[t]here are many beneficed priests in the Plantation." Backing up his complaint with evidence, he then listed twenty-four names and the fees those individuals charged for their services, services including marriages, christenings, "extreme unction," burials, and "churning butter." Furthermore, according to Phillips, "there are also vagrant friars who wander about and liv on the county" (names also supplied) and, even more remarkably, seven of the London Companies (Ironmongers, Salters, Drapers, Vintners, Fishmongers, Grocers, and Skinners) had permitted masshouses to be erected on their lands (Mahaffy 1900, 643–44). While Phillips does not mention masshouses on the other Company lands, such as that of the Mercers, it is probable that unofficial masshouses were in operation in areas long associated with worship practices, possibly utilizing field altars or continuing to deploy older religious buildings.

One of the Companies that openly permitted masshouses and Catholic worship on their lands was the Skinners. The Skinners failed to attract many incoming settlers, no doubt because they drew the worst lot when the lands were divided up. Straddling the Sperrin Mountains, the 49,000 acres granted to the Skinners lacked ready access to cultivable lands, was wholly landlocked, and was interspersed with Native and church lands (Curl 1986, 285–87). While they could physically access the fisheries of the River Roe, all rights to the fish themselves had been granted to Sir Thomas Phillips. Sir Edward Doddington, Phillips's brother-in-law, held the charge as the Skinners' Company agent and as such was responsible for building a manor house and bawn from which to discharge his duties. Pragmatically, Doddington focused his energies on the O'Cahan tower house he had already captured and held, re-edifying it and building his manor house immediately adjacent. Unusually, this tower house was appended to a house of worship, a twelfth-century Augustinian priory for which the O'Cahans served as patrons. Still extant inside the chancel of the surviving priory buildings is a remarkable canopied stone effigy tomb. Erected probably in the late fifteenth century to commemorate a mercenary O'Cahan (the sculpted human effigy atop the tomb is clad in the garb of a Highland warrior), the tomb would have been understood as a clearly Gaelic and Catholic object in the early seventeenth century. Such Catholic iconographic representations were frequently the target of Protestant reformers, yet the effigy tomb was left in situ. Clearly visible to the few Protestant worshippers who might have come to the rededicated church, it is also conceivable that the manor house incumbents turned a blind eye to other visitors to this sacred site, even as their manor home was built up against the very fabric of the church.

Sir Edward Doddington died in 1618, but his wife Lady Ann Beresford Doddington (later Cooke) remained mostly in residence until her death in the 1670s (Hamlin and Brannon 2003, 263; Brannon 1985a). Daughter of Tristram Beresford, the deal-making, swindling mayor of Coleraine, Lady Ann may have learned the importance of strategic positioning from a young age. Her widow's inheritance was more than on shaky ground, given the stark demographics on the Skinners' lands. According to Phillips, in 1622 there were a scant twelve British men in residence on the whole of the Company's

Figure 2.2. Surviving fifteenth-century effigy tomb, Dungiven Priory and Bawn.
Photograph by Audrey Horning, 2018.

proportion, versus 348 Irish (Moody 1939a, 218). Yet Lady Ann retained her hold. Her successful strategy was revealed in a complaint lodged against her in 1641: "Lady Cooke brought in no English, but was a great fosterer of Irish Papists" (Mahaffy 1901, 291). The degree to which her brother-in-law, Sir Thomas Phillips, willingly overlooked her open flaunting of plantation expectations is worth considering. Insofar as Phillips lived just over five miles away from Dungiven and that he made it his business to catalog the failing of the companies, he could hardly have been unaware of the comings and goings at Dungiven, and of Lady Ann's pragmatic machinations.

CONCLUSION

For centuries, the success of the Londonderry Plantation has been presumed, notwithstanding some notable hiccups along the way. Historical memory sees the existence of the present-day county of Londonderry as a physical marker of British rule, and as such it is little surprise that in contemporary Northern Ireland, it remains a contested space. The principal city of the Londonderry Plantation, the settlement now officially known as Derry-Londonderry, saw significant levels of violence during the thirty years of the Troubles (1968–1998), and continues to be a flashpoint as Northern Ireland negotiates its (mostly) post-conflict peace. Given this contemporary context, then, the documentary, archaeological, and cartographic evidence for rather more complicated private lives in the early seventeenth-century Londonderry Plantation villages and towns gains greater significance in its capacity to force a reconsideration of longstanding narratives of division and conflict. The private lives of Irish, English, and Scottish individuals and families may have been marked by anxiety and uncertainty in the face of political, social, and economic upheaval and the ever-present threat of violence. Yet those private lives, to judge particularly from the material evidence, not only overlapped but were wholly entangled. Everyday life demanded uneasy alliances, as between Anthony Mahue and his maidservant, between Lady Ann and her Irish Catholic tenants, between Mr. and Mrs. Browne and their Irish neighbors, and between the drinkers who shared social space in one of Moneymore's many alehouses.

NOTES

1. My thanks to the editors for the invitation to contribute to this volume, and for their patience. Research incorporated in this chapter benefitted from funding from the

Arts and Humanities Research Council, the Leverhulme Trust, the (former) Environment and Heritage Service of Northern Ireland (now Historic Environment Division), Queen's University Belfast, William & Mary, and the input of many colleagues, including Nick Brannon, Colm Donnelly, Paul Logue, Rachel Tracey, Elizabeth FitzPatrick, Ruairí Ó Baoill, Robert Heslip, Helen Perry, Colin Breen, Colin Rynne, and Sean Connolly. I am grateful to Roisin Doherty of the Tower Museum, Derry-Londonderry, for access to the archaeological materials from the 1970s and 1980s excavations, and to former City archaeologist, Dr Brian Lacey, for his support, encouragement, and fortitude.

2. See http://www.greatparchmentbook.org/wp-content/uploads/2017/01/BBC-History-Raven.png for this and other Raven maps.

3. Mercers' Acts of Court 1595–1629, Mercers' Hall, London.

4. G. Canning, 1616, *Letter*, 15 Jan 1616, Ironmongers Records, London Metropolitan Archive.

5. Woodkerne is an English term derived from the Irish term *ceithearnaigh*, which could mean both peasant and foot soldier.

6. Drapers' Company Records, Public Record Office of Northern Ireland [PRONI] D3632/A105).

7. Smithes and Springham Report, Carter MSS, Public Record Office of Northern Ireland Mic 9B/12B.

8. The materials have only recently been regrouped and housed securely in a facility overseen by the Tower Museum Derry-Londonderry. I am beginning a project to analyze this material.

REFERENCES

Abraham, A. S. K. 1986. *Fragments of Decorative Plasterwork from Dungiven Priory, Co. Londonderry*. Unpublished undergraduate archaeology project, Belfast: Queen's University Belfast.

Blades, Brooke S. 1986. "English Villages in the Londonderry Plantation." *Post-Medieval Archaeology 20*(1): 257–69.

Boyle, E. M. F-G. 1911. "Records of the Town of Limavady: 1609–1804." *Journal of the Royal Society of Antiquaries Ireland Ser. 6 1*(2): 157–74.

Brannon, N., and B. Blades. 1980. "Dungiven Bawn Re-Edified." *Ulster Journal of Archaeology 43*: 91–96.

Brannon, N. F. 1985a. "Archaeological Excavations at Dungiven Priory and Bawn." *Benbradagh 15*: 15–18.

———. 1985b. "Excavations in New Row, Coleraine." In G. Egan, "Post-Medieval Britain in 1984." *Post-Medieval Archaeology 19*: 168.

———. 1988. "Where History and Archaeology Unite: Coleraine, County Londonderry." In *Pieces of the Past*, edited by Ann Hamlin and Chris Lynn, 78. Belfast: Her Majesty's Stationery Office.

Breen, Colin. 2012. *Dunluce Castle: History and Archaeology*. Dublin: Four Courts Press.

Brewer, J. S., and W. Bullen, eds. 1867–1873. *Calendar of the Carew Manuscripts Preserved in the Archepiscopal Library at Lambeth*. London: Longmans Green.

Chart, D. A., ed. 1928. *Londonderry and the London Companies 1609–1629, Being a Survey and Other Documents Submitted to King Charles 1 by Sir Thomas Phillips*. Belfast: His Majesty's Stationery Office.

Clendenning, Kieran. 2004. "The Brownlow Family and the Development of the Town of Lurgan in the Seventeenth Century: English Origin and the Ulstr Plantation, Part 1." *Seanchas Armhacha 20*(1): 100–123.

Curl, James Stevens. 1986. *The Londonderry Plantation*. London: Phillimore.

———. 2000. *The Honourable the Irish Society and the Plantation of Ulster, 1608–2000*. London: Phillimore.

Day, Angelique Day, and Patrick McWilliams. 1991. *Ordnance Survey Memoirs of Ireland: Parishes of Londonderry IX*. Belfast: Institute for Irish Studies.

Donnelly, Colm, Emily Murray, and Paul Logue. 2007. "Excavating with Time Team at Castle Hill, Dungannon, Co. Tyrone." *Archaeology Ireland 21*(4): 16–19.

Flavin, Susan. 2014. *Consumption and Culture in Sixteenth-Century Ireland*. Woodbridge: Boydell Press.

Gillespie, Raymond. 1987. *Conspiracy: Ulster Plots and Plotters in 1615*. Belfast: Institute for Irish Studies.

———. 2009. "The Problems of Plantations: Material Culture and Social Change in Early Modern Ireland." In *Plantation Ireland: Settlement and Material Culture, c. 1550–1700*, edited by James Lyttleton and Colin, 43–60. Dublin: Four Courts Press.

Grew, F., and M. deNeergaard. 1988. "Shoes and Pattens." In *Medieval Finds from London Excavations 2*. Woodbridge: Museum of London and Boydell Press.

Hamlin, Ann, and Nick Brannon. 2003. "Northern Ireland: The Afterlife of Monastic Buildings." In *The Archaeology of Reformation 1480–1580*, edited by David Gaimster and Roberta Gilchrist, 252–66. Leeds: Maney.

Henshall, A. S., W. A. Seaby, A. T. Lucas, A. G. Smith, and A. Connor. 1961/1962. "The Dungiven Costume." *Ulster Journal of Archaeology 24/25*: 119–42.

Hill, Rev. G. 1970 [1877]. *An Historical Account of the Plantation in Ulster at the Commencement of the Seventeenth Century 1608–1620*. Shannon: Irish University Press.

Horning, Audrey. 2001. "'Dwelling Houses in the Old Irish Barbarous Manner': Archaeological Evidence for Gaelic Architecture in an Ulster Plantation Village." In *Gaelic Ireland, c.1250–c.1650: Land, Lordship & Settlement*, edited by Paul J. Duffy, David Edwards, and Elizabeth Fitzpatrick, 375–96. Dublin: Four Courts Press.

———. 2013a. *Ireland in the Virginian Sea: Colonialism in the British Atlantic*. Chapel Hill: University of North Carolina Press.

———. 2013b. "*Leim an Mhadaigh*: Exploring 'Unwanted' Histories of the Atlantic World." In *Exploring Atlantic Transitions*, edited by Peter Pope and Shannon Lewis-Simpson, 93–102. Woodbridge: Boydell Press.

———. 2014. "Clothing and Colonialism: The Dungiven Costume and the Fashioning of Early Modern Identities." *Journal of Social Archaeology 14*(3): 296–318.

———. 2018. "Minding the Gaps: Exploring the Intersection of Political Economy, Colonial Ideologies, and Cultural Practice in Early Modern Ireland." *Post-Medieval Archaeology 52*(1): 4–20.

Hunter, Robert J. 2011. *Strabane Barony during the Plantation 1607–1641*. Belfast: Ulster Historical Foundation.

———. 2012. *The Ulster Port Books 1612–1615*. Belfast: Ulster Historical Foundation.

Lacy, Brian. 1981. "Two Seventeenth-Century Houses at Linenhall Street, Londonderry." *Ulster Folklife 27*: 57–62.

Lennon, Colm. 2019. "Catholicism and the Ulster Plantation Towns." In *Society and Administration in Ulster's Plantation Towns*, edited by Brendan Scott, 158–166. Dublin: Four Courts Press.

Logue, Paul. 2018. "All Things to All Men: Aodh Ó Néill and the Construction of Identity." In *Becoming and Belonging in Ireland 1200–1600: Essays in Identity and Cultural Practice*, edited by Eve Campbell, Elizabeth FitzPatrick, and Audrey Horning, 269–92. Cork: University of Cork Press.

Lucas, A. T. 1956. "Footwear in Ireland." *Journal of the County Louth Archaeological Society 13*(4): 309–94.

Mahaffy, Robert Pentland, ed. 1900. *Calendar of State Papers Relating to Ireland of the Reign of Charles I, 1625–1632*. London: Her Majesty's Stationery Office.

———, ed. 1901. *Calendar of State Papers Relating to Ireland of the Reign of Charles I, 1633–1647*. London: Her Majesty's Stationery Office.

Mahue, Anthony. 1874 (1615). "Examination of Anthony Mahue, taken before Sir Thomas Phillips, 24 April." In *Calendar of State Papers Relating to Ireland of the Reign of James I, 1615–1625*, edited by C. W. Russell and J. Prendergast, 48. London: Longman.

McGrath, Brid. 2019. "Starting from Scratch: the First Thirty Years of Coleraine's Development." In *Society and Administration in Ulster's Plantation Towns*, edited by Brendan Scott, 36–56. Dublin: Four Courts Press.

Miller, Orloff. 1991. *Archaeological Investigations at Salterstown, County Londonderry, Northern Ireland*. PhD dissertation, University of Pennsylvania.

Moody, Terence W. 1939a. *The Londonderry Plantation*. Belfast: William Mullan and Son.

———. 1939b. "Sir Thomas Phillips of Limavady, Servitor." *Irish Historical Studies 1*(3): 251–72.

Ó Baoill, Ruairí. 2013. *Island City: The Archaeology of Derry/Londonderry*. Belfast: Northern Ireland Environment Agency and Derry City Council.

O'Keeffe, John. 2008. *The Archaeology of the Later Historical Cultural Landscape in Northern Ireland: Developing Historic Landscape Investigation for the Management of the Archaeological Resource: A Case Study of the Ards, County Down, Coleraine*. PhD thesis, University of Ulster, Faculty of Life and Health Sciences.

O'Sullivan, Catherine. 2004. *Hospitality in Medieval Ireland 900–1500*. Dublin: Four Courts Press.

Palmer, Patricia. 2003. "Interpreters and the Politics of Translation and Traduction in Sixteenth-Century Ireland." *Irish Historical Studies 33*(131): 257–77.

Pender, Séamus. 1939. *A Census of Ireland, Circa 1659: with Supplementary Material from the Poll Money Ordinances (1660–1661).* Dublin: Stationery Office.

Robinson, Philip, and Nick Brannon. 1982. "A Seventeenth-Century House in New Row, Coleraine." *Ulster Journal of Archaeology 45*: 173–77.

Russell, C. W., and J. P. Prendergast. 1877. *Calendar of State Papers relating to Ireland, of the reign of James I, 1611–1614: preserved in the Great Britain Public Record Office.* London: Longman and Sons.

———. 1880. *Calendar of State Papers relating to Ireland, of the reign of James I, 1615–1625: preserved in the Great Britain Public Record Office.* London: Longman and Sons.

Simms, Katherine. 1978. "Guesting and Feasting in Gaelic Ireland." *Journal of the Royal Society of Antiquaries of Ireland 108*: 67–100.

Thomas, Avril. 1995. *Derry-Londonderry.* Irish Historic Towns Atlas 15. Dublin: Royal Irish Academy.

Tracey, Rachel. 2017. *From Garrison to Atlantic Port: Material Culture, Conflict & Identity in Early Modern Carrickfergus.* PhD thesis, Queen's University Belfast.

Tracey, Rachel, and Audrey Horning. 2019. "Ulster Plantation Towns: An Archaeology of Rhetoric and Reality." In *Society and Administration in Ulster's Plantation Towns*, edited by Brendan Scott, 6–19. Dublin: Four Courts Press.

Chapter Three

"Bible, Bath, and Broom"

Constructing Race Womanhood in The Chicago Defender

Anna S. Agbe-Davies

Nannie Burroughs was a leader in the national movement on the part of African American women to simultaneously uplift their communities and hold America to its ideals regarding equality and freedom. A reporter, describing her approach, explained: "Nannie Burroughs is a matter of fact woman, and lays chief stress of emphasis on the old fashion virtues of goodness and usefulness. The Bible, bath and broom is her motto. Her appeal is to the average girl, who, by her own character and effort, must make her way through an unfriendly world" (*The Chicago Defender* 1926a).

For Burroughs and her early twentieth-century compatriots, the values of Race[1] womanhood compelled her to care for needy individuals and advance the general public good (Pickens 1921). What was good for the girls she served at the National Training School for Girls (NTSG) was good for society. Likewise, the nation needed reform—a racist patriarchy was no fit society for "the average girl." In their rights work, what they may have called "Race work," women like Burroughs achieved their ends, in part, by making what had been private public, and vice versa. In fact, an examination of their world suggests that the convenient fiction that "public" and "private" are opposites is underpinned by the very fact of their inter-penetration and entanglement. Furthermore, the real-life messiness of these supposedly clear-cut realms created room for African American women to navigate the hurdles before them.

This chapter examines the strategies of African American women through the lens of a single publication, *The Chicago Defender*, an African American newspaper with a wide local and national circulation. I wish to understand how this medium promulgated the ideas that underlay women's Race work and also examine the paper's content for instances where women responded to ideas about "public" and "private" themes—whether using by those categories or contesting them. I focus here on a section that later became "the Woman's Page," where the content includes society announcements, church, arts, and educational news, advertisements, a relationship advice column, and news related to racial "uplift."[2]

I've highlighted Burroughs's alliterative motto "Bible, bath, and broom" because it speaks to the spiritual, corporeal, and material dimensions of her program. It also provides a multi-scalar, inward to outward structure for this chapter. Here, I consider how gender ideologies at work in twentieth-century America operated at multiple scales from private to public, guiding "the average girl" through an unfriendly world. This chapter examines, in turn: the inner self; the body; personal relationships; the worlds of work; and the public sphere. However, part of my argument is that these arenas are inseparable from one another. The public *was* the private; the personal *was* political.

Defender publisher Robert S. Abbott's lifelong mission was to end racial discrimination. It was at the center of his paper's "Platform for America" (see, e.g., *The Chicago Defender* 1922a, b). In exhorting other members of the Race to do what they could for the struggle, he wrote in part, "[people ought to] so conduct themselves as to reflect credit upon themselves, by so doing it will disarm those who are endeavoring to discredit our Race" (*The Chicago Defender* 1917). His advice included instructions for appropriate clothing to wear on the street, how to maintain the exterior of one's home, and standards for the use of city infrastructure and marketplaces. Clearly material culture and its capacity to convey meaning was not far from the minds of early twentieth-century African American influencers in the media and in centers of institutional power.

A photo published by the Detroit Urban League—a branch of the nationwide organization dedicated to the betterment of conditions for African Americans—made the point visually. In the photo, reproduced by Victoria Wolcott (2001, 58) in her book *Remaking Respectability*, a person, notably for our purposes a woman, is shown in two scenes side by side. One image is clearly meant to be a "don't." The subject slouches in a loose-fitting housedress, surrounded by a disorderly assemblage of cleaning supplies. The image contrasts with a "do." Her clothing here is formal; she primly holds a newspaper in her lap. The contrast resonates with the themes espoused by organizations like the NTSG, which sought to train young women "for service, not servants."

The objects in the picture with the woman speak to the scales addressed here: mind; body; dress; relations; home; world. Objects tell a story and Race leaders wanted the narrative to be one of respectability and uplift. I have been engaged in archaeological research for several years (Agbe-Davies

2010, 2011) at the site of the former Phyllis Wheatley Home for Girls—an institution with many of the same aims as Burroughs's school. So I, too, am concerned with the role of material culture in meaning-making.

I've chosen to focus this study of the *Defender* on the year 1926, the year that the Phyllis Wheatley Home for Girls moved to its final location on Chicago's Southside. The women who operated, sponsored, lived in, and were served by the Home would have been intimately familiar with the notions related to a woman's role, racial justice, etc., promulgated by the National Training School for Girls and expressed in the *Defender*. Many of the supporters, staff, and beneficiaries of both institutions were likely readers of the newspaper.

The year 1926 is meaningful for other reasons as well. Nearly a decade had passed since the Great Northern Drive, an effort by the publisher of the *Defender* to inspire a mass exodus of African Americans from the rural south to the urban north for improved opportunities including employment, voting rights, and education. It was five years after a major "riot"—part of the Red Summer in which, over the course of thirteen days, twenty-three black Chicagoans were killed and "clashes developed from sudden and spontaneous assaults into organized raids against life and property" that left about 1,000 people "homeless and destitute" (Scott 1919; Chicago Commission on Race Relations 1922, 1, 7). Furthermore, 1926 sits in the middle of a decade in which the "old fashioned virtues" of womanhood were confronted on the pages of the *Defender* by the idea of the "modern girl" (see also Chatelain 2015). It is a fruitful moment to examine in terms of the eventments of individual daily life and the *longue durée* of nations.

With this analysis, I resist the urge to compare ideologies circulating in African America with those at large in the wider nation. Rather than rein-scribing the categorical (racial) distinctions operating in that historical moment, here I am re-centering that which is African American (Watkins 2019). The problem for this chapter is not "what makes African American women's manipulation of the public/private divide distinctive or different?" Instead, I ask, "what did that manipulation *do*?" and "What were the consequences of these moves?" (Agbe-Davies 2017). My attempt parallels the insistence of Abbott (the *Defender*'s publisher) that people of European descent be designated "white" in his paper—mirroring the treatment of "colored" or "Negro" people in the white press. With this, he flipped the usual relationship between marked and unmarked, rendering whiteness the Other, if only for a while. The beliefs and actions of the women we're interested in were rooted as much in the imperative to survive and resist white supremacy and male domination as they are in African American traditions or early twentieth-century gender norms. So, this project aims to understand these patterns as a way of *doing* rather than a way of *being*.

The contributions in this volume contest or play with the idea of a public/ private divide, and this chapter is no exception. Although I have set up a sequence that purports to move from the innermost (private) self to the wider (public) world, in fact the "private" realm of morality and cultivation was an essential component of a woman's public persona. Likewise, it is impossible to discuss the professional and service roles of women without reference to their most intimately held beliefs. The structure employed here is necessary simply to impose order on a phenomenon that continually folds in upon itself even as it opens up into increasingly wider domains. As with paradise, "The further up and the further in you go, the bigger everything gets. The inside is larger than the outside" (Lewis 1956).

THE INNER SELF

Religion and spirituality strictly defined appear only sparingly on the women's pages. Occasional news stories call attention to the relative openness or lack of race prejudice on the part of a particular faith tradition. But in general, there is little commentary on religious policy, and also little reference to theology or doctrine in discussions of individual morality. Church news is mainly about (men's) leadership: the comings and goings of ministers and the selection of lay leaders, the purchase of houses of worship and the sponsorship of missions overseas. Women appear as workers in the church. They raise money for charitable projects, host visiting dignitaries, and provide social services for women and children. Such work is an important part of a woman's biography. It often features prominently in an obituary, or in stories about a woman's accomplishments. "Mrs. Bundy was a devoted Christian worker, with a record of 68 years of active church life." She is described, as such women often were, as "well known in church circles" (*The Chicago Defender* 1926b).

The tone of stories about women's roles in religious organizations emphasizes efficacy and dedication more than piety, self-sacrifice, or goodness. The work of the church sometimes included saving souls, locally or abroad, but more often it addressed needs of this lifetime. Women looking for guidance on spiritual matters would have found little on that subject printed on the page dedicated to their interests.

Strangely (or perhaps not), matters of right and wrong seldom emerge in the paper's coverage of religion, theology, doctrine, or philosophy. Rather, questions of right and wrong are frequently framed in terms of desirable outcomes, not good vs. evil. We see this pattern in the letters written to Princess Mysteria, the *Defender*'s advice columnist.[3] The problems people came to her with had to do with marital (or extra-marital as the case may be) disputes, conflicts between parents and children, dilemmas about how to treat those the letter writers held most dear. The girl who quarrels with her minister fiancé about wanting to see shows and go out dancing is urged to consider the effect of this disagreement on their relationship, and whether his objections will stifle her happiness, rather than whether dancing itself is moral (Princess Mysteria, August 7, 1926, 5 "Bess").[4]

Princess Mysteria's advice is pragmatic in the sense that the term is usually understood. That is, it was results-oriented. Consider the following dilemma:

> I am a woman, 30 years of age, am single, but am going with a married man old enough to be my father. He is very good to me, has furnished a house for me and gives me anything I want. . . . He does not want me to associate with any other man, but I am really in love with a single man whom I have kept company with for about two years. He is also nice to me. . . . The one I love wants me to marry him. . . . The married man knows of the single one and has threatened to kill me. . . . What must I do, Princess? (Princess Mysteria July 10, 1926, 5 "Unhappy")

Princess Mysteria presents her solution as a choice among competing consequences. Furthermore, her solutions are relational; what matters are your dealings with other people. So, although she explains to the writer that she will always be "Unhappy" until she is "pure in heart," instead of grounding the solution in arbitrary rules about fidelity or chastity, Princess Mysteria examines the specific situation, advising her correspondent that

> You can make your own living if you are any woman at all. Thousands of women are doing so and would gladly continue to do so rather than do what you are doing. My advice to you is to make a complete new start, give the married man his house and furnishings back and begin all over.

Finally, Princess Mysteria's advice is contextual. For example, she had no orthodox position on divorce; for some people seeking her advice it is a solution, for others, a cop-out. The difference is made by the circumstances of the marriage. With her relativism and her emphasis on context and consequences, we find in Princess Mysteria a vision of moral behavior rooted in experience rather than abstractions, an embodied morality which shares a great deal with an embodied sense of decorum.

Manners are the public expression of private cultivation. The cultivated self is a closely held thing; it exists within and through one's own body. And yet, it manifests in utterances and behavior. It can only be known, be meaningful, in public. Nannie Burroughs once gave a speech in which she offered an example of this connection between inner and outer virtue. She recalled traveling on a street car and witnessing

> A miss about sixteen entered a car with one of her friends. A seat built for two was unoccupied, but a woman had laid a package (it was meat, I think) on it. She

did not move it when the two girls came in. One of the girls looked at the space occupied by the meat, while her friend took a seat on the other side. She stood for a minute and then, without saying a word, sat down. She soon whispered to her friend . . . and both laughed heartily. The woman should have moved the meat. . . . She would have, perhaps had the girl been white,[5] but the girl should have gently rebuked her insolence by saying, "Pardon me, is this your package?" (*The Chicago Defender* 1914, 4).

Burroughs presents this public behavior as an indicator of the (private) failure of parents, especially mothers, who "are failing to teach their children good manners."

The overall message in the *Defender* about personal probity is that it is earned (or lost) rather than being an inherent quality of a person. It may require effort, but by the same token, self-improvement is possible. There is no talk of predestination or even incorrigibility. And with respect to the changing standards of the twentieth century, both "old fashioned girls" and "flappers" or "modern girls" could be ladies.[6] It is perfectly okay to love dancing; likewise, there is no shame in being a homebody or cherishing the "oldfashioned" virtues. Readers could rest assured that both kinds of women can be good mothers

> regardless of the outward appearance and conduct of the modern girl, she will provide and love her child as good as the old-time mothers did. . . . [A]fter careful study there has been no difference in the way the mother whose dresses touch above her knees and the mother whose dress touch her shoe tops in caring for her child. "The new mother hood seems to be thriving through the Jazz ages and perhaps it is better for the child," the doctor [Ruth Andrus of the Institute for Child Welfare Research, Columbia University] said." (*The Chicago Defender* 1926c)

It was important to know whether the modern transformations of women's roles could cause harm to children within the privacy of the family, for fear that those children would then become a public burden.

THE BODY

Related to morals and manners, cultivation and self-presentation, are the many ways that women learn to move, manipulate, and dress their bodies. Sometimes, these are inculcated by formal training in practices signaling serious cultural capital. Women and girls featuring on the *Defender*'s pages trained their bodies in this way most noticeably in pursuit of the arts. A number of announcements describe young women seeking voice training, especially overseas. Sometimes these stories make explicit that racism in American artistic circles was what prompted them to continue their education abroad. Further underlining the importance of *learning* in the development of the cultivated self, poise and composure are implicitly adult traits. When they occur in younger girls, people take note. A girl pianist's poise is one of the remarkable elements of her recital. A pair of junior high school students win high praise for their victory in an elocution contest sponsored by the Interstate Literary Association, in which their competitors were high school and college students. Notably, the girls spoke on Booker T. Washington and Frederick Douglass, and reprised their speeches for both a *citizens'* forum in Lawrence and the *citizenship* league of Topeka. Their proper, adult comportment reinforced and provided an important frame for their verbal arguments regarding the assertion of rights (*The Chicago Defender* 1926d).

Movement and postures could literally embody all kinds of social meanings. Take, for instance, the Charleston, a dance that played on white America's fascination with African American art forms. The craze was at peak popularity in the mid-1920s, and featured prominently in discussions of bodily movement and everything that it entails. The dance signified the modern girl. Although some were still suspicious of this girl, as hinted at above, no stigma or whiff of impropriety attached to the dance itself. The Charleston was respectable enough that it could still feature in descriptions of children's parties. The movements of the dance were relevant, however. A labor analyst assessing the value and utility of women in the workplace states unequivocally that while "old maids" made the best workers, young girls were best suited to tasks that require quick movements "like the Charleston" (*The Chicago Defender* 1926e).

The Charleston was invoked in contexts beyond that of the dance itself. In an advertisement for toothpaste, the unseen narrator says of a smiling African American woman, hair bobbed and flanked by dancing figures, "And I Learned How to Charleston from Her!" The advertising copy continues, "Glorious teeth, one of the greatest gifts to the Race, can be kept white and glistening with Colgate" (*The Chicago Defender* 1926f). It is a rare example of a racially non-specific product marketed to a racialized consumer. In an era where black likenesses were used to simultaneously capture white consumers' attention and degrade black people, this company flattered the African American consumer with assertions of superiority and depictions that highlighted, in celebratory fashion, the physical features of blackness and cultural forms with roots in African American practice.

Colgate is one of many preparations advertised to improve people's bodies. Medicines to clean the inside of the body, especially the liver and kidneys, promise greater energy and also improved looks. These include cures especially for women, such as Lydia Pinkham's tonic. In ads that frequently feature customer testimonials, women are urged to try a product that would enable them to work harder and to effectively care for their families. Weight loss preparations constitute an area of internal *and* external improvement. These formulas, unlike women's tonics, are designed to improve one's appearance (as measured by popularity and attractiveness to men), rather than one's health or stamina.

But a woman's relationship with personal care products is not only private. The use of these consumer goods can potentially shape personal and professional relationships. Significant attention is given to cleaning products such as soaps and shampoos. These products for cleansing the outside of the body frame the problem as one of causing offense to others by being untidy to look at, or giving off an unpleasant odor, rather than one's own health or preferences. The soaps and powders furthermore promise to project an air of daintiness and gentility, sophistication, even, when one selected fine products with desirable qualities: "Soothing, beguiling—giving that same luxurious, fragrant feeling you used to pay fantastic imported-soap prices for!" (*The Chicago Defender* 1926g). As for the connection between these products for the body and the world of work, recall that ads for these consumer products (hose, wigs, cosmetics, etc.) frequently include an appeal for agents to sell these goods locally. An individual woman thus engaged with the marketplace not only as a private consumer, but potentially as a public advocate for Race interests and as a promoter and sales agent for a given product.

The most prominent advertisements, especially in terms of column inches, are those for hair and skin preparations designed specifically for African American users. These include items especially suited to, for example, darker complexions or curly hair, as well as preparations intended to change or mask these features. Vendors of such goods addressed their African American clientele directly and explicitly. Some ads used language we may read as coded—promising to "soften" "coarse" or "wiry" hair, or to fix "uneven" pigmentation. But these products were not only to fix "problems" specific to African American bodies. Additional culprits included dandruff, psoriasis, and hair loss or breakage. In fact, hair growth seems to have been a more urgent need than hair straightness.

Ads for hair products were directed at men as well as women. Endorsements from Race celebrities attested to the quality of these products. "Hi-Ja helps me wonderfully in keeping my hair in perfect condition [says a petite star of the Ebony Follies, continuing that their hair dressing and beauty soap are] absolutely necessary to any woman who wishes her hair to be ever pretty and always admired." She goes on, "my husband . . . also finds Hi-Ja Quinine

Hair Dressing indispensable" (*The Chicago Defender* 1926h), echoing the sentiment of many ads that these products are not only for women.

Non-medical skin preparations can be further broken down into cleansers, makeup, and skin lighteners. Makeup brands appealed to women's desire to find shades suited to their complexions. Just as hair preparations had uses beyond changing African Americans' hair to resemble that of "the other group," bleaching creams like Golden Peacock promised whiter skin in the headlines, but described other remedies the treatment would provide:

> No more blackheads, no more sallow skin, no more freckles! Science has made a new discovery which clears and whitens your skin with amazing quickness. Almost over night you can clear your skin of freckles, pimples, redness, roughness, blotches, muddiness or any blemish. Soon your complexion takes on that clear, smooth beauty that everyone envies and admires." (*The Chicago Defender* 1926i)

So, it makes sense to situate the "problem" of skin color among a host of other concerns, and not assume that it was the only one motivating those looking to change their appearance.

Advertisements for hair and skin care products frequently appeal to Race solidarity. They highlight the role of African American entrepreneurs in developing toiletries tailored to African American desires. The copy for a product line sold by Mamie Hightower (a fictional figure no doubt modeled on Madam C. J. Walker) read in part:

> Every reader of this paper has heard of Madame Mamie Hightower, benefactress of Our Race. Madame Hightower is devoting her life to the creation of preparations which will glorify the beauty of our womanhood and place us in our rightful position among the peoples of the world. (*The Chicago Defender* 1926j)

Makeup was about so much more than one's personal appearance. As indicated here, it could also promote the interests of the Race at large. In addition, opportunities to sell these goods as local agents are framed as a way for a woman to earn a good and independent living. Agents were especially needed, the ad continues, if the readers' local druggist showed insufficient interest in the purchasing power of "our Group," and failed to stock the products that members of the Race desired.

Moving outward from the surface of the body itself, we come next to clothing and related items such as jewelry and other accessories.[7] Advertisements for dresses emphasize materials, design, and especially *cost* over the kinds of durable embellishments—like decorative fasteners—that an archaeologist like me would be likely to find. Likewise, ads for other dress products (hose, shoes, jewelry, and watches) emphasize cost, quality, and the ability to order "Cash On Delivery" in order to fully inspect the product before buying.

The Charleston dance style mentioned above had a significant impact on the fashions with which women clothed their bodies. More generally, the dress of a flapper—short skirted and uncorseted—signified a whole host of ideas about modern women and girls. But the flapper was not necessarily out of step with the mainstream either ideologically or sartorially. In news stories and features, women presented as paragons of womanhood and sobriety are photographed in outfits that expose the leg. Indeed all of the advertisements for ready-made dresses depict the shorter, freer style, for example, with "Latest Flared Skirt" and "NEW TWO WAY COLLAR," in colors like Lipstick Red (*The Chicago Defender* 1926k). Franklin-Smith and Co., a Chicago-based firm, even sold a dress design called "The Charleston" (*The Chicago Defender* 1926l).

The above items were suitable for everyday wear. Fancy dress norms were another matter. Information about these can be discovered in society notices, especially descriptions of wedding parties. In such stories, the men's clothing is only occasionally described, often simply in terms of color and the degree to which it set off the women's costumes. Again, fabric, color, and cut rule the day, more than the "hard parts" such as fasteners and the like. Some of the reporting concerning women's attire includes dress items that were also heirlooms or gifts, such as fine jewelry, handkerchiefs, and purses, for example: "The groom's present to the bride was a platinum and diamond pin" (*The Chicago Defender* 1926m). Thus the stories indicate how private histories and relationships could be put on display and made legible to a much wider public.

Dress is a fertile ground for contestation between men and women. A number of disputes between romantic partners described in Princess Mysteria's lonely hearts column include women complaining that they cannot get adequate clothing. As a consequence, they are forced to stay home, unable to work or socialize. Clothes facilitated sociability on many levels (Princess Mysteria March 13, 1926, 5 "S. J. J."). From this it follows that deprivation was an effective form of control. While employment was the norm for African American women in Chicago at this time (as we shall see below), because a woman's income was often essential to support her family, in the consumer sphere, employment is frequently framed as an opportunity for independence *from* other family members.

INTIMATE OTHERS

A number of women writing to Princess Mysteria describe their romantic relationships as relations of dependence. They are reluctant to leave partners who provide shelter, clothing, and other things that they deem necessary. Both married women and unmarried women express this dilemma. As noted above, Princess Mysteria's advice is very pragmatic, she is less concerned with the abstract morality of the exchange, or the mentions of sex outside of marriage, than she is with the social chaos caused by infidelity, the bad example parents could be setting for their children (who, furthermore, may be placed in harm's way), and the damage that impermanence and ambiguity can do to an individual's psyche. Her frequent advice is often a version of: many women work to support themselves, if you feel trapped in a sexual relationship, marital or otherwise, the best way out is to find a job that allows you to provide for your own material needs and wants.

Although not a frequent topic outside of Princess Mysteria's advice column, the articles on the Women's Page occasionally did concede that female sexuality exists. The most clear-cut example is the announcement of a new sociological study by a Dr. Katherine B. Davis, of the bureau of social hygiene, "to ascertain what is the normal woman's sex life from infancy to old age." Her proposal included the use of questionnaires to address pressing concerns about birth control, sex knowledge, and the best age for marriage, among other topics (*The Chicago Defender* 1926n).[8]

However, sexuality appears in the paper, more often than not, as a problem to be managed rather than as a simple fact of life. In one telling column, Princess Mysteria addresses what could be called a case of dementia-induced hypersexuality by the letter writer's mother. Princess Mysteria counsels the daughter in much the same way she would the mother of a wayward child. Tellingly, she marks the mother's behavior as that of a "female," but not that of a "woman." In doing so, she draws a distinction between the immoderate and the cultivated self—the latter being a true woman (Princess Mysteria, December 25, 1926, "Worried Daughter"). Princess Mysteria acknowledges women as sexual beings while freely and frequently reminding readers of the existence of a sexual double standard. As she explains it, it remains a woman's responsibility to control herself and, if needed, to curb the male instinct. Furthermore, she observes that men and women face different consequences for similar actions. At times, she appears to commiserate with women trapped in this bind, but for the most part her advice centers on how to navigate this unfair landscape.

A theme that is almost invisible in the *Defender* (but is the subtext of much of the literature circulated by the women engaged in projects like the NTSG) is the idea that one woman's personal (sexual) virtue might have consequences for other African American women if her actions were to reinforce negative racial stereotypes. Standards must be upheld for the sake of oneself and one's family, but also for the Race at large (Davis 1922). These ideas are absent in Princess Mysteria's column, and find very little mention anywhere on the Women's Page. I would argue that the lacuna is actually meaningful. This matter, affecting the public lives of African Americans nationwide, is nonetheless not to be spoken of publicly. If addressed at all on these pages, the problem of virtue is displaced across class lines: the mores of the impoverished are to be improved, full stop. The effect on the reputation of all African Americans is left as subtext.

On the other hand, Princess Mysteria is very explicit about the need for parents, especially mothers, to protect their daughters from problematic scenarios, encounters, and persons. She cuts considerable slack for mothers who go overboard in their strict discipline because of the seriousness of the problems a young girl could face by what is usually termed "compromising her virtue."

> Why do you think your parents forbade him [an older man with another sweet-heart] the welcome of their home? Did you think it was in order that you could sneak out and meet him secretly? . . . It is a man's nature to seek that which has been forbidden him. . . . Your lover does not respect you or he would not allow you to meet him clandestinely against your parents' wishes and with the conscious knowledge that the community in which you live is ashamed of you. (Princes Mysteria, May 22, 1926)

So we see that she scolds wayward daughters, not for having fallen, but for going against the wisdom of their elders and for disrupting the social fabric. And she stops short of deeming such young women "bad" girls. Inexperience and poor judgment, not flaws of character, make them vulnerable, rather than wicked. The solution is education and firm guidance, not punishment.

In such an environment, one might expect to see women pretending to be married. So it seems a bit strange that the paper offers many more instances of secret marriages than sham marriages. The arrangements are usually between young partners, often while still in school. Neither the belated marriage announcements that families make when the marriage is finally revealed nor the letters to Princess Mysteria delve into the question of *why* one would keep a marriage a secret. One suspects that parental disapproval plays a role. In some instances, young people appear to have feared the loss of educational opportunities or access to resources if the marriage is revealed (Murray 1987). For example, there was the high school graduation at which an eighteen-year-old girl finally admitted to her parents that she had been married for over a year (*The Chicago Defender* 1926o). The letters are mostly about whether to reveal the fact of such a liaison, or the difficulties arising because the commitment has not been made public, not whether this is an advisable strategy.

As for conditions within marriages, or other household relationships, domestic violence appears only sparingly on the Women's Page. This is probably because little in the way of hard news is reported in that section of the paper. Most of the instances appear in Princess Mysteria's column. Physical violence within a marriage was more frequently perpetrated by men against their female partners. Some women did strike back and in at least one instance a husband writes asking how to diffuse his wife's violent behavior without resorting to violence himself. Princess Mysteria often counsels that meeting violence with violence was not a solution. She reminds her readers that law enforcement and courts are one important means of preserving personal safety, yet she does not always recommend this course of action. Frequently she suggests divorce or some other form of separation—removing oneself from the situation rather than trying to punish or change the perpetrator. She scolds women who stay in abusive homes, observing that such treatment progressively breaks down the self and is thus a wasting of one's life.

Mothering is another important intimate relationship that dominates the Women's Page. According to Princess Mysteria, children born out of wedlock should bear no stigma, though she is less sanguine about the parents. Her oft-repeated phrase is that "there are no illegitimate children, only illegitimate parents." Outside of her column, there is little indication of the dilemmas faced by mothers without husbands.

Conversely, the problems of wives without children come to the fore in advertisements. For example, one medicine promises to fulfill a woman's desire for "A Baby in [Her] Home." Even more commonly advertised products are those that purport to alleviate the toll that rearing a baby (and caring for a family) takes on a woman, such as the patent medicines described above. These ads promising renewed energy for mothers acknowledge the fact, seldom addressed even implicitly, that the care women provide to the people they love is nonetheless *work*. It is work, even though it takes place inside the home.

THE WORLDS OF WORK

The ideology of the separation of spheres (male:female :: public:private) was alive and well in early twentieth-century Chicago. Families generally preferred to keep women out of the work force and at home.[9] Work outside the home was not usually desirable, though as noted above, it may have been better to work, even in an undesirable occupation, than to be compromised in some way. Even so, in the *Defender* women's employment outside of the home is a common scapegoat for juvenile delinquency as well as poor infant and child health. The ads that promised to restore women's energy for "work" refer to family care, not financial support through employment.

Wedding announcements offer a clear indicator that, ideally, women's work is inside the home. The professional lives of women with careers—teachers, social workers, and office staff—are acknowledged in these stories, but more often than not in the past tense. Women who worked through their married lives were often highly trained professionals (doctors, educators, and lawyers), artists (especially in musical performance), or owners of their own businesses (such as catering or dressmaking). It is worth noting that this last career track bears the closest resemblance to the kinds of tasks that women perform for their families: food preparation; hostessing; caring for the home and its contents. These roles also gesture toward the realm in which the vast majority of African American women could find work, but seldom saw represented on the *Defender*'s pages: domestic service.

Women who remained at home were visibly responsible for the acquisition and upkeep of the family's possessions as well as providing hospitality to visitors. Party and society announcements in the newspaper acknowledge this work, to the point that an announcement for a men's club meeting that names a male host stands out to the attentive reader. Women whose families could afford to hired other women to perform household labor, but the credit went to the woman of the house. Women decorated their homes in ways that are publicly commented upon, whether describing relatively permanent household furnishings or ephemeral party decorations such as flowers or favors for guests.

The home was a private place that ideally belonged only to its family, however frequently they entertained guests and publicized that fact in the *Defender*. Nevertheless, housing conditions in Chicago were artificially constrained by restrictive covenants that severely limited where African American families could live. Therefore, crowding and higher costs plagued many families, who sought to alleviate the problem by taking in roomers or "doubling up." Frequently, women mediated these relationships. Renting a portion of the family's private space to roomers could be a path to financial stability. However, roomers were also a potential threat. News of thefts by roomers and the looming specter of marital infidelity—real or imagined—stalked these hybrid public/private relationships.

In the *Defender*, women are understood to be the economic stewards of their homes, even in their role as consumers. On their economy rests the financial security of the other members of their household. A woman who does not work outside the home nevertheless contributes to its economic stability by being a thrifty and resourceful consumer.

As already noted, Burroughs declared that her school was about preparing young women for "service, not [to be] servants," yet most of the African American women who were employed at mid-century (in Chicago anyway) worked as servants in private homes. Drake and Cayton, using the U.S. Census of 1930, found that only a little over 9 percent of employed Negro women had pierced the "job ceiling" and worked in professional, business or clerical positions; 55 percent of working women worked as servants (Drake and Cayton 1993 [1945], 226). Service work is nearly invisible in the *Defender*. The people whose lives featured on the Women's Page are usually engaged in so-called "clean work," if they work for money at all. A significant number of women clearly saw their volunteer work, in churches and charitable institutions for example, as a full-time vocation.

THE WIDER WORLD

There are at least two "wider worlds" that I wish to consider in this chapter. The first consists of people with whom one has no ongoing relationship: strangers, a group that includes the woman on the streetcar who one might never see again. A subset (yet simultaneously over-arching category of public—and one of which readers of the Women's Page would have been excruciatingly aware) was white America. Encounters with these two categories-of-person were often in the context of employment outside the home or of social activism.

The mothering responsibilities of adult women are projected into the public sphere when they are employed as teachers, school administrators, and social workers. Women's volunteer efforts reflected in the paper frequently center on the welfare of children (and other vulnerable groups: wounded veterans; the elderly). When individual households' care for their children was deemed inadequate, women (employed or volunteer) stepped into the breach, financing and operating children's homes, soliciting donations for everything from Christmas baskets to medical facilities; doing care work at a community scale (Chatelain 2015). Patricia Hill Collins (1987) includes such advocacy and service in her concept of "other mothers."

Advocates also sought to open up other fields for African American women. For example, trade groups and civic organizations sponsored job fairs to connect willing employers with African Americans eager for new opportunities, highlighting the underutilization of black women's talent. News stories point out that while the (domestic) service industry could absorb many women, at the time, few spaces existed in more desirable and lucrative industrial and commercial employment (*The Chicago Defender* 1926p, see also Drake and

Cayton 1993 [1945]). Women like Burroughs and the sponsors of the Phyllis Wheatley Home for Girls sought to dignify all forms of work. Some did so by professionalizing and organizing the work force. In their estimation, it was in part the *private* nature of domestic service that made its workers so prone to exploitation and abuse (Princess Mysteria, October 2, 1926, 5 "Billie"). Organizing was one technique for taking private labor public.

The *Defender* took other aspects of private life public as well. Via its pages, the achievements of the Race could be more widely known. The stories about Race pioneers in the professions or the public sector were directed primarily toward other African Americans, however, the echo of the achievements chronicled in the paper were likely to reach white ears as well. And, indeed, the *Defender* was careful to note those occasions when African Americans appeared in the white press in a favorable light, or when they were received with common human courtesy in situations where the rules of Jim Crow might still normally apply.

Consumption, conspicuous and otherwise, is another arena in which the achievements of Race people (in terms of wealth and taste) could be made public. Hundreds of single-sentence entries in the "Society" column depict women motoring to vacation cottages, to the Indianapolis 500, or to conventions and fairs. Automobile trips undertaken by women traveling alone or in single-sex groups were not so unusual. On these journeys, the means of transport as well as the destinations attested to the wealth of the participants. The gift of a car from a husband to a wife occasionally appeared in the Society section, while other, presumably equally expensive, presents went unmentioned. Some women even ventured abroad, either on a grand tour or to study with international experts in their chosen fields—opportunities that were generally unavailable to Race women in the United States.

A significant number of journeys were to visit friends and relatives. Announcing these events in the "Society" column served to make these otherwise private relations public. These entries demonstrated networks that connected the participants in the Great Migration to people "back home" and advertised the cosmopolitan experiences of world travelers. Of course, the other reason for selecting private automobile travel, and for "visiting" far-flung family and friends, was to avoid the indignities of segregated interstate travel and lodging. Refused public accommodation, Race people turned to private options. Reports of people refused service and the strenuous efforts of, for example, conference organizers trying to connect attendees with home stays or charter private trains (*The Chicago Defender* 1926q) demonstrate how pervasive the problem was, holding a mirror up to America, should it care to notice.

Conventions were the ultimate assertion of the right to be in public and to function as a member of the public. As seen in the pages of the *Defender*, African Americans congregated to work for the public good. These conventions were intended to change American society, often by engaging with its institutions: the church; the various levels of government; schools; or the judicial system.[10] For women participants, conventions might be the closest they came to engaging with the public sphere as political actors. Although women had the right to vote, and African Americans were an important constituency in Chicago, little news about electoral politics appears on the Women's Page. Much more common are explicit calls to voluntary action and service in defense of the Race and the civil rights of its members.

One example of this "privatized" public advocacy is reflected in the stories about business bureaus and chambers of commerce that sought to create alliances among African American business owners. Reports of celebratory events like the United States Sesquicentennial described opportunities to put the progress of the Race on display. Exhibits of inventions and artistic performances emphasized the accomplishments of a group of people still thought of as only recently removed from slavery. Men usually ran conventions of the various Christian denominations, but women held important leadership roles as heads of committees for mission work, child welfare, etc. Women, in their capacity as mothers to the Race, occasionally banded together with other women "(white)," in interracial organizations focused on topics of mutual interest (youth welfare, infant health, Christian missionary work abroad), or directly addressed race relations and racial inequality (*The Chicago Defender* 1926r, 1926s).

SO WHAT?

With this chapter I have argued that all of the ostensibly different "scales" I describe in fact inform one another, that the contents of the Women's Page reflect a continual challenge to the neat private/public dichotomy. Women could deploy the apparatus of each concept (dress, social relationships, etc.) strategically, but playing with the boundaries between them also produced effective results. By bringing what was ostensibly private into public view, and conversely taking public concerns into their own hands as individual citizens, Race women accomplished a number of goals. They protected the most vulnerable members of society. They learned about new technologies and commodities while simultaneously projecting respectability and good taste. These women also articulated a vision for women's equality and dignity within their families and in their places of employment.

Many have argued that the *Defender* was an important agent in the production of an imagined community—a national African American community that transcended the local, was informed about developments in far-off locations, and that was aware of the challenges faced by its members, individually and collectively. This chapter has shown that the paper was no less important for producing a community of Race women without whom the transformations of the coming decades, what in hindsight we can call the long Civil Rights movement, would have been impossible. These intersecting discourses (both national and local) were about how to be a woman and how to be a citizen—in other words, how to be a credit to, as well as an advocate for, the Race.

Princess Mysteria's column is in many ways the inverse of the rest of the Women's Page: it revealed women's struggles, their human frailties, rather than projecting the ideal woman. Was this because the content was (to all appearances) generated by the public, rather than a publisher, editorial board, or society reporter? This question is still relevant in the twenty-first century. A rush of commentary and scholarship has examined the way that African American women have used social media platforms to reveal hidden abuses, to insert themselves into public spaces, to see and be seen. Campaigns like #sayhername focus national attention on the deadly racism and sexism that seem to be otherwise easily ignored in polite company (Brown et al. 2017). Women of color from ordinary backgrounds, like the creators of #metoo, have found the leverage by which to challenge and even topple powerful corporate leaders, high government officials, and popular entertainers who would otherwise have continued to, quite frankly, direct the fates of nations (Afzal and Wallace 2019).

The Bible, bath, and broom are more powerful tools than Burroughs perhaps let on. By assisting the average girl as she develops the art of navigating among these domains, one can hope to transform an unfriendly world. The inside is larger than the outside.

NOTES

1. Early twentieth-century publications by and for African Americans often used the label "Race" self-referentially, instead of or alongside other contemporaneous labels like "colored" or "Negro."

2. Uplift as a concept encompassed such topics as racial advancement, civic participation, correct behavior, refinement, and the withering of racial discrimination that would presumably ensue.

3. Princess Mysteria was the stage and pen name of Vauleda Strodder, a spiritualist and performer whose advice column "Princess Mysteria's Advice to the Wise and Otherwise" ran for the ten years before her death in 1930 (*The Chicago Defender* 1930).

4. As it happens, this day's column included one of the rare references to Christian spirituality. A "discouraged, motherless girl" asks for readers' prayers. Although, even here, the efficacy of prayer is in the encouragement that it offers the letter-writer,

rather than the intervention of a Higher Power (Princess Mysteria August 7, 1926, 5 "Faith").

5. We will return to the significance of Burroughs's speculation on the role that race may have played in this encounter.

6. An observer praises the NTSG for having "no flappers," continuing, "The girls are neatly and becomingly dressed." However, in claiming that "You can never build the womanhood of a strong and sterling race upon the basis of the flapper," he appears to be referencing the term's association with frivolity and "extravagant displays" rather than modern attitudes toward a woman's place and abilities (*The Chicago Defender* 1926a, 5).

7. In between the categories of clothing (draped on the body) and body preparations (applied to or within the body) there are things like charms, incense, and other products that enhance the body, especially its attractiveness.

8. Incidentally, this article appeared directly under "Defends Modern Girl," discussed earlier (*The Chicago Defender* 1926c).

9. Although much had changed in the intervening years, later, in 1940, 38 percent of African American women were housewives. Nearly 36 percent were in the labor market (working or looking for work) (Drake and Cayton 1993 [1945], 215).

10. For the ongoing study of the nineteenth-century antecedents of this work, see http://coloredconventions.org/.

REFERENCES

Afzal, Sarah, and Paige Wallace. 2019. "#MeToo as a Node on the Feminist Mesh." *South Central Review 36*(2): 131–55.

Agbe-Davies, Anna S. 2010. "Archaeology as a Tool to Illuminate and Support Community Struggles in the Black Metropolis of the Twentieth and Twenty-First Centuries." *Public Archaeology 9*(4): 171–93.

——. 2011. "Reaching for Freedom, Seizing Responsibility: Archaeology at the Phyllis Wheatley Home for Girls, Chicago." In *The Materiality of Freedom: Archaeologies of Postemancipation Life*, edited by J. A. Barnes. Columbia: University of South Carolina Press.

——. 2017. "Where Tradition and Pragmatism Meet: African Diaspora Archaeology at the Crossroads." *Historical Archaeology 51*(1): 9–27.

Brown, Melissa, Rashawn Ray, Ed Summers, and Neil Fraistat. 2017. "SayHerName: A Case Study of Intersectional Social Media Activism." *Ethnic and Racial Studies 40*(11): 1831–46.

Chatelain, Marcia. 2015. *South Side Girls: Growing up in the Great Migration*. Durham: Duke University Press.

Chicago Commission on Race Relations. 1922. *The Negro in Chicago: A Study of Race Relations and a Race Riot*. Chicago: The University of Chicago.

Chicago Defender, The. 1914. "Nannie H. Burroughs on Ill-Bred Youngsters." April 11, p. 4.

——. 1917. "Things That Should be Considered." October 20, p. 12.

——. 1922a. "Defender's Platform for America." February 25, p. 16.

——. 1922b. "Defender's Platform for America." April 1, p. 12.

——. 1926a. "Praises Work of Training School." August 21, p. 5.

——. 1926b. "Widow of the Rev. Jason Bundy Dies at Age of 81." January 16, p. 5.

——. 1926c. "Defends Modern Girl." December 4, p. 6.

——. 1926d. "Young Girls Win Oratory Contest: 12-Year-Old High School Pupils Triumph over College Students." February 20, p. 5.

——. 1926e. "Says Old Maids Ablest Workers." May 1, p. 5.

——. 1926f. [Untitled display ad.]. June 19, p. 5.

——. 1926g. [Untitled display ad.]. May 22, p. 5.

——. 1926h. [Untitled display ad.]. July 31, p. 5.

——. 1926i. [Untitled display ad.]. August 7, p. 5.

——. 1926j. [Untitled display ad.]. November 27, p. 4a.

——. 1926k. [Untitled display ad.]. March 6, p. 5.

——. 1926l. [Untitled display ad.]. August 28, p. 5.

——. 1926m. "Society Throngs Spring Wedding." May 22, p. 5.

——. 1926n. "To Study Sex Life." December 4, p. 5.

——. 1926o. "Keeps Wedding Secret for Almost a Year." June 19, p. 5.

——. 1926p. "Equal Rights League Petitions the President." June 5, p. 5.

——. 1926q. "Baptists Hold Meet in S.C." June 26, p. 5.

——. 1926r. "Women of Both Races in Meet." December 4, p. 5.

——. 1926s. "Baptists Hold Annual Missionary Convention." November 27, p. a4.

——. 1930. "Princess Mysteria Pens Last 'Advice to the Wise.'" March 22, p. 1.

Collins, Patricia Hill. 1987. "The Meaning of Motherhood in Black Culture and Black Mother-Daughter Relationships." *Sage* 4(2): 3–10.

Davis, Elizabeth Lindsay. 1922. *The Story of the Illinois Federation of Colored Women's Clubs*. New York: G. K. Hall & Co.

Drake, St. Clair, and Horace A. Cayton. 1993 [1945]. *Black Metropolis: A Study of Negro Life in a Northern City*. Chicago: University of Chicago Press.

Lewis, C. S. 1956. *The Last Battle*. New York: Collier Books.

Murray, Pauli. 1987. *Song in a Weary Throat: An American Pilgrimage*. New York: Harper & Row.

Pickens, William 1921. *Nannie Burroughs and the School of the Three B's*. New York: [Publisher not identified].

Princess Mysteria. 1926. "Princess Mysteria's Advice to the Wise and Otherwise" in *The Chicago Defender*.

Scott, Emmett J., edited. 1919. "Letters of Negro Migrants of 1916–1918." *Journal of Negro History* 4(3): 290–340.

Watkins, Rachel J. 2019. The Role of Black Feminist Theory in Critiquing Scientific Practices and Concepts of Race. Invited talk, Department of Anthropology, the University of North Carolina, Chapel Hill.

Wolcott, Victoria W. 2001. *Remaking Respectability: African American Women in Interwar Detroit*. Chapel Hill: University of North Carolina Press.

Chapter Four

The Warmth of the Hearth

Andean Domestic Life among Colonial Textile Mill Workers

Rachel Corr

In 1661 Diego Masaquisa, an indigenous Ecuadorian man, told a judge about how he was forced into unpaid labor.[1] Masaquisa was a worker on one of the estates owned by the Spaniard Antonio Lopez de Galarza, who ran a large textile mill in the region. At the time of his declaration, Masaquisa said he had worked on the estate for three years without pay. He agreed to work there only after the estate managers took him to the mill, where he saw other indigenous men being whipped, and they told him that he too would be sent to the mill if he didn't agree to serve as a laborer on the estate. As an estate worker, he had to stay up all night guarding the crops from the manager's dogs, and he stated: "and so that I don't suffer being whipped, I can't spend even one night with my wife and children, or know the warmth of the hearth during the time of the worst rains."[2]

The reference to family and "the warmth of the hearth" captures the simultaneous longing for the intimacy of home-space and family. The domestic lives of indigenous people were disrupted by forced labor in the textile economy, which included the large estates associated with textile mills. Ecuador's Andean indigenous population includes the descendants of many people who were enslaved in large textile mills (called *obrajes*) during the colonial period, which lasted from 1534 to 1822. While mines in the central and southern Andes supplied silver to the Spanish Empire, a secondary market developed in the northern Andes to supply cloth to populated mining centers. Most mill owners were of Spanish descent,[3] while labor was drawn from the native population—the indigenous people of the central and northern highlands of Ecuador. Colonial documents refer to the native Andeans as *indios* (Indians), as will be seen in the testimonies I present here. In the towns surrounding the mills, these indigenous families had their plots of land and huts, where private life took place. During most of the colonial period, the indigenous population was divided into sectors under the rule of native lords or chiefs called *caciques*. Spanish colonial administrators required these chiefs to send their subjects into the mills, so the chiefs would order other indigenous authorities to round up laborers. Sometimes native authorities would go into people's homes to take men or boys as workers in the mills. Chiefs who did not meet Spanish colonial demands for laborers were jailed. There are colonial reports of workers being chained to looms, and mills with jails or dungeons inside. Some workers died due to the hunger and brutal treatment they experienced.

In this chapter I focus on the historical testimonies of indigenous mill workers to understand the link between private, domestic lives and public socioeconomic settings as families tried to adapt to forced labor in the textile economy. The main source for the material I use is a seventeenth-century criminal investigation of the large textile mill of San Ildefonso, involving over 150 indigenous witnesses, in which the sharing of personal stories became a call for legal action. The mill was located in the town of Pelileo, in the central sierra of Ecuador, which I learned was more diverse in the seventeenth century than it is today. The population surrounding the mill included African slaves, Spaniards, mestizos, and different groups of indigenous people. Indigenous men and boys of the town were forced to work in the mill, as were African slaves, although, unfortunately, the Africans' testimonies were not recorded in the record of the criminal investigation.

In the mid-seventeenth century the textile mill of San Ildefonso was owned by the heiress Maria de Vera Mendoza, and her husband, Antonio Lopez de Galarza, oversaw operations, even after her death. In 1661 Galarza was the target of a five-year investigation into abuses against the Indians, and the legal commission carrying out the investigation recorded the testimonies of indigenous mill workers and their families. Most of the testimonies detail punishments and complain of lack of pay, and by the end of the investigation Galarza was forced to settle accounts with more than a thousand indigenous workers, and some of the (white) mill foremen were sent to jail. In the records of testimonies, the private, intimate aspects of the native workers' lives were inserted into the legal record as part of the investigation; the workers thereby linked home life with one of Ecuador's largest and longest-lasting textile mills.

I focus here on two aspects of the indigenous people's testimonies that fall within the domain of the intimate: the expression of emotions (private sentiments) and statements about domestic life. The expression of emotions reveals affective ties among people, both kin and non-kin. The references to domestic life are most clearly seen in descriptions of the act of feeding and food sharing, and highlight women's contributions to nourishing their families, sustaining the workforce, and trying to keep their families together. When discussing food, the workers and their families made statements that took the form of the Latin American *testimonio:* a genre of personal narrative that gives voice to a marginalized group of people. A common feature of the *testimonio* genre is to make one's personal experience political (Counihan 2013, 175). In their references to food in their declarations, indigenous people linked the intimate, domestic act of feeding to the labor system of the textile industry to show how they experienced and responded to the oppressive conditions. The reading of emotional expressions and specific narratives about family and home life provides us with a richer understanding of the lived experience of the workers, one that moves beyond official histories of the textile economy. Highlighting the activities that linked households and the mill enables us to uncover the unofficial histories of native workers as they struggled to maintain their families in the face of colonial disruptions. Anthropological approaches, which emphasize attention to detail and everyday acts, enable a particularly in-sightful reading of historical documents. I use approaches from scholarship in anthropology and history that focus on emotional expressions, and the anthro-pology of food and foodways, to read into the statements of native workers. Using bits of information from the archival record, we can fill in the silences and imagine the lived experience and private lives of those indigenous people who were affected by the textile economy. Before getting into the details of the testimonies, a brief introduction to the textile economy is necessary.

ECUADOR'S COLONIAL TEXTILE ECONOMY

The Spanish Empire exploited precious metals from South American mines, such as the great silver mine of Potosí, Bolivia. While Ecuador had some mines (Lane 2002), the mainstay of the colonial economy was the textile market that developed to supply cloth to populated centers around mines in Bolivia and Peru. Ecuador's landscape includes high, humid grasslands that are ideal for raising sheep, which were introduced after the Spanish conquest. This landscape, and the existence of a large indigenous population of the central highlands of Ecuador, promoted the development of a wool textile industry based on indigenous labor. Historians estimate that by 1620 there were well over half a million sheep in Ecuador's central sierra (Phelan 1967, 67). A few Spanish or Spanish American elite families formed "obraje dynas-ties" (Gauderman 2003, 72), intermarried, and owned multiple textile mills in different towns. Catholic religious orders also owned large mills, and many individuals owned smaller-scale mills. San Ildefonso was a large textile mill that was founded in 1594 and operated under different owners until around

1890. It remained in the hands of the family of Maria de Vera for generations, until an heir sold it to the Catholic order of Jesuits. The Jesuits controlled the mill until their expulsion from South America in 1767, after which the colonial government took it over. The government eventually auctioned it off to an individual buyer, and it remained under private ownership until its decline in 1890. In this chapter I focus on the lives of indigenous families of Pelileo in the mid-seventeenth century when the mill was run by Galarza, the husband of Maria de Vera.

The economic dependence on textile manufacture to sustain Ecuador's colonial economy led to the proliferation of legal and illegal sweatshops that operated with coerced indigenous labor. Reports from the seventeenth and eighteenth centuries show that illegal practices were widespread, and Spanish Crown policies meant to protect indigenous people were often ignored at mills such as San Ildefonso. In the farm-factory complex described by Nicholas Cushner (1982), mill owners also owned the sheep ranches that supplied wool to the mill, and they could shift indigenous labor from the ranch to the mill. The process of wool production involved many steps, including shearing the sheep, cleaning the wool, beating, carding, spinning, weaving, "fulling" (a process that made the wool softer), and dyeing. Sympathetic Spanish officials and indigenous chiefs alike complained of the abuses against indigenous people in the textile mills and the extreme measures that mothers took to prevent their sons from being forced into these *obrajes.* Some seventeenth-century native leaders complained that women were practicing abortion (Ortiz de la Tabla Ducasse 1977, 486), and an eighteenth-century Spaniard reported that mothers in the northern highland province of Imbabura were blinding male babies to keep them out of the mills.[4] Despite some Spaniards' denunciations of the abuse of native workers, the economic benefit of the mills outweighed the implementation of reforms, and even Crown orders to demolish illegal sweatshops were revoked (Phelan 1967, 78).

What were these abuses? To ensure the quality of the cloth for which San Ildefonso was known, workers were often beaten and whipped for imperfections. Some workers were shackled with leg irons and locked in a dungeon at night. Colonial reports from different parts of highland Ecuador make it clear that the experiences of indigenous people at San Ildefonso were not an exception but part of the common experience of Andeans forced into the service of textile production. The brutality of the punishments of indigenous workers depended on the individual administrators and foremen at any given time, and the seventeenth-century workers discussed here made a distinction between more humane foremen and those who were cruel.

The public and private spheres at San Ildefonso were interlinked in several ways. First, indigenous authorities, who carried special staffs to symbolize their positions in the colonial hierarchy, went into people's homes in the countryside surrounding the mill to forcibly take people to the mill, thereby invading domestic, family space. Second, during the criminal investigation of the Spanish administrator of the mill (Galarza), indigenous laborers gave legal declarations in which they inserted their emotions by voicing private sentiments about the effects of the mill on their families, and their recorded statements then became part of the official record. Finally, everyday domestic acts, such as food preparation, became geared toward the mill as women took rations to their husbands and sons who were locked in the mill in order to prevent them from running away.

THE TESTIMONIES

The legal testimonies for the investigation of San Ildefonso were given by indigenous people speaking Quichua, a northern Andean version of Quechua, the language of the Inca Empire. The commission included an interpreter (and alternate) who translated the words into Spanish, and scribes who then wrote the Spanish version. Sometimes the scribe used the first person "I" for the witness speaking (e.g., "I saw many times. . ."), other times the testimony was recorded using the third person (e.g., "this witness saw. . ."). Criminal trial records, according to Kathryn Burns, "often present a rare subaltern perspective, even the voices of people otherwise unable to represent themselves in writing. But these voices do not come to us unmediated" (2010, 133–34). As Burns cautions, we cannot take the indigenous testimonies contained in colonial archives as the direct words of witnesses, because they are mediated through the voices of scribes who act as "legal ventriloquists" (Guerrero 1997). Certainly some of the testimony was formulaic, as when witnesses apparently referred to themselves as "miserable Indians." However, the personal experiences related here are indigenous people's own stories, despite the translation into Spanish rhetoric. Furthermore, there are examples of indigenous testimonies that seem to follow indigenous speech patterns better than official Spanish legal formulas. Examples of non-formulaic language translated from Quichua include the following testimony in which a Quichua term slipped into the note-taking, suggesting a close following of the witness's words. A native worker, complaining of the mill foreman, stated, "he perpetrates injustices against the Indians, making the weavers deliver six loads of wool when *ñaupa* [Qu., "in the past,"] it was only four [loads], and he has them locked in during the day without letting them outside even to relieve themselves" [my emphasis].[5] The testimonies often included Quichua terms (Qu.) for labor positions, such as *atalpacama* (Qu. one who takes care of chickens) and objects, such as *cocabi* (Qu. food prepared to be carried and eaten later). Such indigenous terms were incorporated into Andean Spanish when discussing activities in which indigenous people engaged. However, the quote above is the only reference I have seen in which the scribe recorded a Quichua reference to time, and I did not see the word *ñaupa* in any other testimony, so this was not a customary recording. Another example of deviation from standard, formulaic Spanish legal language comes from the declaration of Miguel Guaytusa. Guaytusa had spent many years spinning wool in the mill, and told the commission:

> When I was a boy of about ten or eleven years old, I was with my mother in our field, working the land and pulling weeds from the little bit of corn we had planted there. The *alcalde* [indigenous authority] of the mill, Joan Challay, came. Against my will, he forcefully tied my hands, and as I was resisting as best I could, *he tore my poor little shirt* [pobre camisetilla] and poncho that I was wearing, and as my resistance and that of my mother was useless, he finally took me to the mill [My emphasis][6]

Once inside the mill, Guaytusa was untied, whipped, and placed in shackles until he agreed to work there. When this man stated that the authority tore his "poor little shirt," the interpreter used the diminutive—*illa*, which also serves (in both Quichua and Spanish) as a term of endearment—and the witness expressed sympathy for an item of clothing when discussing violence against himself. This unconventional statement gives the declaration a more personal sense and suggests that the narrative is likely more influenced by Quichua speech conventions than Spanish legal rhetoric. Therefore, despite the mediation of the indigenous voice by scribes and interpreters, I interpret the testimonies presented here as accurate renditions of people's experiences, including their inner feelings.

Historical narratives are full of silences, and as Michel-Rolph Trouillot has shown, silences enter the narrative at different stages, including the making of archives. One way to deconstruct historical silences is to reposition available evidence "to generate a new narrative" (Trouillot 1995, 27). The recording of indigenous people's declarations during the 1661 investigation provides us with evidence of their personal experiences. Here I attempt to fill in the blank spaces—that which goes unsaid—by centering the individual, everyday acts mentioned in the testimonies, and imagining the experiences and activities of those involved. Starting with the statements made by indigenous workers and their family members, I extrapolate to consider the significance of the acts—information that is not always recorded. I read the statements as indigenous expressions of how the textile economy impinged on their intimate lives, and how they responded, and I am influenced by scholars who analyze the larger cultural and political significance of everyday domestic activities. For example, archaeologist Elizabeth Newman (2014) not only describes the material evidence of foodways on a hacienda of Puebla, Mexico, but provides possible scenarios of the thoughts and motivations of the individuals who prepared the foods, and the meaning those foods held for them. Scholar bell hooks (2008) analyzes African American women's home-making activities as political acts in which women created an intimate, private world that countered the dehumanizing racism of the dominant white society. Anthropologist Carole Counihan devised an ethnographic methodology of soliciting "food-centered life-histories" as a way to counteract what has been silenced by bringing the "traditionally private sphere of cooking and feeding into the public arena" and showing "the impact of women's experiences on culture and history" (2013, 175). I use the approaches of these scholars in my reading of the recorded testimonies to read into the private lives of the indigenous mill workers and shed light on their histories.

THE VOICE OF EMOTION

The anthropological and historical scholarship on emotions has tended to focus on the social construction of emotions and interpretations of the *expression* of emotions as a product of historical and cultural contexts.[7] However, the emphasis on the socially constructed nature of emotional expressions should not preclude us from considering that the expressions might reflect real, translatable manifestations of people's inner feelings, despite historical and cultural differences.[8] Here I focus on how individuals chose to use emotives in their legal testimonies, thereby inserting private sentiments into the making of official records about labor and criminal activity.

In these testimonies emotions were often expressed through a term that was translated into Spanish as *compasión* (compassion). For example, Christoval Paucar, who worked as a weaver in the mill, told the commission about how he helped another older indigenous man, Hernando Tubon, who was threatened with forced labor in the mill over a debt, unless he got someone to guarantee payment. Paucar agreed to serve as a guarantor in order to keep the elder out of the mill, and the commission recorded his testimony in the third person: "and because he had compassion for him, since [Tubon] was old and for being a relative, although a distant one, he promised he would pay the cost if Tubon couldn't."[9] This declaration reveals emotional bonds as well as the pressure that some men felt to help relatives. Paucar's distant relative was fearful of being locked in the mill to fulfill a debt. Elderly men who did not work fast enough might be beaten or whipped inside the mill, and as a weaver

Paucar would have been aware of this. By taking on the older man's debt, Paucar placed the burden on himself, and complained that he was repeatedly harassed over the money while working in the mill. Other testimonies told of witnesses seeing the injuries on the backs of relatives who had been whipped and stating that it "caused them to feel compassion," that they were "moved by compassion," or that people did some action "out of compassion" or "out of pity" (*de lástima*).

Medical anthropology has, for a long time, paid close attention to emotions, because many cultures conceive of illness as a physical manifestation of emotional states (for examples from the Andes, see Koss-Chino, Leatherman, and Greenway 2003; Tapias 2015). In Latin America, physical manifestations of emotional states were influenced by a combination of Iberian and indigenous traditional understandings of illness, as well as the particular conditions (such as slavery and debt bondage) that created the emotional states. In a study of melancholy among Afro-Brazilian slaves, Kalle Kananoja (2019) traces the history of the illness known as *banzo*. A likely origin for this term is a Kimbundu word, *banza*, meaning "home" or "village." The term "banzo" therefore referred to melancholy, conceived as an illness related to nostalgia for one's homeland. Eventually (by the 1770s), it was associated with blackness, as it was a condition that afflicted slaves. In the San Ildefonso investigation, indigenous workers and their chiefs told the commission that some workers died of "melancholy," among other ailments. One witness described the death of Augustin Hambacho, "who died from grief [*pesadumbre*] and hunger, from finding himself imprisoned, and abandoned by his wife who had run away, and he had no one to give him food, and he was shackled, put there by the authorities for being a bandit, and because of this melancholy he began defecating blood."[10] This same witness attributed compassion on the part of a Spanish ranch owner who freed an indigenous debt peon from the mill and took him to work as a ranch hand. That Spaniard "paid for the sheep that the Indian owed and got him out of the mill out of compassion upon seeing him imprisoned, because the [Indian's] wife begged him to."[11] Despite this effort to get him out of the mill, the worker died within a year of his release, which was attributed to the conditions he experienced in the mill.

Another man blamed his wife's miscarriage on the intense emotions she felt upon seeing his misery in the mill. Matheo Gualpamullo was a forty-year-old shepherd responsible for a large flock of sheep on one of the ranches associated with the mill. According to his testimony, he was charged not only for the sheep that were attacked by predators, but also for those that died of old age, and he claimed that he was charged for more sheep than the actual number that had died. This put him in debt to the mill, and allowed the estate manager to force him into the mill to work off the debt, as was the case with many shepherds. Because he had no experience with the process of textile production, he was whipped three times in one month for not working well. Gualpamullo said that he was

> held to the ground by the hands and feet, and in order to get out of this prison, which was the reason for which his wife, with the emotion [*sentimiento*] that she felt to see him mistreated, lost the baby with which she was pregnant and very advanced. She had to bring to the manager. . . a pair of oxen that this witness had, so that [the manager] would send him out [of the mill], which he did, and allow him to work off the rest of the debt on the ranch.[12]

In this statement Gualpamullo drew on understandings of the effects of emotion on people's bodies, in this case his pregnant wife, and then described the desperate measures that his distraught wife took to free him from the mill. According to witnesses, several wives tried to free their husbands and sons from the mill by bringing gifts of (uncooked) food products or livestock to the managers. Gualpamullo's wife paid with draft animals, necessary for ploughing the fields of indigenous families so that they could grow crops and feed themselves, just so that her husband could work off his debt outside of the mill.

In fact, the mill owners of colonial Ecuador benefited from this familial love, exploiting affective ties to get free labor. By taking children to the mill, they likely knew that parents would volunteer to help. The judge who led the investigation at San Ildefonso, Luis Joseph Merlo de la Fuente, said that due to the cruel treatment of children in the mill, the parents

> not only went to help them, but due to natural love that moved them, to take the whippings that they wanted to give to their children; the father, letting them punish him for the son, four or five times with twelve to twenty lashes, and the mother in the same way receiving a few more, preferring to take this and suffer the pain to prevent something even worse, that their children would runaway out of fear of the mill, as others have, and [their parents] cried in their absence.[13]

The Spanish judge, like the indigenous witnesses, made references to emotions that "moved" people, thereby linking private sentiments and affective family ties as the basis for actions with respect to the textile economy.

DOMESTIC LIFE AND FOODWAYS

The testimonies of indigenous men tell how they had to balance their obligations to their families with their need for self-liberation from the mill. Ventura

Cunamasi told the commission that his chief forced him into the mill, where he was made to work in the task of dyeing the wool cloth. He was whipped for not dyeing it well. He ran away, but was caught and brought back. The commission recorded his testimony:

> and having the chance to run a way again he went with his wife and family for two or three months to Ambato [the capital of the province] and other places so that in his absence they wouldn't take them and lock them up as he saw them do with the wives and children of Indians who fled; and aside from locking them in they forced them to work until the person returned, and he was captured again and locked up and put to work again with the dye and he ran away another two or three times but they always caught him and locked him up so he decided to stay put . . . and as he saw that there was no way out of the mill, he built his house near the mill chapel to live there, and he didn't bother to run away anymore, not even with his family.[14]

Based on Cunamasi's testimony it is worth considering the difficult choices that indigenous men faced in the colonial textile economy: run away to avoid torture and imprisonment, but place one's wife and children at risk of being taken as substitutes, or stay with one's family and suffer in the mill. Cunamasi refused to abandon his family, and instead brought his home life closer to the mill by building a house there.

The longing for the comforts of home and family were best expressed in the testimony of Diego Masaquisa, quoted at the beginning of this chapter. In Masaquisa's case, the tortures taking place inside the mill were used as a threat to get labor on the associated estate of Chumaqui (figure 4.1). Masaquisa's reference to "the warmth of the hearth" inserts a longing for domestic space within a narrative about economic exploitation related to the mill. It is not just the physical warmth of the fire, since he could build a fire wherever he was stationed. Rather, he made reference to the warmth of the hearth and alluded to the longing for the warmth of intimate familial space. Scholar bell hooks writes of the significance of "homeplace" to African Americans during slavery and later segregation: "In our young minds houses belonged to women, were their special domain, not as property, but as places where all that truly mattered in life took place— the warmth and comfort of shelter, the feeding of our bodies, the nurturing of our souls" (hooks 2008, 176). Many of these women had to work outside of the home, but made efforts to "conserve enough of themselves to provide service (care and nurturance) within their own families and communities" (176). For hooks, this creation of nurturing space in a racist society has a political dimension: "Historically, African-American people believed that the construction of a homeplace, however fragile and tenuous (the slave hut, the wooden shack) had a radical political dimension" (176) because of the feeling of safety and human dignity in that domestic space that women created. Part of the reason that the actions and "service" of women have been erased from official histories is that women's creation of nurturing, domestic space is considered "natural," rather than a conscious choice. Rather, as hooks argues, coming home from working in the fields, or as a cook in a white home, and creating a homeplace is a conscious choice, and therefore the efforts should be recognized as such.

In the seventeenth-century thatch-roofed huts of highland indigenous families, homeplace would have been a space of warmth, food, and comfort,[15] where one could speak one's own native language and communicate freely with family members away from the watchful eyes of Spanish-speaking bosses and priests (and the indigenous middle-men who served them). It would have been a place where bodies were healed, and where some indigenous cultural practices were reproduced. In highland Ecuador, the hearth of indigenous homes continues to serve as an intimate space symbolizing

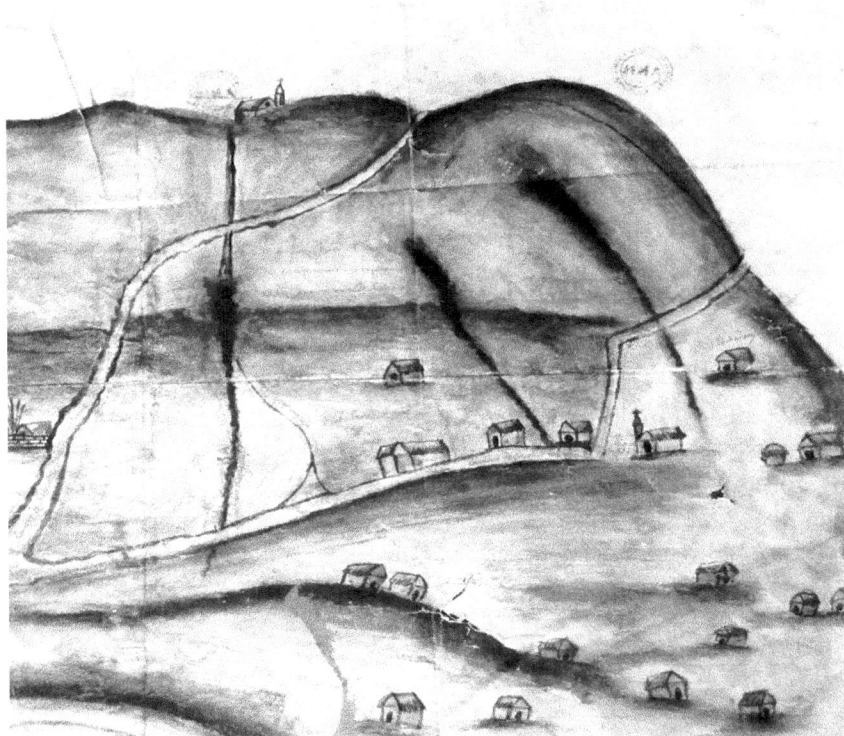

Figure 4.1. Detail of eighteenth-century map of the Hacienda of Chumaqui.
Source: Archivo Nacional del Ecuador Mapas y Planos Código ANH.MP.03.11.24.319.

cooperation, reciprocity, and family unity, which is sustained by female kin (Ferraro 2004, 180). In the statement of Diego Masaquisa, his expression of yearning to be home with his family and "know the warmth of the hearth" hints at the unofficial history of homeplace as a site of restoration of human dignity, of both physical and emotional comfort.

While Diego Masaquisa was forced to work on the mill owner's estate (or face being forced into the mill), other workers were taken and locked inside the mill. If a worker could not enjoy the comfort of home, women could try to send home comforts to them by bringing home cooked meals to the mill, or, in the case of child laborers, by sending a sibling along to accompany the child who was taken by force (Corr 2018, 91–92). Siblings would bring a sense of the intimacy of home to the prison-like mill where some children were taken, therefore, sending younger sisters along to help the brothers who were forced into the mill was a choice that some indigenous mothers made.

Bentura Quillicana had been locked in the mill and forced to work as a wool beater, and had trouble finishing his daily quotas, for which he was whipped, and eventually died from his injuries. According to his co-worker, Bernal Tiban, during his time in the mill Bentura "suffered much hunger, and he only had to eat what his wife brought him, but his wife couldn't come every day because she was busy, he would go without eating unless, out of pity [*de lastima*], his co-workers would share with him what their wives brought them to eat, as happened with this witness, and it's very common."[16]

Tiban's statement highlights the dependence of men on their wives to bring them food. Otherwise, those who were hungry had to accept advances of food from the mill, against their work accounts, sending them into further debt and increasing the time they would be imprisoned there. Although Tiban claimed that it was "common" to share food with those who had none, I only found a few references to such sharing out of pity. This is perhaps because many workers were hungry and probably could not afford to share the little bit of food brought from their homes. Nevertheless, the rare mention of acts of sharing home-cooked foods with a hungry co-worker highlights what Jon Holtzman refers to as food's "rather unique movement between the most intimate and the most public," which gives it symbolic power in people's memories (2006, 373). Although people made references to Bentura's wife, his father claimed that he was quite young. Perhaps people felt sorry for him due to his young age and the brutal treatment he suffered for not meeting his quotas. Those who didn't have family within walking distance to bring them food suffered greatly. Other men told the commission that they would have starved if their wives hadn't brought them food. The foods mentioned in the testimonies include toasted corn, greens, and corn tortillas.

Women not only brought food to their husbands and sons who were locked in the mill, but they also prepared food for more skilled men who helped their husbands with their work assignments. Geronimo Moposita explained that he saw that the administrator would

> give the wool carders six pounds of wool as the quota to card but adding half a pound more he would give them six and a half pounds to card every day, which even the most experienced ones in this trade could hardly finish, and those who weren't experts in the job were bitter, trying to finish their quotas within the day, and in this way it's true that they made use at this time, especially, of helpers, to whom many times this witness saw the wives of such carders bring seasoned guinea pig meat or corn tortillas, as payment for the said help, or they would share what [their wives] brought them to eat or they would pay them when they had half a *real* or one, according to the task, and the spinners would do the same, with which they would escape being whipped for not finishing their assigned tasks.[17]

The Spanish scribes often used the Quichua word "cocabi" to describe the prepared food that people brought to the mill. While corn, tortillas, and greens were commonly mentioned, and probably consumed daily, guinea pig meat was usually reserved for special occasions, and it has served as a protein-rich delicacy for Andeans since pre-Columbian times (Abbots 2011, 207; Krögel 2011, 32–33). It would have been an especially prized food for the skilled helper. From these male references to women's food work, we can fill in the blanks and imagine the wife of the mill worker preparing the food, a technique used by archaeologist Elizabeth Newman in her analysis of foodways on a hacienda in Puebla, Mexico. Newman provides "informed imaginings of what someone living during the time under study would have thought and experienced" (2014, 4). We can imagine the wife taking time from her other daily tasks to select a guinea pig from her household stock. If she prepared roasted guinea pig, this would mean removing the hair and entrails after killing it, then seasoning it, and slowly roasting it over the fire, before wrapping it to take to the mill as compensation for the man who helped her husband, so that her husband would not suffer being whipped for not completing his tasks. The wives of men assigned to spin wool would sometimes stay to help their husbands after bringing the food to the mill.

The everyday activities of men and women, such as men's hard labor ploughing the fields to grow crops to feed their families, and women's preparation of food, took on meaning in these historical testimonies precisely because indigenous people were disrupted in their efforts to provide for their families. When one no longer fulfills their "natural" roles as spouses or parents, the extra efforts required to do so become clear. Consider the

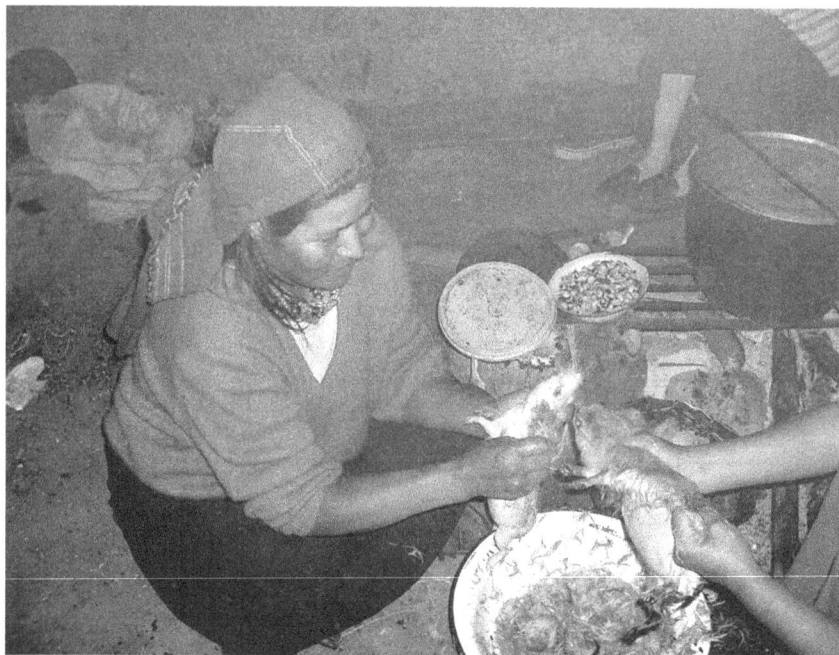

Figure 4.2. **Indigenous woman preparing to roast guinea pig over the fire, modern Cantón Pelileo.**
Photograph by Alejandro Gonzalez, 2004.

following declaration from a man whose wife had run a way and abandoned him, but then returned: "about two years ago his wife came back, and she helps him as best she can, with a morsel [bocado] of food, and if it weren't for her he would perish once and for all in this mill."[18] While several men gave statements that their wives brought them food, this testimony of a man who had been abandoned for years speaks of a "morsel," perhaps a gloss of a Quichua statement that used a diminutive/term of endearment to reflect the appreciation for the little bit of food that the worker enjoyed after his wife came back to him.

Men who were locked in the mill were at the mercy of their wives' ability, and in some cases, their willingness, to bring them food. For those wives who made the long trek to bring food to the mill, we can fill in the historical silences by acknowledging their activities, their labor and their efforts to provide home-cooked meals, and a little sense of comfort, to husbands. This was also an effort to prevent the break-up of their families, since some women feared that their husbands would run away under the pressure. In her discussion of black women's history of service to their communities, bell hooks uses the example of Fredrick Douglass's recollection of his mother, who had been hired as a field hand by a white man who lived far from Douglass's home. After working the fields all day, she would walk a great distance at night just to sleep next to her son, only to be back in the fields by sunrise or suffer being whipped. For hooks this act not only resisted slave codes, but provided a brief moment in which a black child could feel humanized and valued. Like the slave mother who had to be in the fields by sunrise, but trekked for miles at night just to be with her child when he slept, Andean women's journeys to bring food to the mill are part of the history of struggle to maintain intimate family relationships in a racist society. Indigenous men were defined as laborers and treated in inhumane ways, despite the de jure paternalistic Crown protections. The efforts of those indigenous women to counter that inhumane treatment in small, everyday ways, such as bringing food to a skilled worker who would help her husband reach his quota, are part of the historical experience of everyday life.

CONCLUSION

I have focused here on seventeenth-century indigenous people's testimonies about their experiences in one colonial textile mill, but abuses of indigenous mill workers occurred throughout the highland towns of central and northern Ecuador in the seventeenth and eighteenth centuries. Recent studies in family history call for attention to how families responded to global and local historical transformations, how they experienced social, economic, and political pressures at the household level, and how families, in turn, shaped historical patterns. In their introduction to a collection of articles titled "Centering Families in Atlantic History," Julie Hardwick, Sarah M. S. Pearsall, and Karin Wulf take the household as their unit of analysis and state: "Certainly families were affected by economic, political, or cultural structures of many kinds, but they made choices and pursued strategies that, in thousands or tens of thousands of repetitions, shaped those same patterns" (Hardwick, Pearsall and Wulf, 2013, 206). In colonial Ecuador, individual and family decisions to leave one's home community in order to escape the indigenous labor draft and tribute requirements occurred in thousands of repetitions, leading to the disruption and recreation of indigenous communities (Powers 1995). Within families, people's household positions and kinship and gender roles shaped how people experienced and responded to historical transformations. Many individuals chose to run away: men abandoned wives, wives abandoned husbands, and children ran away from home, leading to the disintegration of indigenous families. I have chosen to focus here on people who chose to stay, on the voices of those who struggled every day to keep their families together. The textile economy operated in such a way that it invaded intimate indigenous spaces: indigenous authorities took people from their corn fields and their homes. Individual men and women tried to maintain their families by maintaining a sense of home for those locked in the mill; women would send siblings to accompany child laborers, and bring home-cooked meals to their husbands and their helpers, and some men built homes close to the mill to keep their families nearby. The criminal investigation of one mill administrator allowed workers to come forward and express their feelings about how the mill affected them emotionally. In my reading of these testimonies I placed indigenous statements about affective ties with family, compassion for others, and small every day acts of feeding and food sharing at the center of the narrative about the colonial textile industry. By focusing on mundane, everyday domestic tasks we recover voices and learn about domestic and family history. Exploring how these public (legal and economic) and private (emotional, domestic) spheres were intertwined gives us a deeper understanding of the historical experience of native Andean people.

NOTES

1. This chapter grew out of a larger research project on the indigenous history of Pelileo, Ecuador, the results of which are published in my book *Interwoven* (Corr 2018). I gratefully acknowledge the National Endowment for the Humanities Fellowship and the American Philosophical Society Franklin Grant that supported the research, and Dra. Rocío Pazmiño Acuña, director of the National Archive of Ecuador, and staff for their generous assistance.

2. Archivo Nacional del Ecuador, Obrajes 8-X-1661 folio 186 recto-verso. Subsequent testimonies are from the same source, which uses both first- and third-person narratives.

3. There were some indigenous lords (caciques) who owned textile mills, but for the most part the owners were of European background. The industry was regulated by the Spanish Crown.

4. Archivo General de Indias (AGI) Quito 133n.26 9-VIII-1737; see also Hu 2017.

5. Archivo Nacional del Ecuador (ANE) Obrajes 1666 fol. 493 v.

6. ANE Obrajes 1661 fol.172 r.

7. Space does not permit an overview of this literature, but for discussions of the relationship between inner feelings, culture, and emotional expressions, see Abu-Lughod and Lutz 1990; Plamper et al. 2010; Villa-Flores and Lipsett-Rivera 2014.

8. While I acknowledge the influence of culture on emotional expressions, I argue that we can still empathize with how people feel, even if they are from cultures or historical periods that are very different from our own. For example, Renato Rosaldo (1984) has written that he came to understand the rage that grieving Ilon-

got headhunters felt at the death of a loved one only after he experienced similar emotions, despite radically different means of expression available in each culture. For a discussion of the pitfalls of reducing emotions to political context, see Harkin 2003, 266–68.

9. ANE Obrajes 8-X-1661 fol. 115v.-116r.

10. ANE Obrajes 1666 fol 419r.

11. ANE Obrajes 1666 fol. 420r.

12. ANE Obrajes 1661 fol. 237 v.

13. AGI Quito 13, R. 13, No.38; 1666–11–15 "Estado de la encomienda de Pelileo y agravios a sus indios." Digital document accessed through PARES. Image 30.

14. ANE Obrajes 8-X-1661fol. 60r.-61r.

15. Homes were, sometimes, spaces of domestic violence as well, but a discussion of domestic violence is beyond the scope of this chapter.

16. ANE Obrajes 1661 fol. 49r.

17. ANE Obrajes 1661 fol. 335v.

18. ANE Obrajes 1666 fol. 41v.-45r.

REFERENCES

Abbots, Emma-Jayne. 2011. "'It Doesn't Taste as Good from the Pet Shop': Guinea Pig Consumption and the Performance of Transnational Kin and Class Relations in Highland Ecuador and New York City." *Food, Culture, and Society 14*(2): 205–23.

Abu-Lughod, Lila, and Catherine A. Lutz. 1990. "Introduction: Emotion, Discourse, and the Politics of Everyday Life." In *Language and the Politics of Emotion*, edited by Catherine A. Lutz and Lila Abu-Lughod, 1–23. New York: Cambridge University Press.

Burns, Kathryn. 2010. *Into the Archive: Writing and Power in Colonial Peru*. Durham, NC: Duke University Press.

Corr, Rachel. 2018. *Interwoven: Andean Lives in Colonial Ecuador's Textile Economy*. Tucson: University of Arizona Press.

Counihan, Carole. 2013. "Mexicanas' Food Voice and Differential Consciousness in the San Luis Valley of Colorado." In *Food and Culture: A Reader*, third edition, edited by Carole Counihan and Penny Van Esterik, 172–86. New York: Routledge, 2013.

Cushner, Nicholas P. 1982. *Farm and Factory: The Jesuits and the Development of Agrarian Capitalism in Colonial Quito 1600–1767*. Albany: State University of New York Press.

Ferraro, Emilia. 2004. *Reciprocidad, don y deuda: relaciones y formas de intercambio en los Andes ecuatorianos*. La comunidad de Pesillo. Quito: Abya-Yala.

Gauderman, Kimberly. 2003. *Women's Lives in Colonial Quito: Gender, Law, and Economy in Spanish America*. Austin: University of Texas Press.

Guerrero, Andrés. 1997. "The Construction of a Ventriloquist's Image: Liberal Discourse and the 'Miserable Indian Race' in 19th Century Ecuador." *Journal of Latin American Studies 20*(3): 555–90.

Hardwick, Julie, Sarah M. S. Pearsall, and Karin Wulf. 2013. "Introduction: Centering Families in Atlantic Histories." *William and Mary Quarterly 70*(2): 205–24.

Harkin, Michael. 2003. "Feeling and Thinking in Memory and Forgetting: Toward an Ethnohistory of the Emotions." *Ethnohistory 50*(2): 261–84.

Holtzman, Jon D. 2006. "Food and Memory." *Annual Review of Anthropology 35*: 361–78.

hooks, bell. 2008. "Homeplace: A Site of Resistance." In *Philosophy and the City*, edited by Sharon M. Meagher, 175–83. Albany: SUNY.

Hu, Di. 2017. "The Revolutionary Power of Andean Folk Tales." Sapiens.org (http://www.sapiens.org/archaeology/andeanfolktalesrevolutionarypower/). Wenner-Gren Foundation.

Kananoja, Kalle. 2019. "Melancholy, Race and Slavery in the Early Modern Southern Atlantic World." In *Encountering Crises of the Mind: Madness, Culture and Society, 1200s–1900s*, edited by Tuomas Laine-Frigren, Jari Eilola, and Markku Hokkanen, 88–112. Leiden: Brill.

Koss-Chioino, Joan, Thomas Leatherman, and Christine Greenway, eds. 2003. *Medical Pluralism in the Andes.* New York: Routledge.

Krögel, Alison. 2011. *Food, Power, and Resistance in the Andes: Exploring Quechua Verbal and Visual Narratives.* Lanham: Lexington Books.

Lane, Kris. 2002. *Quito 1599: City and Colony in Transition.* Albuquerque: University of New Mexico Press.

Newman, Elizabeth Terese. 2014. *Biography of a Hacienda: Work and Revolution in Rural Mexico.* Tucson: University of Arizona Press.

Ortiz de la Tabla Ducasse, Javier. 1977. "El obraje colonial ecuatoriano." *Revista de Indias 37*(149–50): 471–541. Madrid: CSIC.

Plamper, Jan, William Reddy, Barbara Rosenwein, and Peter Stearns. 2010. "The History of Emotions: An Interview with William Reddy, Barbara Rosenwein, and Peter Stearns." *History and Theory 49*(2): 237–65.

Phelan, John Leddy. 1967. *The Kingdom of Quito in the Seventeenth Century: Bureaucratic Politics in the Spanish Empire.* Madison: University of Wisconsin Press.

Powers, Karen Vieira. 1995. *Andean Journeys: Migration, Ethnogenesis, and the State in Colonial Quito.* Albuquerque: University of New Mexico Press.

Rosaldo, Renato I. 1984 "Grief and a Headhunter's Rage: On the Cultural Force of Emotions." In *Text, Play, and Story*, edited by Edward M. Bruner, 178–95. Prospect Heights: Waveland Press.

Tapias, Maria. 2015. *Embodied Protests: Emotions and Women's Health in Bolivia.* Urbana: University of Illinois Press.

Trouillot, Michel-Rolph. 1995. *Silencing the Past: Power and the Production of History.* Boston: Beacon Press.

Tyrer, Robson Brines. 1976. "The Demographic and Economic History of the Audiencia de Quito: Indian Population and the Textile Industry, 1600–1800." PhD dissertation, University of California Berkeley.

Villa-Flores, Javier, and Sonya Lipsett-Rivera. 2014. "Introduction." In *Emotions and Daily Life in Colonial Mexico*, edited by Javier Villa-Flores and Sonia Lipsett-Rivera, 1–14. Albuquerque: University of New Mexico Press.

Chapter Five

Friends of the Family

Gender, Kinship, and Elite Colonial Networks in Early Twentieth-Century North India

Jacqueline H. Fewkes

Readers of historical studies of early twentieth-century north Indian trade might easily, and regrettably, form the impression that the historical trade routes were populated only by men, as the primary agents discussed are usually all male.[1] In my own previous work, for example, I have written about historical trade in Ladakh (a region in northern Indian), as conducted by men: cosmopolitan Arghun traders from Ladakh who acted as "middlemen" between Central and South Asian trade systems, British colonial officers manning Indian tax posts to collect revenue for the empire, and local *kiraiyakash* ("ponymen"), villagers who owned livestock and worked with animals to transport global commodities over the Himalayan and Karakorum mountains (Fewkes 2008). Yet, a number of women, many unnamed and most rarely recognized in histories, were also an integral part of this historical economic and political system. Some of these women were traders' wives, whose marriages represented alliances between local and foreign trading networks; others were British colonial official's wives, whose family members served in roles throughout the British Empire. Many more of all ages were the family members and domestic staff who helped run the *caravanserai* sites that simultaneously acted as inns, tax posts, and trade depots for travelers in the region. Households populated by both women and men in the ethnic enclave neighborhoods of South and Central Asian trading entrepôts represented a community's settled history in the region, a crucial signifier of stability that furthered participants' economic interests and political influence. In these and other ways the success of historical South/Central Asian trading communities was ensured through the participation of both genders.

Considering the omission of these women's roles in common historical narratives, I have come to think more carefully about how, while historical South Asian colonial and economic power is often framed in terms of public—and frequently male—interactions, consideration of the private in the form of kinship relations and domestic spheres in elite families can help develop alternative perspectives on the topic that demonstrate the porosity of public/private spheres in this historical context. In this chapter I explore the kinship networks of Ladakhi trading elites and British colonial officials in late nineteenth- and early twentieth-century South Asia to better understand the dynamics of colonial relations—both political and economic—during the time period. Using published biographies, material culture, archival documents, and first-person accounts from ethnographic interviews as evidence, in this chapter I trace the kinship networks of Indian and British communities in the late nineteenth and early twentieth centuries. As I will demonstrate, elite trading communities in historical Ladakh formed internationally oriented networks in colonial South Asia, making the "private" role of the family central to trade networks that extended beyond the region. Kinship networks were also significant structures in contemporaneous elite British colonial families; British kinship networks helped to maintain colonial power within social, political, and economic arenas. These two systems of transnational kinship groups—separate yet associated—represent a subtext of colonial interactions that contributed to the complexities of social relations in colonial South Asia and provide a perspective that highlights the interplay between public/private spaces and gender roles within the historical colonial system.

CONSIDERING KINSHIP

Varied anthropological perspectives on the study of kinship have accumulated over the last two centuries, leading Marilyn Strathern to aptly observe that "[a]nyone writing about kinship today does so in the middle of a long anthropological conversation" (Strathern 2014, 43). To participate fully in that conversation a few distilled highlights are worth reviewing. Late nineteenth-century social organization studies on kinship were considered central to the disciplinary approach, contributing to the problematic social evolutionary perspective of the time period (e.g., Morgan 1871 and 1877). Kinship studies were reshaped in the twentieth century, becoming synonymous with structuralism as a fundamental structure of human society in the work of Claude Lévi-Straus (1949), and later deconstructed by post-structuralist anthropologists who sought to explore the fluid and sometimes ambiguous meanings of human kinship practices. The topic became central to late twentieth-century feminist anthropology studies in which the authors debunked notions of universal gender roles through cross-cultural kinship studies (e.g., Ornter 1974; Rosaldo 1974). Scholars of globalization in the same time period explored how kinship networks were not merely resilient in the face of global flows, but could organize those flows (e.g., Gardner 1995; Georges 1990) and take on expanded symbolic roles in global diasporas (e.g., Baumann 1995). More recent debates about kinship have caused further dissection, division, and intersections of the concept. Marshall Sahlins discusses kinship as a "mutuality of being" that goes beyond a biological/cultural dichotomy (Sahlins 2011a, b); while kinship may indeed be either biologically or socially produced, Sahlins notes that even something as fundamentally biological as human reproduction is "symbolically formulated and culturally variable" (Sahlins 2011a, 3). Responses to Sahlins, and in turn to Sahlins's respondents, have therefore not just questioned what we—both humans in general (experientially) and anthropologists (academically)—can "do" with kinship, but sought to rekindle earlier fundamental debates about what kinship is and is not (see Kronenfeld 2012). Strathern has followed up this discussion with a fundamentally ethnographic question, asking, even if we agree on what kinship is, how do we, as anthropologists, describe it (Strathern 2014, 45)? According to Strathern an anthropological description of kinship takes into account relations, relationships, cultural order, and knowledge (Strathern 2014), suggesting its study requires both a phenomenological and epistemological focus. Parallel to this disciplinary conversation most individual anthropologists seem to carry on with a somewhat dualistic approach to the topic, continuing to teach structuralist kinship charting to their students in introductory classes (recalling with varying degrees of precision classic studies on ideas such as the "Iroquois system"), while reconstructing and deconstructing the topic in their own work more broadly.

Of particular interest to the focus of this chapter are the ways in which studies of kinship systems allow scholars to newly consider the concept of the public/private divide. Social science discourses about public/private frequently are situated within the public sphere, forming the private largely in opposition to the public, following the classic construction of the public sphere developed by Jurgen Habermas as a space in which public opinion develops (Habermas 1991). Habermas's notion of the public sphere focused on the relationships between societies and states, and the intertwining between these two bodies (Fraser 1990), a version of the public sphere that underlies many academic conversations about public vs. private (e.g., Joseph 1997).

Others have provided an alternative route for conceptualizing the public/private, such as the early feminist anthropology scholars of kinship who deconstructed the public and private as absolute categories, working from the private (or domestic sphere) "outward." In "Feminism and Kinship Theory" Anna Tsing and Sylvia Yanagisako (1983) discuss a number of examples of anthropological works that do just this. Their work suggests how kinship relationships in a well-defined "domestic" sphere, that seemingly strengthens a public/private dichotomy, may also create economic opportunities for women that extended their spheres of influences far outside of the home, negotiating new forms of class and gender privilege (Tsing and Yanagisako 1983, 512). Thus, a focus on kinship can help complicate notions of a public/private divide, while maintaining the political and economic implications associated the terms.

KINSHIP AND TRADE IN COLONIAL SOUTH ASIA

While historical South Asian colonial power is often framed in terms of public, and frequently male, interactions, there is a great deal of scholarship in South Asia on caste—and by extension kin—based associations of traders. In nineteenth- and early twentieth-century British South Asia, merchant caste communities in Hindu communities were often formulated along lineage alliances. Kin groups were particularly central to the social organization of trade networks, for, as Claude Markovits comments, "virtually all merchant firms were family firms or 'partnerships' between two families of the same caste, often related by marriage" (Markovits 2008, 310–11). This arrangement was longstanding, as Markovits also notes that a study of late eighteenth-century trading firms reveals similar features, to the degree that "the identity of the family and that of the firm was synonymous to such an extent that there was no specific term for the latter" (Markovits 2008, 310–11). These communities were found outside of South Asia, and Scott Levi has documented Indian family firms operating throughout Central Asia in the nineteenth century, that may have existed as early as the fifteenth or sixteenth centuries (Levi 1999, 486). The kinship bonds within and between the family firms had symbolic value in securing trust with customers and trade partners, making familial ties in Indian trading communities what David Rudner has called "a family firm's greatest intangible asset" (Levi 1999, 491; Rudner 1994, 109).

A major group identity feature of the trade networks in Ladakh—a trade entrepôt posed between South and Central Asia—was based on kinship groupings as well. However, the Ladakhi trading communities discussed here were quite different from those discussed in the studies mentioned above. They were predominantly Muslim, did not have caste-based associations, and members of elite trading families moved between multiple regions, marrying into local families. Elite Ladakhi trading families were diverse, with kin group bonds that deliberately linked families across religious, cultural, and geographic boundaries. Thus in her historical study of trade in Ladakh Janet Rizvi has concluded that Ladakhi traders formed a "more amorphous community" than their caste-based counterparts in British Indian trading communities (Rizvi 1999, 16). Yet there are still a number of similarities between caste-based South Asian family firms and the kin groups within Ladakhi trading networks. As I have documented in previous works, Ladakhi trade families similarly depended upon kinship bonds to create bonds of trust, facilitate travel, maximize capital, and consolidate power (Fewkes 2008; Fewkes and Khan 2016).

These Ladakhi families were not the only other kin-based groups functioning in early twentieth-century colonial South Asia. As I will discuss in the next sections, two systems of transnational kinship groups, elite north Indians and British colonial officials, formed a social landscape for the economic and political events of the time period. Tracing the manner in which some of these ties were formed and represented during the time period helps us to understand the complexities of social relations in colonial South Asia, as well as the role that women played in this system.

TRADE FAMILIES AND THE
LADAKHI COSMOPOLITAN ELITES

A variety of Ladakhi families were involved with the late nineteenth- and early twentieth-century lucrative trans-regional trade (see Fewkes 2008; Fewkes and Khan 2016). For example, in villages throughout the region *kiraiyakash* acted as transporters for goods across the mountain terrain, moving international commodities between south and central Asia on the backs of ponies, yaks, and *dzo* (a yak-cow hybrid). An integral part of the trade system, as the region lacked rail transport and motorable roads in many areas, *kiraiyakash* labor was intimately linked to household structures and relationships. In ethnographic interviews, many former *kiraiyakash* recalled the economic functions of household productivity during the early twentieth century. The domestic sphere was a commercial site where all family members—male and female—might be involved in caring for and breeding transport animals. Sons were encouraged to learn Uighur as a second (or even third) language in order to communicate with Yarkendi traders and increase the potential for their participation in supplying labor and transit goods; they would frequently travel with their fathers to help with the work, receiving on-the-job training while increasing their household income.

Another community in Ladakh involved in trade during the same time period was composed of elite international trading families. Frequently called the "Arghun" community in Ladakh and recognized by specific family names outside the region, they had economically complex trading roles, and their kinship networks were used deliberately as a strategy to increase trading opportunities. Most of the families in this trading network—Khans, Khwojas, Shahs, and others frequently mentioned in interviews with former traders—had families that spanned across regional and national boundaries, with members of the family spread out and married in towns presently in India, China, and Pakistan. Through these networks the Arghuns of Ladakh were responsible for the distribution of a wide variety of commodities in historical South and Central Asia, including items such as carpets, cloth, dyes, medicines, drugs, weaponry, household items, jewelry, and other dry goods (Khan Family Papers, 1900–1948).

Similar to the *kiraiyakash,* elite urban trading families in Ladakh often built their businesses around household settings with multi-generational involvement and training. Although their homes were frequently the sites of, or adjacent to, their *caravanserai*—spaces that functioned as inns, trading locations, and government tax posts—business did not simply take place in the households of these elites; commercial interests of their families fundamentally formed their households. To illustrate, in a series of interviews in Ladakh with one Arghun family whose recent ancestors were elite traders I learned about a man named Bahauddin Khan, who had originally come from Central Asia to Ladakh with his father in the late nineteenth century. According to family oral tradition, he was instructed by his family to stay in the area and establish a branch of the family business in the town of Leh, in the northern Indian region of Ladakh. Like his father and grandfather before him, Bahauddin Khan engaged in an inter-ethnic marriage; he married a woman from the Ladakhi community and established a local household that was also an outpost of his family's firm.

Several themes associated with Bahauddin Khan's marriage highlight the significance of kinship practices among the historical Ladakh Arghun traders. Such former traders' reminiscences clearly demonstrate that heterosexual marriage functioned as a business-building tool for their forebears. While historical trade and colonial power in South Asia are often framed in terms of male interactions, cursory consideration of these kinship relations plainly reveals that female members of these families played a crucial role in the formulation of connections, as women linked families together.

The resulting social relationships were central to their trading role, as Ladakhi Arghun traders were generally middlemen in a complex inter-regional trade system that enabled international commerce to link several parts of Asia. As trade intermediaries the Ladakhi Arghuns did not produce their own goods or purchase a majority of their trade goods for their own use. Instead these trading elites transferred goods between neighboring regions by arranging the transport of goods for others (using the labor of the *kiraiyakash*), financing shipments for retail in various areas, representing distributors to retailers in multiple markets, acting as tax representatives for those outside the region, and/or providing commerce support services for their colleagues in the international trading networks (Khan Family Papers 1900–1948). Kinship relations formed by marriage therefore had both vertical and horizontal implications for these diverse trading roles. The strategy of kinship expansion through local marriages established economically significant vertical descent groups, assuring that trading families would have descendants native to a variety of trading areas, able to fluently speak multiple languages, including the local languages of the region. Multiple kin histories recounted by the descendants of former traders during interviews demonstrate that the horizontal ties formed by these historical marriages functioned as a social contract between families, which meant that Arghun traders such as the Khans who married local women were able to secure social relations with their wives' natal families, aligning local interests with those of their family. Households that were simultaneously local and internationally oriented created powerful kinship networks that secured trust between the international interests of the families such as the Khans and local family partners who supported—financially, politically, and socially—their trading interests in the Ladakh region. Networks of such relations allowed trading middlemen to function efficiently as intermediaries, as demonstrated in a 1931 account by Nicholas Roerich, a Russian traveler in early twentieth-century Chinese Central Asia. While traveling Roerich met a customs officer[2] in Yarkend who told him that he was the "brother" (which also could have referred to a close cousin in this context) of one customs official in Kashgar and another in Leh, all of whom had a third brother who headed "a big trading establishment in distant Lhasa" (Roerich 1931, 86). It is easy to perceive how a trade middleman from Lhasa could facilitate shipments from Leh to Yarkend to Kashgar with his brothers in charge of the customs paperwork at each stop. Thus, as many of the former traders I have interviewed confirmed, international families such as the Khans, Khwojas, and Shahs had strong motivation to maintain family connections throughout South and Central Asia, in the trading towns of Khotan, Lahore, Leh, Lhasa, Srinagar, Yarkend, Kashgar, etc. Their local marriages were linked to an intricate web of kin-based international social networks that reinforced their political power and economic strength.

These international elite trading families would also intermarry with each other to further strengthen their international influence, while maintaining their distinct business identities through patrilineal succession. Bahauddin Khan's grandson, for example, was later married to a woman from another major trading family, the Khwojas, who had similar kinship networks throughout the region. According to interviews with former traders, many of the early twentieth-century international families lived in the same neighborhoods of larger towns such as Yarkend. While these neighborhoods were frequently discussed by my interviewees as ethnic enclaves in accounts about the time period (e.g., the "Kashmiri quarters" in Yarkend), those who lived there in their youth (before the partition of India and Pakistan) reported that social interactions in these neighborhoods most frequently occurred only between those who were related. Thus individual elite trading households were best able to maintain close personal social ties to both local and non-local households through marriage.

As I have argued in other works (Fewkes and McLaughlin 2007; Fewkes 2012), Ladakhi Arghun communities were necessarily cosmopolitan; their roles as trading intermediaries depended on their adept movement between cultures, acting as cultural brokers between the diverse Asian and European communities involved in nineteenth- to twentieth-century Central and South Asian trade. Elite Ladakhi traders' work depended on their abilities to translate between multiple languages, scripts, calendrics, and currencies, as well as keeping up with international news (Khan Family Papers 1900–1948). Their business correspondence demonstrated that they had to navigate between local, regional, and nationally oriented social networks to function effectively in markets where taxation and distribution norms varied greatly. Material culture from the time period and commercial receipts suggest that these traders' aesthetic tastes were shaped by transnational political associations and access to global commodities, and in turn informed fashion and commerce in various local markets.[3] Trading middlemen were thus not simply men who acted as financial intermediaries; they were the faces of extensive multi-gendered international kinship networks that formed, reinforced, and represented a cosmopolitan worldview—a sense of being at home anywhere—that facilitated negotiation between diverse cultural communities of South and Central Asia.

BRITISH COLONIAL FAMILIES
AND THE FAMILY BUSINESS

While the economic significance of South Asian kinship networks in colonial India are widely recognized in historical scholarship, British colonial kinship networks are less commonly discussed. Functioning in complementary fashion to the Ladakhi kinship networks described above, British kinship networks also established and maintained power positions within political and economic structures.

For example, we can look at Sir Henry Mortimer Durand, the Foreign Secretary of India (1884–1894), who was responsible for the negotiation of the Durand Line, a boundary between Afghanistan and then India. Durand's work in Afghanistan made possible the lucrative colonial trade along the Leh

Treaty Route in Ladakh during the late nineteenth century (Roerich 1931, 7). Sir Henry Mortimer Durand's initial appointment was facilitated by the influence of his father, Sir Henry Marion Durand, whose role in the colonial administration had included (among other jobs) Resident of Bhopal, serving in the military in the First Anglo-Afghan War, and later appointment as Lieutenant General of the Punjab (Durand 1883). Durand's kinship advantage was not (only) due to unofficial influence and social networks; the official procedures for filling British colonial governmental positions before the 1920s gave preference to individuals with kinship connections in British Asia. Durand entered the Indian Civil Service in 1873; in 1860 the entrance exams for the Civil Service in British Asia were written to include a section on parentage information, which was taken into consideration for appointments (Coates 1988, 76–78). Kinship information was collected this way on the exam until August 1921; even after 1921 the entrance exams would continue a de facto favoring of the descendants of British Indian officials, army personnel, and civil servants, due to the children's familiarity with the history, customs, and languages of the region (Coates 1988, 76–78, 491, and 538). Terrance Creagh Coen, a member of the Indian Civil Service, wrote in his memoirs of the colonial political system that while education and linguistic skills were important for political appointments in early twentieth-century colonial India,

> it cannot be denied that the claim which above all weighed was relationship to a member or retired member of the sendee [*sic*]. Reading the history of India, one comes across the same surname among politicals again and again, from the earliest times. Four officers, serving in 1947, well illustrate this tendency. Russell [Lt.- Col. A.A. Russell] represented the last of five generations in direct descent from Claud Russell (b. 1732) who joined the Company's service at Madras in 1752, and whose successors served in India in the Army, Civil Service and lastly Political Service. Cotton [Major Sir J. H. Cotton] was descended from five generations, father and son, of Indian Civil Servants. Hancock's father and grandfather, like him, were political officers in Kathiawar, while his great-grandfather was Adjutant- [General of the then Bombay Army. St. John's]: father and grandfather (whom we have already met in Kashmir) were military political officers who reached the rank of first-class Residents. Thus in this service, appointment by nomination, which was abolished for the Indian Civil Service in the mid-nineteenth century, survived. (Coen 1971, 34–35)

Thus Coen corroborates that kinship was the basis for hiring within colonial posts long after the practice had officially ceased.

Similar to the kinship networks of the Ladakhi traders, those of British colonial officials such as Durand's seem, at first glance, to be patrilineal, handed down from father to son; it is only upon closer inspection that women's kinship roles through matrilineal and affinal relationships are notable. Sir Henry

Mortimer Durand's advantageous parentage information would not only have included his father's work, but also, through his mother, his maternal grandfather's (Major-General Sir John MacAskill) position in the Indian army and perhaps even his guardian's son's wife's father, MacCallam More Duke of Argyll, who was Secretary of State for India from 1869 to 1874 (MacInnes 1899; Sykes 1977, 13–17). Later his career would be supported by his wife's family, including her father, Teignmouth Sandys, who was a civilian judge in the Bengal presidency, and other relations gained through his sisters' marriages to various British colonial civil servants and military (Durand Family Papers 1870–1914; Gadru 1973, 317; Sykes 1977, 25, 34, 48, and 128).

Another example of such British kinship connections is that of the Younghusband family. The famous explorer Sir Francis Edward Younghusband who acted as an explorer, political agent, mapper, and Resident Officer for the British colonial government had a father and brother who both served in the British Indian Army, paving his way to start in the same career (French 1994). Through his maternal kinship relations Younghusband's family had extensive economic influence in the region; his maternal uncle, Robert Shaw, was a tea plantation owner who had formed caravans to trade his tea in Yarkend, traveling through Leh as the first documented British visitor in Yarkend (Shaw 1871). Shaw's status in the region was such that he was part of the British expedition to meet the revolutionary leader Yakub Beg and establish alliances in non-Chinese controlled Central Asia; he later became a British resident in Ladakh (Shaw 1871; French 1994; Seaver 1952). Thus families such as Younghusband's were able to represent and forward their financial interests through kinship-based connections with influence in the political realm.

British kinship networks also functioned to support power more indirectly, providing an additional symbolic element to public events and ceremonies. For example, Charles Nuckolls notes that Governor-General Lord Hardinge's plans for the 1911 Delhi Durbar (a sumptuous political ceremony where Indian rulers publicly pledged loyalty to King George V as "King-Emperor of India") were formed in large part by his personal interest in maintaining the status of his grandfather, Lord Henry Hardinge, a previous Governor-General of India (Nuckolls 1990, 554).

British colonial kinship networks were, like their elite Ladakhi counterparts, frequently transnational in nature, providing individuals with the linguistic skills and cultural knowledge that would aid in their careers. George Macartney, who became a British consular officer in Kashgar in 1908, was well connected patrilineally; his father was descended from the George Macartney of the eighteenth century who was both a governor of Madras and the first British ambassador to China. It was his mother's family, however, that provided the cultural knowledge that contributed to his success in the political service; Macartney was raised in Nanking speaking both English and Chinese as his mother was Chinese (and reportedly a descendent of a Taiping prince who had led a rebellion against the British government; see Skrine and Nightingale 1973, 3). Early exposure to a variety of Asian languages may have facilitated his study of other languages—listed by his contemporaries as Russian, German, Persian, Hindustani, and Turki [*sic*]—later in college, which would help his career as he first came to Kashgar as an interpreter for Younghusband in 1890 (Skrine and Nightingale 1973). Sir Clarmont Percival Skrine, British Consul-General in Kashgar from 1922 to 1924, noted the role of Macartney's familial connections as common knowledge, writing,

> [t]hanks to Macartney's services as interpreter and his knowledge of Chinese customs he and Younghusband established friendly personal relations with the Taotai and his officials. Macartney was almost certainly helped by his father's position in London and by the fact that Halliday Macartney has accompanied the Marquis Tseng as secretary and aide in his successful negotiation of the Treaty of St. Petersburg. (Skrine and Nightingale 1973, 27)

Skrine and others writing in the twentieth century clearly understood Macartney's successes in relation to a well-known system of kinship networks, in this case due to his patrilineal connections. The connections and skills from his matrilineal kin were less commonly discussed openly due to attitudes about British men marrying Asian women during the time period.[4] As several British officers during the time period had lost their jobs for marrying Asian women from families of a lower social status—e.g., L. M. King, assistant to the Chengtu consulate-general in the early 1920s, who was forced out of his post after his marriage to an unnamed Tibetan woman (Coates 1988, 418–23)—colonial recognition of Macartney's maternal family's elite status was essential to the political careers of members of the Macartney family.

Overall, we can see that kinship patterns within British kin groups were not haphazard; they were the result of social gate-keeping strategies that reinforced colonial British economic and political interests, as well as social expectations about the relationships formed between two families through marriage. Thus British kinship networks reproduced and reinforced colonial power within the social, political, and economic arenas of Asia.

LADAKHI/BRITISH KINSHIP ENCOUNTERS— RESISTANCE AND IMPLICATIONS

These elite Ladakhi and British communities formed parallel kinship networks in the late nineteenth and early twentieth centuries. Interactions between the two complimentary systems[5] of transnational kinship groups represent a significant subtext of colonial interactions that is worth considering in more detail. To return to Sahlin's and Strathern's earlier points about kinship as a way of both knowing the world and being in the world, these two kinship networks were not just about having access to local knowledge and power but shaped what it meant to exist in colonial India. What were the social implications of the interplay between these types of kinship groups, and how can we observe the relationship between the intimate spaces of the home and public forums of colonial power?

An anecdote from the life of Sir Henry Mortimer Durand provides a glimpse of possible answers to these questions. As mentioned earlier, Durand had lived in Bhopal as a child while his father, Sir Henry Marion Durand, had been the British Resident of the Bhopal Agency. In his biography Sykes includes excerpts from Durand's autobiography, including a section where Durand reminisces about his childhood in Bhopal, and links those experiences to his later work as Foreign Secretary of India, when meeting with a ruler in Bhopal named Shah Jehan Begum.[6] Durand wrote:

> My father held the Bhopal Agency for about four years [. . .] Many years later, when I was Foreign Secretary in India, the Bhopal State was under the rule of [Sikander Begum's] daughter, the Shah Jehan Begum, a capable and high-spirited lady. She, too, ruled the State well, but she married a man who gave some trouble to the Indian Government, and I had once to speak to her about him. I tried to do so as gently as possible, all my sympathies being with the Begum, but she turned upon me hotly. "You!" she said. "You speak to me like that! You were born in my State, and I remember you as a little *baba*—that high. I looked upon you as my small brother then. And now you come and lecture me as if you were the Great Lord Sahib! Oh wonderful, wonderful! If you had your father's *akl* (brains) you would know what nonsense it all is—utter nonsense—just a make-up of my enemies." I answered, and then tried to turn the conversation by asking whether a fine piece of embroidery I saw in the room was Bhopal work. She said "No, it was not."
> "Has Bhopal any special manufacture of the kind?"
> "No, it has only one standard industry, for which it is famous."
> "What is that?"
> "Lies!"
> She was a charming lady, the Shah Jehan, but not easy to "lecture." (Sykes 1977, 5–6)

As demonstrated in his account, Durand's appointment as Foreign Secretary may have been enabled by the connections and skills that he gained from his kinship networks, but the efficacy of his role was also shaped by the multigenerational relationships between elite Indian and British families.

Figure 5.1.   The Begum of Bhopal, Shah Jahan Begum of Bhopal, who ruled from 1868 to 1901 (b.1838–d.1901).
GCSI, Nov.1872, by Bourne and Shepard. Reprinted with permission, © British Library Board; Lee-Warner Collection, Shelfmark: Photo 2/3(1).

His knowledge of Shah Jehan's mother influenced his understanding of the ruler's role, while Shah Jehan in turn was able to deliberately transform his official "lecture" into a more personal encounter due to their shared family histories and use of kinship terms such as "little brother." As in the situation described above, any negotiating group composed of British officials and high-status elites in colonial Asia had a potential history of interactions with each other's kinship groups that could shape their expectations of each other, and subsequent course of their interactions.

Although difficult to excavate from formal historical records, hints these types of interactions occur in the Khan Archives documents in a pair of letters exchanged between John William Thomson-Glover and Bahauddin Khan in 1938 (Khan Family Papers 1900–1948). Thomson-Glover—who had formerly acted as the assistant to the British Resident in Leh from 1919 to 1923 and the Consul-General at Kashgar (linked to Ladakh through trade) from 1933 to 1936—was at the time the British Resident of Kashmir (Great Britain 1945, 202). Khan is the same individual discussed earlier in this chapter, the head of an affluent family who were elite traders and members of the Ladakhi Arghun community. In these letters Khan and Thomson-Glover discussed both business and personal affairs. The initial letter from Thomson-Glover, as shown in figure 5.2, reads:

My dear Bahauddin, Thank you for your letter of 11th February. I don't know whether I will get to Leh this summer or not. I would like to—have you any good pony for polo. If we come Mrs. Thomson Glover will want to play. I saw your son when I arrived here he does not look very fit. S.C.O. complained you had removed your package, drawn a refund, & kept them outside of Leh. Is

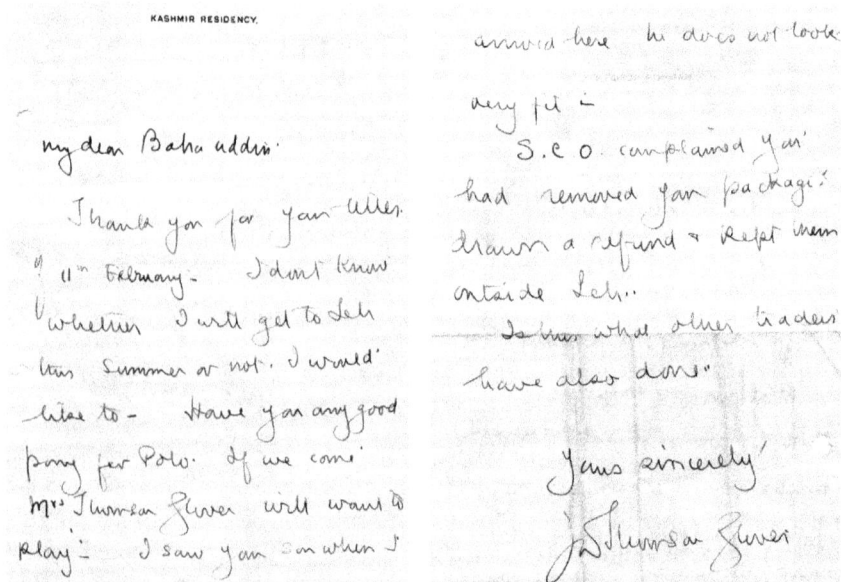

Figure 5.2.   Letter from Thomson-Glover to Bahauddin Khan, early 1930s. Khan Family Archives 1900–1948.
Photograph by Jacqueline H. Fewkes, 2000.

this what other traders have also done. Yours sincerely, J. W. Thomson-Glover (Khan Family Archives 1900–1948)

While Thomson-Glover's letter sounds at first like a casual note between colleagues—with discussion of vacation plans, sports, and children—in its conclusion he alludes to a serious matter in which his status would have been significantly different from that of Khan's: colonial trade regulations. When Thomson-Glover mentions the complaints of the SCO (State Customs Officer), he is referring to a reported problem with customs refunds for duty goods, a major source of revenue and arena of political control for the British in the region,[7] as well as a source of wealth for Ladakhi middlemen. Khan would have "drawn a refund" on a package by cashing in a customs invoice;[8] the question in this letter is whether he was receiving an improper customs duty refund and if this was a common practice.

The tone of the question that Thomson-Glover poses to Khan at the end of his letter is ambiguous. Is this a confidential inquiry from one friend to another about the realities of business arrangements, or a demand from the government official for a colonial subject to justify his behavior? While Khan's response was not preserved in his own documents, there is a typed draft of his reply with edit marks that suggests it was later re-typed and a new version sent.[9] The formality of Khan's reply—typed, proofread, and recomposed in contrast to Thomson-Glover's brief handwritten informal note—suggests that it was read as the latter. Khan's word choices in the draft supports this as well, as he uses the formal colonial title "mem Sahib"[10] for Mrs. Thomson-Glover and includes a plea that he was one of a group of "poor traders" victimized by the SCO in question.

Yet, Khan also includes more personal material in his response to Mr. Thomson-Glover, writing in response about his son's health and discussing ponies for Mrs. Thomson-Glover's polo. These topics suggest that the two families may have been personally acquainted and even socialized with each other in the past, a distinct possibility as Thomson-Glover's wife[11] is known to have resided with him at most of his postings, and the couple enjoyed an active sporting life in the Himalayan region. Indeed, Peter Fleming notes in his memoirs of travels in Central Asia that while living in Kashgar Mrs. Thomson-Glover frequently enjoyed organizing polo games with a "Hunza company of Gilgit Scouts" who acted as guards at the consulate, and that her sporting events set the tone for social relations at the consulate (Fleming 1936, 325–26).

These two letters illustrate the blurring of boundaries between public and private lives in colonial South Asia. In this exchange we are given a sense—perhaps just a hint—of the ways in which multi-generational and multi-gendered social relations contributed to complex sets of political and economic expectations. While not expressed in more formal political and economic documents, these relations shaped trading practices of both British colonial officials and elite Ladakhi traders.

CONCLUSION

As we have seen, both elite South Asian and British colonial families used kinship as a tool to represent their economic and political interests in the early twentieth century. The public world of colonial offices, customs posts, palaces, and sporting arenas was closely linked to the private homes and family lives of both parties. Recognizing these kinship groups as a common foundation for political and economic networks in the early twentieth century advances a few significant insights.

First, this approach brings into focus historical accounts of women's roles—albeit still frequently unnamed—in colonial South Asia. As the conversation between Shah Jehan Begum and Sir Henry Durand demonstrates, individual women occupied positions of power within the system; women such as Shah Jehan Begum, Ella Sandys Durand, Mrs. Thomson-Glover, the wife of Bahauddin Khan, and many others were not simply adjuncts, but rather actors in colonial political and economic events. The numerous unnamed women in this kinship system—wives, mothers, sisters, and domestic employees—are also recognized as having played central roles, binding together families and communities, to provide family firms with their most valuable "intangible asset."

Second, consideration of kinship relations suggests that in colonial interactions in places such as Ladakh, participants may have had a longer history of social relations, with more complex sets of expectations and understandings, than that overtly expressed in the formal documents of the time period. Strathern's aforementioned call for attention to the relations, relationships, cultural order, and knowledge of kin-based structures has expanded our understandings of possible social interactions between British residents, agents, and other colonial officials with high status communities in Asia, including the elite traders of Ladakh and Central Asia. Kinship relationships influenced multi-generational and multi-gendered social relations between British and Indian elites, creating sets of expectations and understandings that informed their political and economic interactions.

Finally, recognizing that core colonial practices in Asian trade—taxation, the political role of residents in princely states, etc.—crucially depended on arrangements associated with intimate household affairs, this expansion of perspectives on colonial social order allows us to question contemporary assumptions about the boundaries between public and private in this historical setting. This version of history allows for a re-reading of colonial affairs, prompting a perspective of the past that facilitates consideration of a more nuanced, and intimate, version of colonial rule.

NOTES

1. This chapter focuses on a part of my larger work on the ethnohistory of Ladakh, published in part in my book *Trade and Contemporary Society Along the Silk Route: An Ethnohistory of Ladakh* (2008) and in several articles/book chapters (e.g., Fewkes 2012, Fewkes and Khan 2016). This work was supported by funding from the Library of Congress Florence Tan Moeson Fellowship, American Historical Association, Duke University Libraries, University of Pennsylvania, and Florida Atlantic University. I am grateful for the research support of Abdul Nasir Khan, the Khan Manzil family, the staff of the Duke University David M. Rubenstein Rare Book and Manuscript Library, and the British Library Asian and African Studies Reading Room staff.

2. Roerich uses the term *aksakal*, which literally means "elder" in Turkic languages such as Uighur, as a title for custom officers in these towns.

3. For more details about the material culture associated with this community and time period, see Fewkes and Khan 2016.

4. See for example Ghosh 2006 for more on this topic.

5. These systems were largely separate, although as noted in Macartney's biography British colonial officials did sometimes marry elites from the communities in which they worked, further extending colonial influence through kinship networks. Another example of this is given by Coen, who notes that Col. Sir Robert Warburton, who was a military political agent at Khyber, was the son of a British artillery officer who married an "Afghan princess" (Coen 1971, 47). The negative impact of marrying non-elite Asians (e.g., Coates 1988, 41–423) could also be considered a facet of the comingling of these systems.

6. Sultan Jehan Begum is the author of a fascinating autobiography titled *Gauhar-e-Iqbal*, in which she wrote about her work, and detailed several interactions with the Durand family in the volume, although not this one (Begum 1912). She confirmed that Sir Henry Marion Durand closely advised her mother, Nawab Shah Jehan Begum, as did Sir Henry Mortimer later (Begum 1912, 18). Sir Henry Mortimer Durand's wife Ella Durand (née Sandys) also visited socially with Nawab Shah Begum (Begum 1912, 130). Although Begum did not mention any British children in the section on her childhood, she did record that a significant portion of her schooling was spent on English language education, which was regularly tested by visiting British agents (Begum 1912, 26–28).

7. By 1938 the British colonial government of India relied heavily on customs income from duty goods from Central Asia. In response to political unrest local administrators had been given permission in 1919 to use land revenues, which had previously supported the British colonial economy, for civic expenses; import revenues

were therefore a crucial source of income to offset national losses for the colonial government (Tomlinson 1982).

8. Customs invoices were refunded through a late nineteenth-century treaty intended to stimulate trans-Karakorum trade between British India and Chinese Central Asia. Goods sold in either area outside of Ladakh were eligible for a lower tax rate than those sold in Ladakh. Thus government officials at an entry customs post sealed goods designated for transport only, not for sale in Ladakh, with a stamp to prohibit tampering. Officials recorded the weight, contents, and value of each sealed package, and traders paid full taxes. Once the goods reached the government customs check-post at their point of departure from Ladakh the sealed packages were inspected to confirm that all items were still in transit. The State Customs Officer (SCO) or another representative of the British Joint Commissioner's office would then refund the paid taxes.

9. I have included Thomson-Glover's letter here, but have decided not to share an image of Khan's reply draft. While I would like to share the document to bring forward his voice, I am also aware that it was a private draft that, unlike Thomson-Glover's letter, was not intended for public dissemination. It is not clear what—if any—of the content Khan ultimately included in the finalized missive sent to Thomson-Glover.

10. "Mem Sahib" is the female equivalent of the colonial title "Sahib," which is frequently translated as a term for respect such as "sir," but in the context of colonial India is most clearly a signifier of unequal power relations.

11. Although she is referred to as "Mrs. Thomson-Glover" in most of these sources this was probably Norah Valentine Thomson-Glover (née Traill) who was John William Thomson-Glover's second wife. They were married in 1933.

REFERENCES

Baumann, Gerd. 1995. "Managing a Polyethnic Milieu: Kinship and Interaction in a London Suburb." *Journal of the Royal Anthropological Institute 1*: 725–41.

Begum, Nawab Sultan Jahan. 1912. *An Account of My Life: (Gohur-i-Ikbal.) By Her Highness Nawab Sultan Jahan Begam, Ruler of Bhopal.* Translated by C.H. Payne. London: John Murray.

Coates, P. D. 1988. *China Consuls: British Consular Officers, 1843–1943.* Hong Kong: Oxford University Press.

Coen, Sir Terence Creagh. 1971. *The Indian Political Service: A Study in Indirect Rule.* London: Chatto and Windus.

Durand Family Papers. 1840–1917. School of Oriental and African Studies (SOAS) Archives, University of London. GB 102 PP MS 55.

Durand, Henry Mortimer. 1883. *The Life of Major-General Sir Henry Marion Durand, KCSI, CB, of the Royal Engineers.* London: W. H. Allen.

Fewkes, Jacqueline H. 2008. *Trade and Contemporary Society Along the Silk Route: An Ethnohistory of Ladakh.* London: Routledge.

———. 2012. "Living in the Material World: Cosmopolitanism and Trade in Early Twentieth Century Ladakh." *Modern Asian Studies 46*(2): 259–81.

Fewkes, Jacqueline H., and Abdul Nasir Khan. 2016. "Manuscripts, Material Culture, and Ephemera of the Silk Route: Artifacts of Early Twentieth Century Ladakhi Trade Between South and Central Asia." *Asian Highlands Perspectives 39*: 73–127.

Fewkes, Jacqueline H., and Amy McLaughlin. 2007, June. "Negotiating Cultural/Conceptual Boundaries: Cosmopolitanism as Process." Paper presented at "Cosmopolitanism Past and Present" conference, University of Dundee (UK).

Fleming, Peter. 1936. *A Journey from Peking to Kashmir: News from Tartary.* New York: Charles Scribner's Sons.

Fraser, Nancy H. 1990. "Rethinking the Public Sphere: A Contribution to the Critique of Actually Existing Democracy." *Social Text 25/26*: 56–80.

French, Patrick. 1994. *Younghusband: The Last Great Imperial Adventurer.* London: Harper Collins.

Gadru, S. N., ed. 1973. *Kashmir Papers: British Intervention in Kashmir.* Srinagar: Freethought Literature Company.

Gardner, Katy. 1995. *Global Migrants, Local Lives: Travel and Transformation in Rural Bangladesh.* Oxford: Clarendon Press.

Georges, Eugenia. 1990. *The Making of a Transnational Community. Migration, Development, and Cultural Change in the Dominican Republic.* New York: Columbia University Press.

Ghosh, Durba. 2006. *Sex and the Family in Colonial India: The Making of Empire.* Cambridge: Cambridge University Press.

Great Britain. 1945. *The India Office and Burma Office List.* Digital version, University of California.

Habermas, Jürgen. 1991. *The Structural Transformation of the Public Sphere.* Boston: MIT Press.

Joseph, Suad. 1997. "The Public/Private: The Imagined Boundary in the Imagined Nation/State/Community: The Lebanese Case." *Feminist Review* [Special Issue, Citizenship: Pushing the Boundaries] *57*: 73–92.

Khan Family Papers. 1900–1948. *Trade Correspondence, Accounts, and Receipts Archive.* Copies in storage with Jacqueline H. Fewkes at Harriet L. Wilkes Honors College, Florida Atlantic University.

Kronenfeld, David. 2012. "What Kinship Is Not—Schneider, Sahlins, and Shapiro." *The Journal of the Royal Anthropological Institute 18*(3): 678–80.

Levi, Scott. 1999. "The Indian Merchant Diaspora in Early Modern Central Asia and Iran." *Iranian Studies 32*(4): 483–512.

Lévi-Strauss, Claude. 1949. *The Elementary Structures of Kinship (Les Structures Élémentaires de la Parenté).* Paris: Mouton/Maison des Sciences de l'Homme.

MacInnes, John. 1899. *The Brave Sons of Skye.* London: Eyre and Spottiswoode.

Markovits, Claude. 2008. *The Global World of Indian Merchants, 1750–1947: Traders of Sind from Bukhara to Panama.* Cambridge: Cambridge University Press.

Morgan, Lewis Henry 1871. *Systems of Consanguinity and Affinity of the Human Family.* Washington: Smithsonian Institution.

———. 1877. *Ancient Society, or Researches in the Lines of Human Progress from Savagery, through Barbarism, to Civilization.* London: Macmillan.

Nuckolls, Charles W. 1990. "The Durbar Incident." *Modern Asian Studies* 24(3): 529–59.

Ortner, Sherry. 1974. "Is Female to Male as Nature Is to Culture?" In *Woman, Culture, and Society*, edited by M. Rosaldo and L. Lamphere, 67–88. Stanford: Stanford University Press.

Risseeuw, Carla. 1992. "Gender, Kinship and State Formation: Case of Sri Lanka under Colonial Rule." *Economic and Political Weekly* 27(43/44): WS46–WS54.

Rizvi, Janet. 1999. *Trans-Himalayan Caravans.* New Delhi: Oxford University Press.

Roerich, George N. 1931. *Trails to Inmost Asia: Five Years of Exploration with the Roerich Central Asian Expedition.* New Haven: Yale University Press.

Rosaldo, Michelle Z. 1974. "Woman, Culture, and Society: A Theoretical Overview." In *Woman, Culture, and Society*, edited by M. Rosaldo and L. Lamphere, 17–42. Stanford: Stanford University Press.

Rudner, David West. 1994. *Caste and Capitalism in Colonial India: The Nattukottai Chettiars.* Berkeley: University of California.

Sahlins, Marshall. 2011a. "What Kinship Is (Part One)." *The Journal of the Royal Anthropological Institute* 17(1): 2–19.

———. 2011b. "What Kinship Is (Part Two)." *The Journal of the Royal Anthropological Institute* 17(2): 227–42.

Seaver, George. 1952. *Francis Younghusband: Explorer and Mystic.* London: John Murray.

Shapiro, Warren. 2012. "Extensionism and the Nature of Kinship." *The Journal of the Royal Anthropological Institute* 18(1): 191–93.

Shaw, Robert. 1871. *Visits to High Tartary, Yarkand and Kashgar (Formerly Chinese Tartary), and Return Journey over the Karakoram Pass.* London, UK: John Murray.

Skrine, C. P., and Pamela Nightingale. 1973. *Macartney at Kashgar. New Light on British, Chinese and Russian activities in Sinkiang, 1890–1918.* London: Methuen.

Strathern, Marilyn. 2014. "Kinship as a Relation." *L'Homme* (210): 43–61.

Sykes, Percy Molesworth. 1977. *The Right Honourable Sir Mortimer Durand: A Biography.* Lahore: al-Biruni.

Tomlinson, Brian R. 1982. "The Political Economy of the Raj: The Decline of Colonialism." *The Journal of Economic History* 42: 133–37.

Tsing, Anna L., and Sylvia J. Yanagisako. 1983. "Feminism and Kinship Theory." *Current Anthropology* 24(4): 511–16.

Chapter Six

Gendering Cosmopolitanism

Intersectional Visibility in Taiwan's Colonial Public Spheres

Melissa J. Brown

Taiwan is home to people of a wide range of ethnolinguistic groups and religious faiths; its government has taken a variety of steps to render all its residents equal before the law, including criminalizing domestic violence in 1997 and legalizing marriage equality in 2019. Women hold high-ranking political positions—president, vice president, mayor of the second largest city (2.8 million residents), and members of parliament (38 percent were women in 2016)—suggesting that women here enjoy a very different status than women elsewhere in the Sinosphere.[1] The contemporary acceptance of women in Taiwan's public sphere has deep roots in women's contributions to Taiwan's extraordinary cosmopolitan history.

Here, after briefly examining how women's social engagements are fundamental to the existence of cosmopolitanism, I discuss two moments in that fluctuating engagement where the swing toward cosmopolitanism depended crucially on ordinary women of populous but politically marginalized groups. These women crossed neo-Confucian ideological boundaries that framed Han 漢 (ethnic Chinese) women as belonging to the "inner" (內 *nei*) quarters, with strict gender divisions of labor: "men plow, women weave" (*nangeng nüzhi* 男耕女織) (e.g., Bray 1997). First, under seventeenth-century Dutch colonialism, aboriginal Austronesian women facilitated the range of sociality across diversity that made that era one high point of cosmopolitanism in Taiwan. Second, from the late nineteenth through early twentieth centuries—under a combination of Qing settler colonialism (1683–1895), Western imperialism (1860–1895), and Japanese imperialism (1895–1945)—a primarily woman-processed product, tea, rapidly became Taiwan's top global export, requiring quotidian public social engagements by local Han women. Finally, I briefly consider implications of how intersectionality—the interwoven and

mutually reinforcing influences of gender and, in this case, indigeneity (con-
strued broadly)—has been crucial to the ebb and flow of cosmopolitanism in
Taiwan's history for rethinking the public-private dichotomy more generally.

GENDERING COSMOPOLITANISM

"Cosmopolitan" is a word like "culture." Both terms have a meaning in popular society implying the sophisticated worldliness derived from elite levels
of wealth that facilitate education and travel. Wealth is crucial, if unstated;
sailors, for example, are not described as cosmopolitan in this sense, even
though they are well traveled. In short, this sense of "cosmopolitan"—like
the term "cultured"—amounts to an elite attribution of being "civilized,"
thus contrasting with an anthropological framework, where all humans have
culture and are potentially cosmopolitan.

Philosophers talk about cosmopolitanism as an ethical orientation or moral
principle that embraces an identity as a "citizen of the world" (from the Greek
kosmopolitês) over other collective identities, especially over identities linked
to membership in a family, clan, city, or nation-state (e.g., Appiah 2006).
An implicit aspect of citizenship—community membership—also allows
describing a *place* as cosmopolitan. And thus there are also terms attributing
civilization to place: cosmopolitan places are "urbane," urban and central,
in opposition to a "rustic" hinterland. Prasenjit Duara's (2015, 21) working
definition of cosmopolitanism as "the idea that all human beings belong non-
exclusively to a single community" asserts the importance of community
and implies the existence of a global public sphere (cf. Appiah 2006, 135).
But consider the tension between the face-to-face social engagement and
public cooperation implicit in the concept of community (Halperin 1998),
on the one hand, and the necessarily "imagined"—thus ambiguously public
and potentially private—character of social interactions across a global scale
(Anderson 1983).

By examining the face-to-face social interactions of ordinary people in their
local community networks, we can see that a place is cosmopolitan when a
significant proportion of people living there have quotidian social interactions
that can be called cosmopolitan (Fewkes 2014, 44–46). Such interactions
require social circumstances that both allow diversity *and* promote communitarian interactions across that diversity. The presence of diversity alone is
not a sufficient condition for cosmopolitanism, as the nationalistic and racist
violence of contemporary identity politics reminds us only too urgently. But
engagement across that diversity—the kind of engagement that builds and
maintains community, the kind of engagement necessary for conversations

and cooperative ventures, the kind of engagement that is the antithesis of ethnically or nationally based violence—may be sufficient. Moreover, the linkages that create a community connect across a public–private continuum.

Any classification of human beings by gender does not fit neatly into the current theoretical framework for cosmopolitanism. Cosmopolitanism, in all its forms, emphasizes (a) individuality, by taking individuals as the basic unit of moral concern; (b) universality, by viewing every individual as having equal moral value; and (c) generality, by holding all individuals—not merely those individuals with whom we share familial, religious, national, or other ties—as worthy of moral concern to every one of us (Taraborrelli 2015, xiv). This framework often assumes progressive steps: first we take individuals as the basic unit, then we view all individuals we know as equally valuable, and finally we grant value to strangers (but see Delanty [2012, 341] who does not assume progression). These moral concerns are primarily theorized as occurring in a public sphere. But, while every society necessarily has ties across gender differences—perhaps because these necessary ties are usually considered as belonging to a private sphere—many patriarchal societies readily accept the moral equivalence of men, despite differences that make them strangers, while simultaneously refusing to recognize women (and other feminized genders) as morally equal to men.

Women are not theorized in the diversity of cosmopolitanism. Although legal and political activists often target so-called women's issues, their proposed standards for ethical behavior indicate an underlying definition of cosmopolitanism as cooperation, enfranchisement, and tolerance across diversity. Literary and sociological approaches often emphasize local adoption of transnational practices—an embracing of multicultural diversity. But "diversity" has become a code word for the exotic—people, practices, and ideas perceived as interesting but unnecessary, as mutually exclusive, and possibly as dangerous to each other (as they compete for limited resources). Perhaps the theoretical omission of women is because we are entirely familiar—within every family and social unit—and thus not exotic.

It is crucial to include women, and gender more broadly, in the diversity across which tolerance and cooperation are measured because cosmopolitanism is necessarily operationalized through gendered categories. Gender exists across all other categorical distinctions among human beings in every society. Consequently, treatment of those low in the gender hierarchy constrains the possibilities for all categories of people—the ultimate intersectionality—and reveals the depth of a society's cosmopolitanism. If an entire category of person—feminine—is treated within households as less than another—masculine—category, how much more difficult must it be to promote notions of equality and tolerance across more "exotic" diversity?

Such cognitive dissonance must affect both people keeping the feminine gender(s) in subordination and people being subordinated. I suggest that the disjuncture between moral arguments and cultural beliefs that people *ought* to be tolerant, on the one hand, and empirical observations that people are *not* tolerant in social practice, on the other, lays down a cognitive framework of human hierarchy (with the primacy of early childhood association) that contributes significantly to whether people in certain times and places *practice* cosmopolitan.

To assess cosmopolitanism, therefore, we need to examine the actual social interactions of a populace, for even widespread cultural beliefs do not necessarily predict actual social behavior (Brown 2007; Lipatov, Brown and Feldman 2011). Literary approaches do consider social interactions, but primarily the social interactions of the male elite. Women and commoners are not excluded *per se* but the "cosmopolis"—a sphere of soft-power influence—is posited as created by the circulation of a literary "great tradition," including Sanskrit (Pollock 2006), Arabic (Ricci 2011), or classical Chinese (Park 2017). Such great traditions are necessarily limited to those classes who can afford education and, in many times and places, to boys and men. Although literary connections among educated men have no doubt contributed to more tolerant cooperation across some differences, a key component—a gendered component—of cosmopolitanism is not adequately considered.

A focus on urbane male elites also raises questions of whether indigenous yet subaltern colonial elites are ever considered culturally cosmopolitan, or "civilized" (e.g., Shih 2001, 97, 134–35, 275). A social approach to cosmopolitanism, by contrast, allows for the potential to find cosmopolitanism within colonialism (e.g., Appiah 2006, 79) because it examines whether empirical interactions between social actors are communitarian—whether they "practice" community—and whether these lived experiences cross lines of difference.[2] In this approach, cosmopolitanism is experienced at the level of ordinary individuals, not primarily among the elite. Thus, everyone's first potential exposure to cosmopolitanism—as a shared social experience—is local, and a person growing up in a cosmopolitan place may be "cosmopolitan" without ever having left that place.

In gendering cosmopolitanism, therefore, we need to recognize the significant differences between an individual who leapfrogs local provincial attitudes to connect to "the world," on the one hand, and a local community where the majority of its members engage across diversity, on the other. Because in patriarchal societies women often are—or are supposed to be—cloistered (to varying degrees), individual women only rarely have the opportunity to individually achieve cosmopolitanism by leapfrogging local conditions. In such instances, both extreme wealth and unusual familial attitudes often obtain. We also need to distinguish between elite women's knowledge of international fashion as signaling that their household is "cosmopolitan" (in the urbane sense) from women's ability to practice communitarian social interactions across recognized diversity in their quotidian lives.[3]

I suggest that it is no mere coincidence that the communitarian engagements across diversity that mark Taiwan's cosmopolitan zeniths—first in the Dutch period and again at the turn of the twenty-first century—have been facilitated by local women. This view is radical because women often are so often precluded from opportunities for cosmopolitan engagement. But the intersection of gender and indigeneity (considered from a broad view that includes localism) has been crucial indeed.

IDENTIFYING COSMOPOLITANISM IN TAIWAN'S HISTORY

Taiwan's geographic location as a massive island only one hundred miles off China's southeastern coast and in line with the Japanese archipelago has repeatedly led to politically strategic positioning. Across Taiwan's recorded history, its populace has been ethnically diverse. The first moment of cosmopolitanism I discuss occurred during the seventeenth century, when Taiwan served as a trade entrepôt. Dutch records from the 1620s show that Taiwan's indigenous peoples spoke dozens of distinct, mutually unintelligible Austronesian languages. Global trade networks brought speakers of at least another half-dozen languages to Taiwan's shores, where the trade among Chinese, Japanese, and Europeans that was forbidden by China and Japan grew for most of the seventeenth century. Multiple colonial efforts exploited diversity and exacerbated tensions within this population. The second moment I discuss is one of nascent cosmopolitanism that emerged with Taiwan's return to global trade after an almost two-hundred-year hiatus. Increases in women's movement into the public sphere obtained from 1860 into the early twentieth century. I focus on these two moments to show intersectional contributions to cosmopolitanism and to consider how cultural assumptions of women as private often veiled women's economic and public-sphere contributions.

First Moment: Marital Networks

From the 1620s through 1661, the Dutch East India Company (VOC) worked to consolidate colonial control over Taiwan, from a foothold in southwestern Taiwan. VOC officials brought in their service Dutch and German missionaries and schoolteachers; German, Dutch, and Portuguese mercenaries; and both free and enslaved Africans. Although the Dutch never numbered more than 1,200, they suppressed endemic Austronesian warfare across southwestern Taiwan.

Their efforts to control the Siraya, who were the Austronesian majority in the Dutch-controlled core area, affected women—disrupting their delayed-fertility and matrilineal marriage system and the female priesthood. These colonial efforts led to increases in the Siraya population size overall and also in the number of women available for marriage during the 1640s and 1650s, a crucial Han immigration period (Brown 2004, 136–53). Dutch censuses suggest the Austronesian population in 1650 was about twenty-six thousand and the Han population in the same year was fifteen thousand; Han grew from a few hundred traders and fishermen in 1622, augmented by thousands of agriculturalists to an estimated twenty-five thousand men by 1661. Han merchants and the VOC recruited Han men to migrate, and both Han and Dutch—and later Austronesians—sponsored Han laborers and farmers to clear forest land for commercial production of rice (in paddy fields) and sugarcane (in dry fields).

Austronesian women played an important role in the dynamics of cosmopolitanism in seventeenth-century Taiwan, first, because there were far more men than women in Dutch Taiwan. Han women were rare, certainly less than 10 percent of the population (European women were even more rare). Yet Dutch sources report many Han and European men were married and had families, and many also record marriages of Austronesian women with Han middlemen, translators, and farmers as well as with Europeans. By 1650, almost half the population under Dutch control was either of mixed Han-Austronesian ancestry or living in mixed Han-Austronesian households.

But a wildly skewed population sex ratio does not, in itself, give women power. Women were important members in their own right of Austronesian public spheres. The Siraya—later the VOC's closest allies—were matrilineal. Their gender division of labor (upon Dutch contact) made farming—via swidden, dry-field agriculture—the province of women and agricultural fields owned by women. Young men left their mothers' homes to live collectively in a men's house with their age-mates, moving through a militarized age-grade system that focused on warfare and hunting, and only moved to their wives' homes to farm and raise children after retirement, when they were in their forties. Siraya women chose their own husbands and shocked both Dutch and Chinese with their willingness to engage in sexual activity, whether married or not. Perhaps their attitude was because they had access to a reliable means of fertility control that preserved not only the life of the woman but her future fertility.[4] Austronesian women's local agricultural expertise and kin networks were probably viewed positively by Han men seeking marriage partners. Austronesian women's presence in publicly visible spaces was striking to seventeenth-century Chinese observers—no doubt for their flagrant disregard of neo-Confucian ideals—not only did Austronesian women work in agricultural fields with men (figure 6.1) but they also danced publicly during festivals (cf. Teng 2004, 152).

耕種

臺邑卓猴羅漢門新吾
等社熟番男婦耕種水
田禾稻至十月間收穫

Figure 6.1. Austronesian Cultivation, 1745. Despite sinicization and one hundred years of colonization, Austronesian women worked in Taiwan's agricultural fields and even plowed. Men are bare chested, women fully clothed.

Source: "Gengzhong" 耕種 (Cultivation), no. 5 in Fanshe caifeng tu 番社采風圖 (Illustrations of Taiwan's savage villages), 1745. Available online from the Institute of History and Philology, Academia Sinica (中央研究院歷史語言研究所), http://saturn.ihp.sinica.edu.tw/~wenwu/taiwan/.

Crucial to Austronesian women's public contributions was the fact that both Dutch and Han invested in learning to speak Siraya and other Austronesian languages. The VOC economically and politically supported missionaries and schoolteachers in many villages so they would learn the local languages. This continued investment, despite clear tensions throughout the Dutch records between VOC officials and missionaries, suggests how fundamental Austronesians were to the Dutch colony—for the deer trade and military control of the southwestern plains. VOC employees often married Christian Austronesian women. Such liaisons were sometimes explicitly stated in mentioning promotions—for example, with German schoolteacher Hendrick Noorden's 1657 promotion to political administrator over the southern territories under Dutch control—a record that is highly suggestive that Austronesian women "played an active part in the network of relations between the [VOC] Company personnel and the indigenous population" (Everts and Milde 2003, 243). Dutch records also show that many Han learned Austronesian languages sufficiently to become middlemen—collecting the tribal tax and holding VOC-licensed monopoly rights to purchase specified goods, such as deerskins or sugar cane. Many Han middlemen had Austronesian wives. These middlemen purchased not only from Austronesians but also from any Han agriculturalists living in their licensed territories, many with Austronesian wives. Such ethnic intermarriage enhanced bilingualism, not only for husband and wife, but even more strongly for their children.

The network of marital ties in Dutch Taiwan had implications for access to resources and implementation of policies—both public-sphere concerns. Remembering the intermarriage of Han and VOC men with women in these villages, it is not so surprising that—despite orders from their VOC superiors in Batavia (Indonesia) to remove all Chinese from Austronesian villages—in 1642, the Taiwan VOC allowed Han to remain in six communities near the Dutch stronghold as well as in the village of Favorlang (some twenty-five miles north in central Taiwan), "because the Dutch civil administration stationed in these villages could keep an eye on their activities" (Heyns 2003, 182).[5] The Dutch administrators and the Han men living in the villages were married into the same matrilineal Austronesian network—they were marital kin!—something the Taiwan VOC knew well but probably did not reveal to their superiors in Batavia.

Marital ties were always local and thus capable of microlevel feedback to larger social pressures. Consequently, Han-Austronesian intermarriage could cause trouble for the Dutch, as these ties did in Favorlang roughly from 1635 to 1645. "Favorlang Chinese"—married to Austronesian women in Favorlang but with their own ties to seafaring Han—were diverting deer and crops to Han smugglers, who circumvented VOC licensing and fees; they were attacking "Dutch Chinese" who had VOC licenses, and the Favorlang Chinese were encouraging Austronesian resistance to Dutch control (Andrade 2005). Marital ties also gave Austronesians access to Dutch and Han networks. VOC governor Van Nuyts, who bungled diplomacy with the Tokugawa shogunate in Japan and left his position in disgrace, was criticized for a long-term liaison with an Austronesian woman (he also had a wife in the Netherlands) (e.g., Blussé 2003b). Such matrilineal connections—to the VOC administration and missionaries, to Han middlemen and agriculturalists—may explain how some Austronesians became registered landlords, sponsoring the clearing of forests and the establishment of agricultural fields by Han in exchange for tenancy rights; the Taiwan VOC allowed and even recorded several instances of such registration, which the Batavia VOC later rejected (Heyns 2003). The one social milieu where Austronesian marital ties appear not to have extended is that of Han merchants in town near the Dutch forts, for these men were wealthy enough to bring Han wives from China (or elsewhere). Yet Han merchants still participated in the interethnic cooperation necessary to identify appropriate land; ensure peaceful access; organize and supply work teams; plant, protect, harvest, and process crops; pay VOC duties; and arrange shipping to the global market.

Interests frequently aligned across differences in native languages and ancestry. In 1652, for a particularly notable example, Han merchants warned the VOC about a rebellion by four or five thousand Han agriculturalists. The warning allowed VOC troops—120 VOC-paid, musket-armed mercenaries and about two thousand Austronesian militia armed with bows and spears—to suppress the uprising, reportedly killing two to three thousand Han (Brown 2004, 40). On the surface, this anecdote may appear to show Han-Dutch cooperation that bypasses marital ties through Austronesian women. But later events are highly suggestive of VOC reliance on Austronesians to verify Han-originated information; thus it is likely that the VOC confirmed this warning before they acted. As regional military power shifted away from the Dutch, their provincialism of never having adequately learned Chinese (or Japanese) put them at a severe disadvantage.

Perhaps the clearest way to see the importance of Austronesian women's networks for Dutch and Han cooperation, and thus to Dutch Taiwan's cosmopolitanism, is to consider what happened when these networks were cut off. As a result of China's Ming–Qing dynastic civil war, the Taiwan VOC expected invasion from Zheng Chenggong.[6] Negotiation attempts failed because the Taiwan VOC's inability to speak, read, and write Chinese left them stuck sending as their lone emissary a man capable in both Dutch and Chinese languages but infamous for his treacherous dealings with Han and Dutch alike (Andrade 2007, 9, 14–15). Indeed, he facilitated Zheng's 1661 invasion with twenty thousand seasoned troops. The invasion cut ties among Dutch, Han, and Austronesians, leaving the Dutch unable to triangulate information, the Han struggling to maintain their livelihoods, and the Austronesians guarded by a suspicious and experienced army.

Such ethnic suspicions made interethnic contact—let alone cooperation—difficult and fraught. During the nine-month siege of the two Dutch strongholds, Zheng reportedly treated defectors well.[7] But the Taiwan VOC treated Han defectors badly—imprisoning, torturing, and murdering many. At least one Han defector brought news that might have allowed the Dutch to defeat Zheng's forces and keep their colony. But unable to verify his information, they contravened his advice, lost a naval battle, and surrendered completely (Andrade 2007). Although in 1652 the Taiwan VOC had used Han merchant information to act against a Han agriculturalist uprising, ten years later the Taiwan VOC could not understand conflicting interests among the Han—Zheng Chenggong's interests versus those of Taiwan's Han merchants, middlemen, and farmers—sufficiently to act cooperatively with any Han. In short, the Taiwan VOC lost Taiwan because its leaders were no longer cosmopolitan.

Speculating about Austronesian conceptions of public and private is problematic, not only because the limited written records of their ideas were compiled by missionaries who sought to change them. Practices and beliefs do not need to coincide; indeed, changing practices often precede and even drive changes in cultural ideas and beliefs (Brown 2004, 2007; Lipatov, Brown, and Feldman 2011). We are on safer ground considering how the documented practices of Austronesian women must have disrupted Han and Dutch gendered notions of public and private space and roles. Dutch colonizers converted Austronesians to Christianity, overthrowing the indigenous woman-led religious practices and pushing newlyweds to settle in their own (neolocal) home and start raising children immediately, but they, like Han, did not disrupt all women's practices in the public sphere. Surely the demography—a population sex-ratio imbalance and much larger proportions of Austronesians to Europeans or, initially at least, Han—combined with Austronesian customs and local knowledge (such as short-term emigration into forest or mountains in the face of aggression) to give Austronesians leverage to maintain women's marital networks and many resource-related public practices, such as agriculture and marketing. It is not unreasonable to suppose that, although patriarchal empires distinguished public from private spheres and associated women with the private or "inner" sphere, neither the dichotomy nor the association of women with private would obtain in matrilineal village-scale societies. Moreover, this colonial and demographic context laid an important foundation, on which later historical developments built, of the visible participation of women in Taiwan's public sphere.

Second Moment: Tea Processing

Taiwan under the rule of China's Qing dynasty showed a marked absence of cross-ethnic tolerance and cooperation. Taiwan's infamous uprisings and rife ethnic violence (e.g., Lamley 1981; Shepherd 1993) were expensive to control, with 159 major incidents between 1684 and 1895 (Chen 1999, 136). Qing administrative management allowed tens of thousands of Han migrants' encroachment on tax-paying Austronesians' land rights and the growth of local Han strong men with ethnic-based militia—allowances attributed to chronic understaffing (Meskill 1979; Shepherd 1993; Chen 1999). Much nineteenth-century colonization included families, so these settlers (largely to northern Taiwan) had fewer marital ties to Austronesian peoples (Brown 2004, 156). By 1800, people of patrilineal Han descent and Han identity across Taiwan—including those with Austronesian matrilineal ancestry—had sufficiently large numbers that most Han men could marry endogamously, even within native-place-of-origin groups at the prefectural or county levels. Interethnic cooperation was no longer necessary for economic production. Despite the existence of mixed Han-Austronesian villages, most Han in Taiwan had little reason to engage with Austronesians at all (though some Han continued to make a living this way).[8] Feuding, often among county-level native-place groups, meant there was little if any cooperation across ethnic-type distinctions even among the Han. The Qing exploited these tensions, keeping their troop (and administrative) expenditures lower by using different ethnic groups' militias to patrol each other, but these policies also fomented local strongmen. By 1860, cosmopolitanism in Taiwan had reached a nadir.

Although the first half of Taiwan's nineteenth century was characterized by an insular focus on Han settler colonialism, the second half brought attention to global markets, further shifting specifics of the ongoing colonial transformation of Taiwan's ecosystems. The British and French used military force to expand "free" trade—that is, freedom for Europeans to trade where they chose in China with minimal Qing taxation. The 1860 unequal treaty opened to international trade two Taiwanese sea ports and, after additional pressure, two more sea ports, the Qing administrative seat in southwestern Taiwan (the old Dutch stronghold), and two northern river ports (Mengjia 艋舺 and Dadaocheng 大稻埕, both now within Taipei City) (Gardella 1999, 167). After losing a war largely fought in northern China, the Qing ceded Taiwan to Japan, whose colony it remained through WWII. Western and Japanese imperialism meant that the focus of Taiwan's peoples was turned externally—first to global trade and later to Japanese imperial trade—an orientation that brought both economic exploitations and benefits. It also necessitated at least minimal cooperative interactions—between Han locals and

European or Japanese merchants—for resource extraction, refinement, and shipping. Cosmopolitanism marginally increased.

Although sugar was a major export throughout the nineteenth century, after 1860 tea rapidly surpassed it.[9] Cooperation among Western merchants, Han merchants, and Han middlemen led to increased incursions into the forested, mountainous Austronesian territories, cutting trees and setting up camphor stills and later planting tea. Indeed, Qing official oversight of developing the tea and camphor trade[10] lay with a bureau intended to subjugate Austronesians and annex their territories (Fuken Ju 撫墾局, lit. pacification and clearing bureau). Local Han militia leaders were often appointed to this bureau, to their profit. In 1888, for example, the Lins of Wufeng received a land grant of several thousand hectares with virgin camphor stands after Lin militia suppressed three Austronesian uprisings.

The global tea trade changed the face of northern Taiwan, including Taipei City, and it dramatically altered the lives of local women—bringing many into the public-sphere side of wage labor. Han women's economic contributions to their households have long been legion—as well as both underestimated and undervalued—but in rural areas, such contributions, often in the form of homemade handicrafts and textiles, did not previously necessitate leaving a prescribed area of household, fields, and water source (Brown 2017; Brown and Satterthwaite-Phillips 2018; cf. Bray 1997). As tea became Taiwan's leading global export during the late nineteenth century, however, Westerners, such as John Dodd, built warehouses and hired Han middlemen to deal with cultivation and processing. Americans and Europeans retreated to handling export shipping when their former compradors outcompeted them at the local level. The river port of Dadaocheng became a boomtown where tea harvested in the hills around the Taipei basin was brought for sorting, processing, and shipment on to the coastal port of Danshui. There was a huge demand for female labor from the rural hills to the river ports because picking tea (leaf by leaf), sorting, and processing (curing) were all traditionally women's work, though men also processed tea. Notably this work occurred in public, as vividly portrayed in a nineteenth-century drawing of men and women working in a public square (figure 6.2).

Women could earn good wages from tea—enough to support themselves and another person or two—and by 1900, thousands were doing so in Dadaocheng on a daily basis (Davidson [1903] 1988, 385–86; Wolf and Gates 2005, 121). This economic organization has major implications not only for household economics and power dynamics but also for communitarian cosmopolitanism. Japanese demographic records from the early twentieth century show that over 90 percent of Han women in towns (91 percent) and rural areas (98 percent) of Taiwan married, but in Dadaocheng almost 23 percent

Figure 6.2. Sorting Tea in Public, 1871. This illustration for a Western newspaper shows an outdoor, public space in northern Taiwan, where Han women are sitting alone, with other women, and with Han men to sort tea. One man, with his shirt open and a turban, may be Austronesian.
Source: Edward (Sung-tie) Greey, 1871, "'Tai-wan'—Formosa," Frank Leslie's Illustrated Newspaper 33(834, 23 September): 28. Available online from the Reed College digital archive, Formosa: Nineteenth century images, https://rdc.reed.edu/c/formosa/s/r?_pp=20&query=tea&s=5ded2bcd5b8394afbf0e4c2b755ac5bf70bcc1bf&p=1&pp=1.

of women never married (Wolf and Gates 2005, 119). This European-like marital pattern may derive from urban life generally (Wolf and Gates 2005, 125, 128)—including wage work in the global tea trade in Dadaocheng and wage work for the myriad workers supporting prostitution in Mengjia—but did work in these different industries bring women into the public with the same frequency?

The wealthiest families claimed achievement of the neo-Confucian patriarchal ideal of keeping women cloistered within their household, except for occasional visits to temples. Historians' accounts of such cloistering often rely on patrilineage genealogies (e.g., Meskill 1979, esp. chap. 13), but genealogies I have seen frequently leave women out entirely, with kinship charts that show fathers giving birth to sons, without any women on the page. Genealogies may record difficult times but usually with an eye to showing moral fortitude, expunging elements not to their credit (Meskill 1979, 65)—including departures from neo-Confucian ideals. But occasional reports—one woman recruiting and leading new troops to rescue her husband and his forces under siege in the mountains, another woman pursuing four legal suits to restore the name of two sons (Meskill 1979, 162–75, 188)—raise questions about where these women learned the necessary skills.

The daily work of women in nonelite households surely took them more frequently outside the house—especially in urban areas to stores or markets (whether buying supplies or selling handicrafts or other goods). However, the employment supported by the sex trade in Mengjia—not only prostitutes and brothel owners, but also seamstresses and silver-platers—was largely carried out behind closed doors. By contrast, the tea industry brought local women into Taiwan's public sphere to such an extraordinary degree that it was note-worthy even to contemporaneous observers. John Davidson, an American journalist who reported on Japan's 1895 colonial take-over of Taiwan, wrote, "During the summer months, nothing is more striking than the crowds of girls"—he estimated a daily average of over twelve thousand—"who at noon and night simply overrun [Dadaocheng]" (Davidson [1903] 1988, 385).

I suggest that the growth of the tea industry was important to the broad acceptance of local women's highly visible expansion in Taiwan's public sphere. Moreover, the tea industry apparently smoothed ethnic tensions among the local Han.[11] And it also extended into smaller towns and the rural hinterland. As the global tea trade pervaded Taiwan society, more and more households—including its female members—necessarily had quotid-ian public engagements—with strangers and with people of different ethnic groups—so fundamental to communitarian cosmopolitanism. Tea remained an important export through 1910.

Subsequently, various colonial policies moved Taiwanese women more into the public sphere. The Japanese government banned footbinding, which it considered barbaric, in 1905 but did not add footbinding to the list of items to be checked during semi-annual police visits until 1915—when they understood that women with bound feet would not work in the paddy fields. Implementation of the ban expanded women's participation in agriculture, as intended (Brown 2004, 95, 161, 232, 265n45), so men could move into manufacturing, construction, clerical work, and other wage labor. Although the 1915 footbinding ban ironically worked against cosmopolitanism in some Austronesian communities (where it resulted in assimilation to a Hoklo Han cultural identity), the ban promoted cosmopolitanism within Hoklo Han communities where footbinding had previously been customary.[12] The ban did move more women to work in agricultural fields and also to work in factories. Other policies kept women in the public-sphere workforce; for ex-ample, in the tobacco monopoly, women had pregnancy leave of more than a month and the right to continue working after marriage (Brown 2010, 270). For Taiwanese women with even a middle school education, there were job opportunities in banks and offices as clerks, and those with a normal school education themselves became teachers (Farris 2004, 340). Although these colonial efforts were explicitly aimed at boosting subaltern productivity, they also had lasting effects on civil society—not only expanding women's quotidian experience in the public sphere across classes and regions of Taiwan, and certainly well beyond what the nineteenth-century tea industry had produced—but also promoting such participation as both proper and "modern."

VISIBILITY IN THE PUBLIC SPHERE AND
THE PRESUMPTION OF WOMEN AS PRIVATE

Both these historical moments provide different ways of looking at the public-private dichotomy. The first moment, because it shows the interaction of matrilineal and patrilineal societies, raises questions about the extent to which the conception of a public-private dichotomy constitutes patriarchal ideology that genders public as male and private as female.[13] In Dutch-era Taiwan, matrilineal marital networks had multiple public ramifications—for access to information, resources, and military alliances. We do not know exactly how any of Taiwan's many Austronesian peoples conceptualized public or private space in the seventeenth century, but Dutch and Chinese historical records indicate that Austronesian *practices* did not privilege one gender in either (what they and we consider) "public" or "private" space.

This first moment also raises questions about the extent to which the concept of a public-private dichotomy is related to large-scale, economically specialized societies. Siraya Austronesian villages during the Dutch period were on the order of 800 to 3,000 people—larger than horticulturalist villages elsewhere in Taiwan, but still small enough for people to recognize other community members on sight (Brown 2004, 145). In such a social context, with buildings that were physically small, often open-aired, and sometimes serving a specific purpose (e.g., sleeping, sugar processing), how "private" is any activity anywhere? Siraya men may not have told Siraya women what was going in the men's huts, but if all the village men in one age grade are party to any particular event there, can such events be characterized as "private"?

A notion of private space implies cloistering in some way. At a village level, even in a large-scale economically specialized society, it is difficult to enforce. But with specialization, it is an economically important distinction: what goods, what information, what time belong to individuals versus to their employers, or belongs to cultivator households versus to their landlord?

Relevant to these questions are the seventeenth-century Dutch reports complaining that Austronesians would not plant surplus rice (rice beyond the needs of their family and village) (Brown 2004, 37–38). Not surprisingly, the VOC saw this refusal as idleness and a fault—and it led them to initiate large-scale immigration of Han farmers and laborers, a tactic that ultimately backfired on their colonial designs. But as grounds for rethinking the public-private distinction, the Austronesian refusal implies a different conception of resources as public versus private.

The second historical moment offers us an invitation to reconsider how—in a large-scale, economically specialized society—the fiction of a strict and a gendered public-private dichotomy was maintained despite women's public-sphere presence and engagement. Han women were not as cloistered anywhere as neo-Confucian ideology said they ought to be or even as cloistered as many people believed they were. An idiom of "helping" veiled not only the economic contributions of women and girls but also their presence in the public sphere. In other words, women worked publicly but received no social credit—a cultural veiling that continues into twenty-first century China (Brown 2017).

Discrepancies in genealogies raise questions about whether cloistering women applied even to the wealthiest of families, but certainly such cloistering was not possible among the nonelite (e.g., documented in Fei and Chang 1945; Gamble 1954). In many parts of the rural PRC where I have interviewed, people expected Han women before 1950—and especially recent brides—to have very limited social engagements outside the household and within the village. There was expected movement between house, pigsty, fields, grinding stone, and the water sources for drinking, cooking, and washing clothing, but not much more. But even assuming these expectations accurately reflect practice, they definitely took women beyond the confines of the "inner quarters." The 1871 image of Han young women processing tea in Taiwan (figure 6.2) is striking in showing them so visibly in the public sphere—in contrast to these neo-Confucian ideals.

Visibility matters. Women's public presence and contributions have to be visible—and accurately socially credited—in order to for women to win power and social status, whether within households or in the political arena. The economic contributions that Chinese women made to households have long been veiled (Bray 1997). Rural Han women, even footbound women, performed agricultural as well as cottage handicraft labor (Brown and Satterthwaite-Phillips 2018). During orally administered structured interviews with 2,737 Chinese women, mostly born between 1915 and 1942 and residing in twenty-two rural Han counties in eleven Chinese provinces, mentioning "work" (*gongzuo* 工作, *zuoshi* 做事, *zuo laodong* 作劳动, *ganhuo* 干活) often elicited some statement that a woman herself, or women in general, did not work, even from women who had done agricultural labor.[14] For example, a woman I call Ms. Li said, "[Before 1949] males did agricultural field work; females didn't go into the fields" (地里的活男的做，女的不下田) (Hunan no. 2101146, b. 1935). So to discover what labor women actually performed, we asked about specific tasks. Ms. Li planted, harvested, and dried sweet potatoes and soybeans for her natal family; she also picked cotton—all labor that required going into agricultural fields. When asked what they were doing if not "work," many such women replied that they were "helping" (*bang-mangle*, 帮忙了). Handicraft labor was also often elided as "helping" mothers or mothers-in-law, who were credited with the product. For example, asked who spun in her marital household, one woman said: "My mother-in-law. My sister-in-law helped her spin" (婆婆，嫂子给帮忙防) (Anhui no. 1101032, b. 1916). In years of interviewing in both Taiwan and the PRC about house-hold- and village-level customs over the sweep of the twentieth century, I have been struck by the distinct difference not only in socially crediting girls' and women's contributions but often even in recognizing the existence of female contributions. In Taiwan, both men and women often acknowledged these contributions (Brown 2004). In the PRC, men did not acknowledge female contributions, women often did not even realize that they had made contributions, and women who did realize could not say so in front of their men (Brown 2017). This idiom of helping may also veil women's presence in the public sphere. If women were in the public sphere not as agents but as "helpers," then were they socially visible? Did the descriptive language of the public sphere even register their physical presence?

Women are necessarily part of quotidian social engagements because women are part of all class and ethnic divisions within a society, so women—especially women of populous marginalized groups—are crucial, if often unacknowledged, contributors to public spheres (Weller 1999). Politically and economically, women's status in the PRC continues to lag that of women in Taiwan (e.g., Farris 2004), so I return to consideration of Taiwanese his-tory to better understand the impact of engaged women on society. I suggest that impact is cosmopolitanism. Ordinary, local women have been crucial to the ebb and flow of cosmopolitanism across Taiwan's history, including its present-day zenith.

The intersectionality of these two moments of Taiwan's cosmopolitan his-tory has implications for rethinking our conceptualization of a public-private dichotomy. The less specialized economy of the Austronesians in the first moment raises questions about whether social space can legitimately be dichotomized between public and private. Austronesian matrilineality raises questions about whether the association of women with a private, or "inner," sphere is patriarchal ideology. And women's public tea processing raises questions about whether ideological associations of women with a private sphere—perhaps using an idiom of "helping"—have veiled women's actual economic contributions and public-sphere presence.

NOTES

1. By contrast, neither the People's Republic of China (PRC) nor Japan has ever had a woman head of state; Korea had one woman president (Park Geun-hye, but she was removed from office for corruption and imprisoned). And women are significantly underrepresented in all three national parliaments: PRC around 25 percent, Japan around 10 percent, and Korea around 17 percent. (About 25 percent of members in the U.S. Congress are women.)

2. Halperin (1988, 1998) defines this approach as "institutional." In contrast, Delanty (2012, 339) defines as it "transactional."

3. At the local level of patriarchal societies, face-to-face interactions between men and women are not usually perceived as engaging across diversity. Women, and feminized genders more broadly, are often taken for granted—as "helpers," for example.

4. Shepherd (1995) discusses seventeenth-century Dutch reports that Siraya externally manipulated a woman's abdomen to cause abortion.

5. The Batavia VOC did not accept these accommodations, so further movement occurred in 1644.

6. The Zheng merchant-marine empire and the VOC had long traded naval attacks, seizures of ships, and cargo on both sides.

7. One German defector taught Zheng how to overcome the defenses of the Dutch stronghold Zeelandia (Andrade 2012, 132–33).

8. Qing documents call Austronesians "savages" (*fan* 番), subdivided into "civilized" (*shou* 熟, lit. cooked) or "wild" (*sheng* 生, lit. raw), by their degree of sinicization and acquiescence to Qing rule (Brown 2004, 2010; Teng 2004).

9. In 1868 sugar was about 60 percent of Taiwan's exports and tea was only 9 percent, by 1876 sugar and tea were both about 46 percent, and by 1881 tea was 60 percent of exports (Gardella 1999, 167).

10. Camphor exports began around 8 percent during the late 1860s, dropped below 1 percent from 1876 through the mid-1880s, and climbed back up to 9 percent during the 1890s, when new chemical techniques used camphor in smokeless gunpowder and in film.

11. Dadaocheng's founding resulted from Quanzhou-descended Han driving Tongan-descended Han out of Mengjia; they joined Zhangzhou-descended Han downstream in what became Dadaocheng (Wolf and Gates 2005, 115).

12. An ethnolinguistic division existed among Han (in Taiwan and southern China) between Hoklo, who bound daughters' feet, and Hakka, who did not.

13. Ortner's (1974) classic essay is an early attempt to consider whether such a dichotomy was "natural," based on the biology of childcare in foraging and horticulturalist societies. Taiwan's matrilineal Austronesians suggest otherwise.

14. See Brown and Satterthwaite-Phillips (2018) for methodology, results, and availability of data.

REFERENCES

Anderson, Benedict. 1983. *Imagined Communities: Reflections on the Origins and Spread of Nationalism*. London: Verso.

Andrade, Tonio. 2005. "Pirates, Pelts, and Promises: The Sino-Dutch Colony of Seventeenth-Century Taiwan and the Aboriginal Village of Favorolang." *Journal of Asian Studies 64*(2): 295–321. doi: 10.1017/S0021911805000793.

———. 2007. "Chinese under European Rule: The Case of Sino-Dutch Mediator He Bin." *Late Imperial China 28*(1): 1–32. doi: 10.1353/late.2007.0006.

———. 2012. "Koxinga's Conquest of Taiwan in Global History: Reflections on the Occasion of the 350th Anniversary." *Late Imperial China 33*(1): 122–40. doi: 10.1353/late.2012.0003.

Appiah, K. Anthony. 2006. *Cosmopolitanism: Ethics in a World of Strangers*. New York: W. W. Norton.

Blussé, Leonard, ed. 2003a. *Around and About Formosa: Essays in Honor of Professor Ts'ao Yung-ho*. Taipei: Ts'ao Yung-ho Foundation for Culture and Education.

———. 2003b. "Bull in a China Shop: Pieter Nuyts in China and Japan (1627–1636)." In Blussé 2003a, 95–110.

Bray, Francesca. 1997. *Technology and Gender: Fabrics of Power in Late Imperial China*. Berkeley: University of California Press.

Brown, Melissa J. 2004. *Is Taiwan Chinese? The Impact of Culture, Power, and Migration on Changing Identities*. Berkeley: University of California Press.

———. 2007. "Ethnic Identity, Cultural Variation, and Processes of Change: Rethinking the Insights of Standardization and Orthopraxy." *Modern China* 33(1): 91–124. doi: 10.1177/0097700406294701.

———. 2010. "Changing Authentic identities: Evidence from Taiwan and China." *Journal of the Royal Anthropological Institute 16*(3): 459–79. doi: 10.1111/j.1467–9655.2010.01634.x.

———. 2017. "Dutiful Help: Masking Rural Women's Economic Contributions." In *Transforming Patriarchy: Chinese Families in the Twenty-First Century*, edited by Gonçalo Santos and Stevan Harrell, 39–58. Seattle: University of Washington Press.

Brown, Melissa J., and Damian Satterthwaite-Phillips. 2018. "Economic Correlates of Footbinding: Implications for the Importance of Chinese Daughters' Labor." *PLOS ONE 13*(9): e0201337. doi: https://doi.org/10.1371/journal.pone.0201337.

Chen, Chiukun. 1999. "From Landlords to Local Strongmen: The Transformation of Local Elites in Mid-Ch'ing Taiwan, 1780–1862." In Rubinstein 1999, 133–62.

Davidson, James W. (1903) 1988. *The Island of Formosa Past and Present*. Reprint, Taipei: Southern Materials Center.

Delanty, Gerard. 2012. "A Cosmopolitan Approach to the Explanation of Social Change: Social Mechanisms, Processes, Modernity." *Sociological Review 60*(2): 333–54. doi: https://doi.org/10.1111/j.1467–954X.2012.02076.x.

Duara, Prasenjit. 2015. *The Crisis of Global Modernity: Asian Traditions and a Sustainable Future*. Cambridge: Cambridge University Press.

Everts, Natalie, and Wouter Milde. 2003. "'We Thanked God for Submitting Us to Such Sore but Tolerable Trials': Hendrick Noorden and His Long Road to Freedom." In Blussé 2003a, 243–72.

Farris, Catherine S. P. 2004. "Women's Liberation under 'East Asian Modernity' in China and Taiwan: Historical, Cultural, and Comparative Perspectives." In *Women in the New Taiwan: Gender Roles and Gender Consciousness in a Changing Society*, edited by Catherine S. P. Farris, Anru Lee, and Murray A. Rubinstein, 325–76. Armonk, NY: M. E. Sharpe.

Fei, Hsiao-tung (Fei Xiaotong) and Chih-I Chang (Zhang Zhiyi). 1945. *Earthbound China: A Study of Rural Economy in Yunnan*. Chicago: University of Chicago Press.

Fewkes, Jaqueline H. 2014. "Living in the Material World: Cosmopolitanism and Trade in Early Twentieth Century Ladakh." In *Sites of Asian Interaction: Ideas, Networks and Mobility*, edited by Tim Harper and Sunil Amrith, 38–59. Cambridge: Cambridge University Press.

Gamble, Sidney D. 1954. *Ting Hsien [Ding Xian]: A North China Rural Community*. New York: Institute of Pacific Relations.

Gardella, Robert. 1999. "From Treaty Ports to Provincial Status, 1860–1894." In Rubinstein 1999, 163–200.

Halperin, Rhoda H. 1988. *Economies across Cultures: Towards a Comparative Science of the Economy*. London: Macmillan Press.

———. 1998. *Practicing Community: Class Culture and Power in an Urban Neighborhood*. Austin: University of Texas Press.

Heyns, Pol. 2003. "Land Rights in Dutch Formosa." In Blussé 2003a, 175–207.

Lamley, Harry J. 1981. "Subethnic Rivalry in the Ch'ing Period." In *The Anthropology of Taiwanese Society,* edited by Emily M. Ahern and Hill Gates, 282–318. Stanford, CA: Stanford University Press.

Lipatov, Mikhail, Melissa J. Brown, and Marcus W. Feldman. 2011. "The Influence of Social Niche on Cultural Niche Construction: Modelling Changes in Belief About Marriage Form in Taiwan." *Philosophical Transactions of the Royal Society, B* (special issue on Human Niche Construction) *366*: 889–900. doi: 10.1098/rstb.2010.0247.

Meskill, Johanna Menzel. 1979. *A Chinese Pioneer Family: The Lins of Wu-feng, Taiwan, 1729–1895*. Princeton, NJ: Princeton University Press.

Ortner, Sherry B. 1974. "Is Female to Male as Nature Is to Culture?" In *Woman, Culture, and Society*, edited by Michelle Zimbalist Rosaldo and Louise Lamphere, 67–88. Stanford, CA: Stanford University Press.

Park, Saeyoung. 2017. "Me, Myself, and My Hegemony: The Work of Making the Chinese World Order a Reality." *Harvard Journal of Asiatic Studies 77*(1): 47–72. doi: 10.1353/jas.2017.0004.

Pollock, Sheldon. 2006. *The Language of the Gods in the World of Men: Sanskrit, Culture, and Power in Premodern India*. Berkeley: University of California Press.

Ricci, Ronit. 2011. *Islam Translated: Literature, Conversion, and the Arabic Cosmopolis of South and Southeast Asia*. Chicago: University of Chicago Press.

Rubinstein, Murray A., ed. 1999. *Taiwan: A New History*. Armonk, NY: M. E. Sharpe.

Shepherd, John Robert. 1993. *Statecraft and Political Economy on the Taiwan Frontier, 1600–1800*. Stanford, CA: Stanford University Press.

———. 1995. *Marriage and Mandatory Abortion among the 17th-Century Siraya*. Arlington, VA: American Anthropological Association.

Shih, Shu-Mei. 2001. *The Lure of the Modern: Writing Modernism in Semicolonial China, 1917–1937*. Berkeley: University of California Press.

Taraborrelli, Angela. 2015. *Contemporary Cosmopolitanism*. Translated by Ian McGilvray. London: Bloomsbury.

Teng, Emma Jinhua. 2004. *Taiwan's Imagined Geography: Chinese Colonial Travel Writing and Pictures, 1683–1895*. Cambridge, MA: Harvard University Asia Center.

Weller, Robert P. 1999. *Alternate Civilities: Democracy and Culture in China and Taiwan*. Boulder, CO: Westview.

Wolf, Arthur P., and Hill Gates. 2005. "Marriage in Taipei City: Reasons for Rethinking Chinese Demography." *International Journal of Asian Studies* 2(1): 111–33. doi: 10.1017/S1479591405000057.

Chapter Seven

Public, Private, and the Politics of Information in Late Colonial Gambia

Niklas Hultin

THE GAMBIA: A "WELL-INFORMED" COLONY

Consider, by way of introduction, two excerpts from the colonial archive.[1] The first excerpt is from October 25, 1957. The Colonial Secretary of the Gambia, based in Bathurst (now Banjul, the capital of the Gambia), wrote to the Colonial Office in London expressing concern over what he described as a new "local political technique" potentially threatening "civil amenities."[2] The official wrote:

> One of the political parties has established the practice of delivering its addresses through amplifiers sited in private quarters adjoining one of our main road intersections . . . there may develop a competition in this matter and . . . louder and better loudspeakers will be booming competitively across the length and breadth of this otherwise peaceful burgh.

After discussing the possibility of some kind of municipal regulation, perhaps imported from another colony, he continued: "If we can grasp this particular nettle before it flourishes, I think that political parties of all complexion would welcome a self-denying ordinance."

The second excerpt comes from an earlier letter, dated September 21, 1948, from the Officer Administering the Gambia in Bathurst to the Secretary of State for the Colonies, concerning the Gambia's internal security and the risk of Communist infiltration. The officer noted:

> the best policy [is] . . . to ensure that the loyalties and contentment of the people . . . can be achieved by improved social services and the full co-operation of the community in development projects. I am of the opinion that a happy,

contended, well informed people with good prospects to look forward to will provide the best answer to Communist propaganda.[3]

These excerpts offer a window into British aspirations for public discourse in British Gambia—a sliver of land that was very much an afterthought in the British Empire and, it being virtually completely surrounded by Senegal, a territory that the British had unsuccessfully tried to trade to the French at the end of the nineteenth century (Perfect 2016, 7). During the twentieth century, Bathurst grew significantly and the British had to contend with the twin pressures of a growing independence movement and the recognition that Banjul, confined to a swampy island at the mouth of the River Gambia, was bursting at its seams. Thus, it comes as no surprise that the loudspeakers caused some dismay as they not only represented Gambian political awareness but also the cramped reality of the "peaceful burgh" of Bathurst. Read in conjunction with the second example concerning Communism, the British viewpoint appears to be something like this: on one hand, a precondition of participation in the public sphere is a form of reserve or temperance and where such is not forthcoming, the law needs to encourage it (through a "self-denying ordinance"). While the content of political expression is obviously a concern (as in the second example regarding Communism), also important is the modality of the expression, including purportedly self-imposed limits thereto. On the other hand, it is important to create a well-informed people as a kind of inoculation against Communism; of course, what counts as well informed is determined by the British and, in their view, is linked to the socio-economic development of the territory more generally.

These two examples—loudspeaker regulation and anti-Communist propaganda—were part of a range of institutions, debates, and promulgations in late colonial Gambia (roughly WWII-era until independence from the British in 1965), with various degrees of interdependence, concerned with information-related issues. They exemplify a colonial information policy in that their work entailed the encouragement of specific kinds of information to be put into motion (or not) which, in turn, was premised on a particular understanding of a Gambian public (or public-in-the-making). As the two examples suggest, Gambians were encouraged to be well informed and expressive, but only up to a point. The raucous environment of competing rallies was looked down upon in favor of a more timid, if not passive, public, something of a pale shadow of what is typically thought of as the public sphere. This understanding, furthermore, hinged on a particular conception of public/private that ignored—or excluded—existing Gambian institutions as a potential such public. In other words, these institutions aimed at creating and regulating a liberal public that, at least in part, was premised on a kind of dismissal of certain forms of public expression. In the British colonial imagination, both private and public, then, incorporated attributions of affect (to the colonized) and with that ideas of the proper time and place for the manifestation of such affect (Stoler 2004). Part of being a good colonized subject was to know when (and how and where and in what way) to be "public" and when (and how and where in what way) to be "private." That a range of practices might fall between what the colonizer deemed legitimately public and private was thus a feature, not a bug.

This chapter examines how the British sought to use information policy to demarcate the public and, in so doing, demarcate the private. The focus of the chapter is on the explicit invocations of a public in two central institutions—the Information Office (part of the colonial government) and the local branch of the British Council (not, technically, a part of the British government; this point is important, as we will see below). Both of these organizations were part of a colonially sanctioned information landscape that included, in part, the African, urban, elite while largely ignoring and excluding other organizations, such as mosques, that nonetheless played a de facto public role in Gambian life. In the section immediately following this introduction, I will first elaborate what I mean by colonial information policy and how it relates to the idea of the colonial public sphere (the two are closely linked but there are some important key differences). The next two sections address the Information Office and the British Council, respectively. The final section will briefly contextualize these two institutions within late colonial Gambian society generally and discuss how these two institutions obscured alternative, indigenous processes of public/private.

COLONIAL INFORMATION POLICY
AND THE COLONIAL PUBLIC SPHERE

Historians and others have spent the better part of two decades problema-tizing the idea of a public sphere in colonial settings (notably sub-Saharan Africa and South Asia), showing justifiable skepticism toward the utility of a term associated primarily with the work of Jürgen Habermas, who based it exclusively on the European experience.[4] In Habermas's original formula-tion, the public sphere exists somewhere between the state and the domestic sphere and is a space where individuals can come together, in their capacity as private individuals, and debate matters of public concern in a rational and critical fashion (unimpeded by considerations of social class). It is commonly noted that such a thing only rarely occurred in colonies and, inasmuch as it did, it did so in a context of racialized colonial domination—hardly a situa-tion that would allow for much open rational-critical debate on the merits of various approaches to public affairs.[5] Thus, part of colonial rule was to create a facsimile of a public sphere that gave a very modest measure of African say in local affairs, without meaningfully questioning colonial rule itself (cf. Ekeh 1975). Examples of this kind of arrangement includes the Schauri (district councils) in German East Africa (Deutsch 2002) and, in the Gambia, the Annual Chiefs Conference (Ceesay 2016; see also below).

Nonetheless, the notion of the public sphere has proven to be analytically useful when applied to a colonial setting, albeit in a modified form. To take two recent examples: in Dass's study of the Indian cinema under late colonialism, the author refers to the public sphere as "a space of contestation rather than consensus" (Dass 2016, 15). And in Hunter's study of the public sphere in late colonial Tanzania, she considers the public sphere as "a sphere of public debate and reflection, recognizing the constraints under which debate took place and the power dynamics at play" (Hunter 2015, 24). In both of these examples, the goal is to uncover the ways that the colonized (Indians and Tanzanians, respectively) sought to participate in, debate, and perhaps even resist colonial politics. This redefining of the public sphere for the colonial context is important precisely because it pushes back against the ease with which the original conception of the public sphere sidelined the structural conditions that made certain kinds of persons' participation (im)possible in the first place. What is less obvious, however, is the amount of regulatory work in which the colonial authorities engaged beyond bluntly repressive censorship and the like—regulatory work aimed precisely at creating such a public irrespective of indigenous institutions and practices. Although the late colonial governments of the Gambia and elsewhere did not employ the term "information policy"—at the time, this term was seen as largely synonymous with wartime propaganda (Braman 2011, 2)—what we see in the above examples from the archive is a need not simply to repress public expression on the part of Gambians. Rather, public expression needs to be regulated so that its worst excesses (as defined by the colonial authorities) are avoided, or, perhaps better put, an unregulated "public" is in fact impossible as such would be nothing more than a riotous crowd (again, in the eyes of the colonial authorities). At the same time, colonialism required a population that is well informed, in possession of the right kind of information that inoculates them, as a public, against the appeals of Communist agitation and the like. While censorship and repression undoubtedly were part of the colonial apparatus in the Gambia, it is thus the case that the colonial authorities' efforts encompassed a wider scope of information-related aims. Braman's (2011, 3) definition of information policy as "decision making and practices with society-wide constitutive effects—involving information creation, processing, flows, access, and use"—is as apt a summary as any of what the colonial authorities sought to do.[6]

This analytical shift from the colonial public sphere to colonial information policy has two additional implications: first, the intertwinement of colonialism and information has been a recurring and important theme in the recent history of European colonialism, with the perhaps most well-known example being Bernard S. Cohn's magisterial study of the knowledge practices of the British in India. "The conquest of India was a conquest of knowledge," Cohn (1996, 16) notes before listing the myriad kinds of information the British created about India (maps, political sketches, and so on). While Cohn was principally concerned with the ways the British created (not just recorded) knowledge to cement their rule, the flipside of this creation is that the resulting knowledge (information) has to be channeled, processed, and used both in and outside India in order to be effective. If colonialism was to a significant extent about the creation of new knowledge about the colonized peoples, customs, and land, it was also—and this is less obvious in Cohn—about putting particular kinds of knowledge into motion both internally and externally. This latter point was captured by Pietz in his essay on the phonograph in Africa. To Pietz, in the twentieth century, and with the advance of new communication technologies, colonialism "discovered a vast new intentional space" (Pietz 1987, 278)—something akin to what we might think of as the information landscape today—that had to be colonized. That is, the colonialism/knowledge nexus is not just about creation but also about propulsion (simultaneously—the two are not really two distinct phases but rather the same processes viewed from different angles).

Secondly, when the British suggest the need for a happy, contended, well-informed people—as in the example at the beginning of this chapter on the need to resist Communist propaganda—they are simultaneously addressing a hypothetical collective (a public) and an actually existing group of individuals. In a sense, the aim of information policy is to bring these two into congruence with each other, to weld the targeted individuals into a "public" as envisioned by the proponents of the information policy (here, the British). Information, of whatever kind and once put into motion, implies "a transformation in the conduct of those who are, or who should be, informed" (Barry 2001, 153). A fitting analogy is that of the "imaginary lay person" (Maranta et al. 2003) in social studies of science, according to which there is an idealized type of person able and willing to process scientific information when presented in an easily digestible form. Of course, the flipside of laity is the expert, reinforcing the idea that some individuals and institutions—here the organizations of British colonialism—are ultimately responsible for the creation and circulation (and non-circulation) of specific kinds of information and, as is the case with the aforementioned Annual Chiefs Conference, the "public" is created at a "downstream" level far removed from actual power and decision making (cf. Cotton and Devine-Wright 2012). This act of creation engenders the public and the private at the same time, as the latter's existence is presumed and rendered manifest in its presence in the former; the drive to create a public assumes in most colonized save for the urban elite, perhaps, the non-existence of the kind of private interior life that is a precondition of the public sphere (cf. Newell 2002, 6). At the same time, Mamdani's (2018, xvi) argument that "colonialism took command of the private domain, defining custom, thereby shaping the terms within which the subjectivity of the colonized" would be produced is more broadly applicable to information policy as well. Thus, in the drive to create a public, colonial information policy in effect creates two different understandings of "private": one that is the staging ground for the public in that it assumes a kind of subjective interiority that is capable of being properly public, and one that is not so much private but lacking the subjectivity to be properly public/private.

Accordingly, this chapter frames the colonial Information Office, the British Council, and other institutions in the Gambia not simply as part of repression (though in some ways they were), nor as evidence of a genuine public sphere (though in some ways they were, perhaps, this as well). The two institutions are different facets of the British drive to forge what they perceived as an appropriate public for the furthering of their political goals. As has been shown for Ghana, Tanzania, and other British colonies, cultivating literacy and, more generally, the right attitude toward literature and international (read: European) literary culture was part of the colonial civilizing mission and a way for elite, principally urban Africans to demonstrate their distinction vis-à-vis the rest of the colonized population (see, e.g., Hunter 2015; Newell, 2002, 2006; Watson 2018). This chapter expands on this insight to show how a greater range of colonial institutions were involved in this work.

THE COLONIAL INFORMATION OFFICE

The British established an Information Office in the Gambia, as in other colonies, to cater to a wide range of information and public relations needs. The establishment of the office came on the heels of a decade of relatively rapid institutional development in the Gambia. The 1920s and 1930s had seen dramatic growth in the size of Bathurst and with that a "flurry of new legislation designed to regulate the flows and people and machines through the city" (Park 2016, 130; see also Ceesay 2016). While much of the colonial government was preoccupied with infrastructural development, especially as the authorities were discussing moving parts of the governmental machinery from central Banjul (on an overcrowded, swampy, island) to the neighboring Cape Point, it also recognized the need to develop the information landscape. This task was given greater urgency during WWII and the looming threat of Communist infiltration during the post-WWII era. In 1956, the Information Officer (IO) shared an alarming anecdote with his superiors in the midst of discussing his plans for the Information office for the coming year. A few years earlier, expensively printed multicolor posters had arrived in Bathurst advertising an "international youth (Communist) rally in Prague."[7] The posters were so attractive (and free), the officer noted, that "one dear old [Gambian] gentleman who was completely taken in wanted me to put one up in the Information Office!"

In a 1958 telegram, the IO enumerated the duties of the office as follows:

> The Administration of the office
> Photography
> Censorship of Films
> Produce the daily "Gambia News Bulletin"
> Repairs to office equipment
> Writes articles to Newpapers [*sic*] Overseas
> Write up part or whole of the Colonial Report and other documents such as the Brochure
> Member of the Colonial Entertainments Committee, Government Caterer, Annual Chiefs Conference.[8]

The IO's responsibilities were thus extensive—arguably too extensive, as a frequent complaint in the correspondence coming out of the Information Office is how out of step the office's responsibilities are compared to its allocated resources.[9]

Such complaints aside, this work had two overarching aims: to cultivate closer ties to the United Kingdom and to engage the public in public affairs (up to a point). In a 1950 directive, the Acting Colonial Secretary instructed the Information Officer that a "keynote of the Government's policy . . . is to increase the participation of the people of the Gambia in the management of their public affairs."[10] One immediate challenge for the IO was that there was not one single audience in the Gambia, but rather a multiplicity of interest groups whose interests and tastes were not always compatible. In a memo written in 1958, the IO complained that "it has been said that the [Gambia News] Bulletin is not interesting enough, but my question 'interesting to whom' has not, to the best of my knowledge, as yet been clearly answered. Often what is of interest to Gambians is of no great interest to Europeans."[11]

In a different letter, the IO stressed that his work "can be as varied as the Public itself with which I am in daily contact."[12] What is striking, of course, is that the IO invokes a public as a single public at the same time as it complains that such does not exist. This invocation arguably tells us more about the intentions and underlying premises of information work rather than the nature of Gambian society at the time.

A further sense of the striated or plural public is conveyed by a response submitted by the colonial government to a questionnaire sent a few years earlier by the Colonial Office in London. The purpose of the questionnaire was to assess the information services in overseas territories (the services were described as consisting of colonial information offices, the British Council, and the BBC).[13] London asked each colonial government to describe the impact of various information strategies on four distinct groups—"leaders of public opinion," the "school and college population," "the newspaper-reading public," and the semi-literate or illiterate public"—with a particular focus on whether or not these strategies strengthened the bond between the United Kingdom and the colony (in this scheme, the small European population in the Gambia did not matter, perhaps because they were presumed to already have strong ties to the United Kingdom).

The governor responded that "as a whole [these services] do have a useful effect in maintaining and strengthening the links of friendship."[14] The British Council is highlighted as particularly effective since not only is a significant proportion of the urban and educated elite members, but the "semi-literate or illiterate public" enjoys film screenings and "illustrated papers." The BBC, in contrast, was largely dismissed by the governor as having few listeners across all groups—though he also cautioned against curtailing the BBC or any other service as "the fact that material is available results in growing interest." It bears noting that there is a particular ontology of information implicit in this statement in that information is somehow automatically generative of interest, if not now at least at some point in the future. This echoes not only Pietz's comments (above) about colonialism "discovering" an "intentional space" to fill with information, but also the understanding of information as taken-for-granted, which effectively flips the burden of receiving and apprehending it to the addressee (here: Gambians) and not the producer (cf. Hultin 2013).

In addition to the above Gambian subgroups, a significant divide with which the IO had to contend was between the Colony and Protectorate. The Colony, consisting of Bathurst and its immediate environs, was institutionally differentiated from the rest of the territory (the Protectorate), reflecting the piecemeal extension of British control past Bathurst in the second half of the nineteenth century. Although Bathurst had been founded in 1816, it was not until 1894 that the British began to organize the rest of the territory into a protectorate and, consistent with the British policy of indirect rule, the British largely governed through the Protectorate's traditional authorities (Ceesay 2016). By the late colonial era, British correspondence contained ample references to the need to bridge the two parts of the territory; to circulate "knowledge of existing conditions in different parts of the country."[15] The gathering and distribution of information about the country's socio-economic and geographical diversity would not only make for better-informed citizens but also provide for, the directive continues, the raw material for Gambians from "differing ways of life . . . to weld themselves together into a consciously united whole."[16] This was not just a one-way street from the capital to the Protectorate, but a two-way street: in the same discussion, another official suggested that films should be made of government activities and local ways of life—such as rice farming—in the Protectorate to be shown in the capital.[17]

The governor's misgivings about the BBC aside, it is clear that a major part of the IO's responsibilities was relaying news from the United Kingdom to the colony. One of the chief vehicles for this was the aforementioned Gambia News Bulletin, or GNB. While readership figures are not available, it appears that it was intended for an African as well as European audience. A few years after the governor's message, the colonial authorities reported its circulation as 2,000 (at the time it was issued three times a week)[18]—a number likely far exceeding the number of Europeans in the Colony, suggesting an indigenous readership.[19] The GNB published local notices as well as international and British news, and the process of acquiring the latter tells us something about the aspirations of the Information Office. At one time, the IO wished that Cable & Wireless would be able to "supply this Office with a regular news service . . . suitable for insertion with the minimum of editing" and, in the same letter, cautioned against using the BBC as their transmission was liable to interference which could lead to "incomplete or indistinct recording of the news [which] can be a little dangerous."[20] While the wish for a minimum of editing was surely in part due to an interest in saving time and labor, the assumption that a re-contextualization of metropolitan news was not necessary, points to the desirability of transcending the immediate local context and fostering an appreciation of supra-local (or Imperial) events and interest (cf. Kalpagam 2002, 37). That is, the goal was to ensure that Gambians imagine themselves as part of the metropolitan British community and feel that they have a stake, if not much of a say, in developments in or related to Britain.

These two goals of enmeshing the Gambian reading public in the greater empire through British news and to inform Gambians about whereabouts in their territory is aptly illustrated by the October 25, 1951, issue of the *Gambia News Bulletin*. This was the day after the British election that returned Winston Churchill and the Conservatives to power, and this result was quite understandably the lead story. This story was followed by a brief notice that Egypt had declined to participate in a Euro-American defense plan. The following section—headlined "Stop press!!"—reported a lost pocket watch and found key ring, both in downtown Bathurst, and offered a reward for the return of the watch. Next were a section on local news, featuring the results of the Legislative Council election, followed by notices regarding the weather, the mail service, radio highlights, and literary, religious, and entertainment events. The final item is a notice of a screening of the film *General Election in Britain* at the British Council in Bathurst, to which we will now turn.

THE BRITISH COUNCIL

The British Council was the Information Office's "partner" in establishing a Gambian public, but this relationship was a somewhat ambivalent one. In the early 1940s, a discussion about the opening of a Bathurst British Council began between the Gambian government, the Colonial Office, and the British Council. This discussion was complicated by the ambiguous status of the British Council vis-à-vis the British government. The British Council had in fact begun as a semi-official body under the Foreign Office in the early 1930s, and there was some discussion of combining it with the British Ministry of Information during the Second World War (Holman 2005).

In an undated memorandum attached to a letter sent to Sir Angus Gillan, who was the head of the British Council's Empire Division, the governor of the Gambia struck a note of caution, suggesting that he was generally in favor of establishing the British Council in the Gambia. But he foresaw

> difficulty in keeping a clear distinction in the African mind between the activities of the British Council and the . . . local . . . government. Public criticism by the Council would, in African circumstances, be impossible. The absence of criticism will be interpreted as tacit agreement with government policy. For this reason . . . there should be a rapid development of the Public Relations side of the work of the Information Officer. It will then be his job to expound and defend local policy, the British Council representative will be able to refer enquirers to him; and with him and not with the Council must always lie the task of conducting governmental apologetics.[21]

The British Council for its part reciprocated the concern, noting that the British Council had a much broader mandate than the Information Office, and argued, for example, that the Council should be based in a building near the Information Office, but "preferably not too near."[22] It had to be "distinct from the Information Bureau [Office] and cater for a different circle which would

include, for example, only the uppermost intellectual fringe of those now using your Bureau."[23]

Two things are important to note about this discussion: first, that it speaks
to a very real institutional separation between the two organizations. Although they can both be considered part of the colonial edifice, the British
Council was ultimately intended to involve Gambians in their activities, in
contrast to the IO which was essentially the spokesperson for the colonial authorities—and, somewhat paradoxically, the latter was seen as having a wider
reach than the former. The establishment of the British Council in Bathurst
was premised on the idea that it would primarily cater to the small, urban,
African elite, along with the few Europeans in the city, whose economic interests were more closely aligned to those of the British. This elite was also
disproportionately Akus, a group that traces its origin to the Krios of Sierra
Leone and who are predominantly Christian, thus not sharing particularly
strong bonds with the majority Muslim Mandinkas and other ethnic groups
of the Protectorate. Second, this premise is reinforced with the assumption
that the "African mind" would not be able to keep the two organizations apart
and the functioning of the public as a place where power can be discussed
and critiqued would be thereby undermined. In this exchange, in other words,
we see a drive by the British to establish a rather rough approximation of a
public sphere in that some public criticism is desirable and should be institutionally shielded from the colonial government—at least insofar as it came
from the urban African elite who, in a sense, could be trusted not to rock the
boat. By way of illustration, a few years earlier, the colonial authorities did
have to contend with one member of the local elite doing precisely that, and
their description of him is telling. In the 1920s, Edward Francis Small, an
educated Aku who was a member of the local chapter of the National Congress of British West Africa (a pro-independence organization), and would
become a leading figure in Gambia's politics leading up to self-government,
was described by the British authorities as a "self-appointed champion of
non-existing grievances felt by an imaginary body of citizens" (quoted in
Langley 1969, 383). In the British imagination the body of citizens drawn
into the British Council was presumably less imaginary indeed.

The British Council was governed by an Advisory Committee of not more
than twenty members, chaired by the British Council representative. Although the Committee was intended to be a cross-section of the community,
its minutes unsurprisingly suggest that the urban African elite and Europeans
dominated the body.[24] Board members included, for example several Gambians from the Banjul Town Council (or who would later serve on it), including
Hannah Mahoney, the only woman on the Bathurst Town Council, and an
outspoken activist on health issues (Fourshey 2019), I. M. Garba-Jahumpa,

who would later be appointed by the governor to the Executive Council and, after the Gambia's independence, became a prominent politician (Perfect 2016, 184–85), and George St. Clair Joof, who would later found the youth-oriented Gambia Peoples' Party (Perfect 2016, 250).[25]

The general membership was in principle open to anyone, but a prospective member had to be supported by two sponsors and pay a fee. Based on the meeting minutes, members were rarely rejected. Membership appears to have been mostly African. In 1946, the total membership was reported as 191 members, of which 142, or roughly 75 percent were African. Among both Europeans and Africans, men outnumbered women about two to one. The gender discrepancy was even starker for the youth membership: out of the 191 members overall, 37 were listed as school boys, but only 2 were school girls. Finally, "town members," which was more or less consistent with the Colony, made up almost 95 percent of the membership.[26] It is not known from the archive if these membership ratios were satisfactory to the British Council in London or the colonial government in Bathurst. The goal was, after all, for the council to be a meeting place "for people of both races" but there was also a perceived need to have European members, perhaps to have a particularly British way of organizing associational life rub off (cf. Sinha 2001).[27] There was thus an echo of the governor's earlier comment that the British Council would serve to strengthen the link of friendship through a kind of clubby manifestation of proper public and private subjectivity.

The activities of the Council were to be free but the discussion of this issue illustrates the limits of the Council's open doors. In one letter, the Council's Director of the Colonies in London rejected deposits for book lending, but hastened to add that the local Council did not have to lend books to what he termed riff-raff and could restrict membership to "suitable persons."[28] The director continued, nevertheless, by noting that "the great thing is to get the books to the people in as large number as possible, and the risk of losing a few books should not be allowed to stand in the way of this object." The question of "riff-raff" was a pervasive one in the deliberations of the British Council, but whatever debate there was consistently broke in favor of being more open. Thus, in a letter concerning the British Council in the Gold Coast, Gillan noted that while there had been an initial push to restrict the membership to the African elite to make it easier to attract European members, the door must "be opened a little wider if we are not to be accused of snobbery."[29]

Considering the membership of the British Council, both its numbers and the discussion surrounding its composition, it is clear that it was predominantly used by, and aimed to, the urban Gambian elite in Bathurst. Insofar as there were efforts to involve the Gambians in the Protectorate, these appear to be minimal and ad-hoc. In July 1946, for example, there was some discussion of a collaboration with the Medical Research Council (a British-funded health research facility) to show movies with titles such as *Make Fruitful the Land*, but it is not clear of anything came of these plans.[30] But within this limited demographic, the Council appears to have been quite successful with a robust membership and hosting a broad range of activities.

The British Council's various activities offer a glimpse of what information was deemed important to the Gambian public. In addition to providing a library (featuring both books and gramophone records), a children's library, and a film series, the Council hosted study groups, theater performances, public outreach events, and art exhibits and lectures. An initial report by the Council Representative describes the library as containing 1,500 books and forty-six periodicals—including the three Gambian newspapers in existence at the time as well as the *Times* and the *Sunday Times*—local government publications, and British Council publications in Arabic, English, and French.[31] There is also a record of an order placed for several Boy Scout periodicals. The latter point is important as there was also a discussion of supporting the Boy Scouts in Bathurst.[32] As Park has shown, the colonial authorities had great hopes that the Boy Scouts would "settle ambitious youths," illustrating how the aspirations of the British Council and the colonial government dovetailed (Park 2016, 303).

In somewhat of a contrast to the Information Office's films, the British Council's films were predominantly focused on the United Kingdom. An overview of films shown in June 1946 lists several themes, each theme made up of several films. The themes are "England," "London (Empire Day)," "Social Services," and "Industry." Each theme was initiated by "British News" and followed by films with titles such as *Walthamstone Nursery School*, *Good Value*, *Health of a Nation*, and *St. Paul's Cathedral*. The gramophone concerts similarly appear to have tapped into a metropolitan standard, focusing on English music and military marches. Plans for the publication of a newspaper, however, appear to have been shelved.

CONCLUSION

The Information Office and the British Council were recognized by the colonial authorities in both London and Bathurst as central planks in the British information strategy, although, as we have seen, the latter very much wanted to keep the formal colonial apparatus at an arm's length even though they were in broad agreement of the aims of the British presence in the Gambia.

What is striking, however, is the complete absence of any kind of associational life on part of the Gambians outside of these institutions in the correspondence. The aforementioned directive from the Acting Colonial Secretary laying out the responsibilities of the Information Office suggested working through "existing voluntary societies"[33]—but there is no further discussion, in the directive of elsewhere, of what these associations are like. It is of course possible that such more specific discussions occurred either off-the-record or that the records thereof have been lost. But given the overall tenor of the discussion, it is likely that what the British had in mind was something like the British Council.

Of course, Gambians in the Colony and Protectorate had a rich associational life relatively independent from the colonial structure (including the British Council) or, in some cases, in response to it. It is well documented that the Gambia had robust trade unions that butted heads with the authorities (see Hughes and Perfect 1989). To this day, the National Museum in Banjul has photographs on display of members of the Gambia's high society joining dinner clubs. Many members of the Gambian urban elite were politically active and at times called for political self-government—in fact, local members of the aforementioned National Congress of British West Africa were also members of the British Council or at least came from the same families (see Langley 1969).

And, of course, there were churches and mosques. Perhaps because the colonial authorities presumably disproportionately interacted with the small Christian minority in Bathurst, the Islamic community is only referenced in passing. There are two possible, and not contradictory, explanations. It could simply be that, as Ceesay (2014) has shown, in terms of the exercise of power, working through traditional forms of authority such as Imams and chiefs was simply not as vital in the Colony as in the Protectorate. It might also be the case that religious institutions were kept at a distance on purpose. A telling example of the latter is offered by Saho: when the Chief Justice of the Supreme Court of the Gambia abolished the Muslim Court in 1929. The governor objected because "at times it was more of a club than a court. It was a meeting place for Muslims, and it was something that they felt was theirs" (quoted in Saho 2018, 78).

It would thus be to overstate things to describe the British Council and (even more so) the Information Office as somehow embodying a kind of public sphere, be it in the ideal Habermasian form or in the sense of a colonial public sphere. They were rather colonial projects intended to bring a certain kind of entity being. And despite the aspiration to include all Gambians, there is an unmistakable line of class running through these examples—seen in the concerns over riff-raff, the eagerness to promote the Boy Scouts, the concerns over uncivil loudspeakers, and the fear that Communism might take hold among those Gambians not benefiting from development.

Another way of putting this latter point is that the British Council and the Information Office were not just attempts to weld Gambians together, and weld them to Britain, but also to weld them as particular kind of public persona. The implication, of course, is that to become that kind of person, some things must be left behind or remain hidden. Thus, if we accept the argument that the British created or sought to create a kind of public through its information policy, it follows that in doing so they also created two different kinds of private spheres: one, that of the tempered reader who partakes in the literary culture of the British Council, for example, and whose activities in the public sphere are seen as the reasoned outcome of a particular kind of private subjectivity, and one that is ill tempered and engages in undisciplined behaviors unmoored from civic British virtues—this latter being less "private" and more "riff-raff."

But at issue is not simply that the institutions of colonialism created or exaggerated distinctions. The consideration of the British Council and the Information Office under the rubric of colonial information policy suggests the underlying drive to take over and control the Gambia's information landscape—even if, in the end, this effort was not successful (it is no coincidence that the aforementioned thorn in the British side, Edward Francis Small, was also the founder of the Gambia's first newspaper). Returning to Pietz, if colonialism is about filling an intentional space with information flows, the semantic content of these flows is less important than the fact that they occur and they then fill, monopolize, and suffuse every channel. Referring to an 1877 newspaper cartoon, Pietz notes that "the flow of the telephonic orator's voice does indeed occupy the phonocentric attention of the members of civilized states and sedentary societies; only the pre-literate savages respond to the novel truth at work here. Their response is perhaps the only possible one: to pursue a line of group flight which takes them altogether outside the frame of representation" (Pietz 1987, 281). Based on my analysis of the archival sources concerning the Gambia herein, I would amend this almost apocalyptic read by Pietz. When the "pre-literate savages" are outside the "frame of reference," it is their information practices, not just their bodies that are thusly occluded.

NOTES

1. An earlier version of this paper was presented at the Fourth Annual New York Area African History Workshop and I am grateful to the attendees for comments. I

also thank the staff of the National Archives of the United Kingdom and the Gambia National Record's Office in Banjul for help in locating documents. These two archives are referred to in the notes below as UKNA and NRO, respectively.

2. Confidential letter from Colonial Secretariat to Colonial Office, October 25, 1957, UKNA, CO 554/1953.

3. Letter from Officer Administering the Government of the Gambia to Secretary of State for the Colonies, September 21, 1948, UKNA, CO 537/2772.

4. See Habermas (1991). See also Calhoun (1992) for an influential introduction to the voluminous literature on the public sphere.

5. Leaving aside questions of whether the public sphere as it purports to be ever really existed in Western Europe and whether it in fact maintained its fiction of unbiased rational-critical debate only through the exclusion of women, ethnic and religious minorities, and the non-propertied. See, for example, Fraser (1992).

6. The exact meaning of the term information policy is fuzzy, though most definitions emphasize the intersection of legal, political, regulatory, technical, and social practices that create, propel, direct, and restrict information. See also Yusof, Basri, and Zin (2010).

7. Letter from Information Office to Financial Secretary, September 8, 1956, NRO, CSO 10/82.

8. Letter from Information Office to Colonial Secretary, July 24, 1958, NRO, CSO 10/83.

9. For example, in a 1956 letter to his superiors, the IO complained that "I have to do the best I can with very small funds and often wornout equipment which I cannot get replaced until long after its useful life is really over. Also that I can only have second rate assistance in my office . . . I feel that this should be recognised and the circumstances appreciated." See Secret letter from Information Office to Financial Secretary, September 8, 1956, NRO, CSO 10/82.

10. Attachment to letter from Acting Colonial Secretary to Information Officer, September 9, 1950, NRO, CSO 10/82.

11. Letter from Information Office to Colonial Secretary, March 27, 1958, NRO, CSO 10/83.

12. Letter from Information Office to Financial Secretary, September 8, 1956, NRO, CSO 10/82.

13. Savingram from Secretary of State for the Colonies to Colonial Secretary, May 6, 1952, NRO, CSO 10/82.

14. Ibid.

15. Attachment to letter from Acting Colonial Secretary to Information Officer, September 9, 1950, NRO, CSO 10/82.

16. Ibid.

17. Letter from Director of Agriculture to the Colonial Secretary, May 12, 1958, NRO, CSO 10/83.

18. Letter from Ministry of Works and Communication to Austrian trade delegation, February 20, 1964, NRO, PWD 3/278.

19. A few years earlier, in 1957, the non-African population of the Colony was 544, of which 222 were British with the remainder being mostly Syrians and Lebanese (Colonial Office 1958, 12).

20. Confidential letter from Information Office to Colonial Secretary, March 27, 1958, NRO, CSO 10/83.

21. Attachment to letter from Professor Ifor Evans to Sir Angus Gillan, November 10, 1942, UKNA, BW 102/1.

22. Letter from W. M. Macmillan to the Governor of the Gambia, October 24, 1944, UKNA, BW 102/1.

23. Ibid.

24. See, e.g., Minutes of the sixth meeting of the British Council Advisory Committees, September 23, 1946, UKNA, BW 102/1.

25. The Banjul Town Council was established by the British in 1946 and its fifteen members were elected from Bathurst's different wards. Several Gambian politicians who would be important in the leadup to independence and thereafter got their start on the Banjul Town Council (Perfect 2016, 19).

26. Extract from the quarterly report second quarter 1946. Gambia office and Bathurst Institute, June 12, 1946, UKNA, BW 102/1.

27. Letter from W. M. Macmillan to the Governor of the Gambia, October 24, 1944, UKNA, BW 102/1.

28. Letter from H. L. Ward Price to British Council representative in Bathurst, November 7, 1946, UKNA, BW 102/1.

29. Letter from Sir Angus Gillan to Sir Charles Jeffries, January 25, 1946, UKNA, BW 102/1.

30. Monthly report for July 1946, Bathurst the Gambia, July 1946, UKNA, BW 102/1.)

31. Extract from the quarterly report second quarter 1946. Gambia office and Bathurst Institute, June 12, 1946, UKNA, BW 102/1.

32. Letter from British Council Representative (Bathurst) to Empire Division Director for Colonies, October 4, 1946, UKNA, BW 102/1.

33. Letter from Acting Colonial Secretary to Information Officer, September 9, 1950, NRO, CSO 10/82.

REFERENCES

Barry, Andrew. 2001. *Political Machines: Governing a Technological Society.* London: The Athlone Press.

Braman, Sandra. 2011. "Defining Information Policy." *Journal of Information Policy* *1*: 1–5.

Calhoun, Craig J., ed. 1992. *Habermas and the Public Sphere*. Cambridge, MA: MIT Press.

Ceesay, Hassoum. 2014. "Chiefs and Protectorate Administration in Colonial Gambia, 1894–1965." In *Leadership in Colonial Africa*, edited by Baba G. Jallow, 23–54. New York: Palgrave Macmillan.

———. 2016. "Chiefs and the Management of Urbanization in Colonial Bathurst, Gambia 1939–1960." *Mande Studies 18*: 75–92.

Cohn, Bernard S. 1996. *Colonialism and Its Forms of Knowledge: The British in India*. Princeton, NJ: Princeton University Press.

Colonial Office. 1958. *The Gambia: Report for the Years 1956 and 1957*. London: Stationery Office.

Cotton, Matthew, and Patrick Devine-Wright. 2012. "Making Electricity Networks 'Visible': Industry Actor Representations of 'Publics' and Public Engagement in Infrastructure Planning." *Public Understanding of Science 21*(1): 17–35.

Dass, Manishita. 2016. *Outside the Lettered City Cinema, Modernity, and the Public Sphere in Late Colonial India*. New York: Oxford University Press.

Deutsch, Jan-Georg. 2002. "Celebrating Power in Everyday Life: The Administration of Law and the Public Sphere in Colonial Tanzania, 1890–1914." *Journal of African Cultural Studies 15*(1): 93–103.

Ekeh, Peter P. 1975. "Colonialism and the Two Publics in Africa: A Theoretical Statement." *Comparative Studies in Society and History 17*(1): 91–112.

Fourshey, Catherine Cymone. 2019. "Women in the Gambia." In *Oxford Research Encyclopedia of African History*, edited by Thomas Spear. Oxford: Oxford University Press. Doi:0.1093/acrefore/9780190277734.013.513.

Fraser, Nancy. 1992. "Rethinking the Public Sphere: A Contribution to the Critique of Actually Existing Democracy." In *Habermas and the Public Sphere*, edited by Craig J. Calhoun, 109–42. Cambridge, MA: MIT Press.

Habermas, Jürgen. 1991. *The Structural Transformation of the Public Sphere: An Inquiry into a Category of Bourgeois Society*. Cambridge, MA: MIT Press.

Holman, Valerie. 2005. "Carefully Concealed Connections: The Ministry of Information and British Publishing, 1939–1946." *Book History 8*(2005): 197–226.

Hughes, Arnold, and David Perfect. 1989. "Trade Unionism in the Gambia." *African Affairs 88*(353): 549–72.

Hultin, Niklas. 2013. "Law, Opacity, and Information in Urban Gambia." *Social Analysis 57*(3): 42–57.

Hunter, Emma. 2015. *Political Thought and the Public Sphere in Tanzania: Freedom, Democracy, and Citizenship in the Era of Decolonization*. Cambridge: Cambridge University Press.

Kalpagam, Uma. 2002. "Colonial Governmentality and the Public Sphere in India." *Journal of Historical Sociology 15*(1): 35–58.

Langley, Ayodele J. 1969. "The Gambia Section of the National Congress of British West Africa." *Africa 39*(4): 382–95.

Mamdani, Mahmood. 2018. *Citizen and Subject: Contemporary Africa and the Legacy of Late Colonialism*. Second edition. Princeton, NJ: Princeton University Press.

Maranta, Alessandro, Michael Guggenheim, Priska Gisler, and Christian Pohl. 2003. "The Reality of Experts and the Imagined Lay Person." *Acta Sociologica 46*(2): 150–65.

Newell, Stephanie. 2002. *Literary Culture in Colonial Ghana: How to Play the Game of Life*. Bloomington, IN: Indiana University Press.

———. 2006. "Entering the Territory of Elites: Literary Activity in Colonial Ghana." In *Africa's Hidden Histories: Everyday Literacy and Making the Self*, edited by Karin Barber, 21–35. Bloomington, IN: Indiana University Press.

Park, Matthew James. 2016. "Heart of Banjul: The History of Banjul, the Gambia, 1816–1965." PhD dissertation, Michigan State University.

Perfect, David. 2016. *Historical Dictionary of the Gambia*. Lanham, MD: Rowman & Littlefield.

Pietz, William. 1987. "The Phonograph in Africa: International Phonocentrism from Stanley to Sarnoff." In *Post-Structuralism and the Question of History*, edited by Derek Attridge, Geoff Bennington, and Robert Young, 263–85. Cambridge: Cambridge University Press.

Saho, Bala S. K. 2018. *Contours of Change: Muslim Courts, Women, and Islamic Society in Colonial Bathurst, the Gambia, 1905–1965*. East Lansing, MI: Michigan State University Press.

Sinha, Mrinalini. 2001. "Britishness, Clubbability, and the Colonial Public Sphere: The Genealogy of an Imperial Institution in Colonial India." *The Journal of British Studies 40*(4): 489–521.

Stoler, Ann Laura. 2004. "Affective States." In *A Companion to the Anthropology of Politics*, edited by David Nugent and Joan Vincent, 4–20. Malden, MA: Blackwell.

Watson, Ruth. 2018. "'My Desire Is to Be the Possessor of All the Best Books in This World of Struggle': Respectability and Literary Materialism in Colonial Ibadan." *Africa: Journal of the International African Institute 88*(2): 312–31.

Yusof, Zawiyah M., Mokmin Basri, and Nor Azan M. Zin. 2010. "Classification of Issues Underlying the Development of Information Policy." *Information Development 26*(3): 204–13.

Conclusion

Reading the Intimate Past

Jacqueline H. Fewkes and Rachel Corr

As we have seen in the chapters throughout this book, the intimacy of every-day lives—experienced through personal sentiments, individual bodies, and family relationship—plays a significant role in the public sphere, blurring the line between the public/private and ultimately drawing attention to the ways in which the two are mutually constitutive. Understanding the entanglements of such experiences in historical contexts can be difficult because information about private lives is often hidden within public, historical records. Nevertheless, the researchers in this volume have been able to apply analytical methods from anthropology to study past people's conceptions of public and private spaces, activities, discourse, and social interactions, reading ethnohistorical and material sources to understand everyday lives.

These chapters have spanned geographic areas to emphasize the deep connections between public and private domains that—as Minette Church points out in the introduction—challenge the very existence of such a divide. They have also addressed the significance of these connections for understanding the past holistically, both historically and in a contemporary sense. Bringing together diverse methods from archaeology and cultural anthropology has enabled us to explore both the factors that reinforce dichotomies between public and private spheres, as well as resistance to this dichotomy through links between private and public realms. Whether revealing the role of affect in constructing imagined public identities or unveiling hidden labor contributions to the public sphere in a cosmopolitan society, using anthropological methods to read the past gives a more realistic picture of history as lived experience.

As this volume draws to a close, we would like to take a moment to address in more detail what the titular "Intimate Past" might entail, and repercussions of the phrase for writing ethnohistories of the public/private. As might be expected, consideration of the intimate past is reflected in much

of this work through a focus on the implications of particular types of relationships; unexpectedly it has also provided the authors with an opportunity
to contemplate the types of knowledge gained by diverse methodological
approaches and promoted careful consideration of associated spaces (both
conceptual and physical).

INTIMATE RELATIONSHIPS AND
THE BLURRING OF PRIVATE/PUBLIC

The most immediate association with the term intimate is that of interpersonal
relationships, particularly those that are close (physically and/or emotionally), exclusive, and private. Aspects of this theme run throughout the book,
as several chapters seek to make the unknown (invisible, muted, and/or
veiled) known, often by revealing relationships such as friendships and kin
relations. Individual inner states, emotions, and feelings are often linked to
these relationships as well as sentiments associated with other social relationships. Sara Ahmed, as Jean Muteba Rahier notes in chapter 1, has written
about the role of emotions in aligning individuals with larger collectivities
(2004); most of the works in this book similarly use the notion of intimate
relations to demonstrate how they have served to orient communal patterns
and shape social interactions in the past. These intimate sentiments and relationships, often effaced in public records and difficult to read in broader historical narratives, are revealed as crucial cultural themes that link the public
and private in varied cultural contexts.

The interior aspects of the intimate—emotions, sentiments, feelings, and
thoughts—play a significant role in a number of chapters in this book. In
his chapter Rahier renders the typically considered "invisible" (feelings of
solidarity) visible by reading the statements left in comment books by tourists at West African slave castles/dungeons. He is able to do this through his
innovative methodology of taking photos of thousands of pages of comments
from the visitors' books at these tourist sites. Rahier's attention to the emotions coded into this written record, coupled with observations of site visitors, reveals the existence of a global black consciousness which is otherwise
hidden. History and personal emotions are closely linked together as African
and African diaspora visitors feel a connection with one another based on a
shared history of oppression. Niklas Hultin's chapter 7, which addresses the
construction of a public by colonial governments in the Gambia, also links
publics to interior lives. As Hultin points out, the British project to create a
particular type of public in the Gambia was founded upon colonial assumptions about the non-existence of a private life for a majority of colonized

people (excluding only a small minority of urban elites), making colonial imaginings of the intimate details of Gambian lives central to the public project. Thus, as Hultin notes, even sentiments such as joy—and their subsequent public expression—were central to this project.

Interpersonal intimacy is a repeated theme as well. Jacqueline H. Fewkes (chapter 5) and Melissa J. Brown (chapter 6) both discuss marriages that crossed social and ethnic categories. Fewkes focuses on the lived of experiences of South Asians under colonialism, through an analysis of relationships between individuals and friendships among elite South Asian and British families. Revealing intimate connections of friendship based on long-term associations between these families, Fewkes contributes to the recent anthropology of empathy as a "humane counterweight" (Ortner 2016, 60) to an emphasis only on otherness and oppression that helps us to better understand the complexity of real human relationships in systems of domination enforced through violence. Similarly, Brown's analysis of the network of interethnic marital ties in Dutch Taiwan demonstrates another way in which marriage relationships function for public-sphere concerns such as trade and politics. Brown argues that through marriage, under seventeenth-century Dutch colonialism in Taiwan, aboriginal Austronesian women facilitated social relations between diverse communities, making the time period a "high point of cosmopolitanism" for the country. Through these studies, we see how humanity pushes through powerful structural differences to reveal relationships that cut across racial, ethnic, class, and religious lines. As Veena Das demonstrates in her article "Engaging the Life of the Other: Love and Everyday Life" (2010), such relationships must be understood not only within the context of histories of domination and conflict on a regional, national, and global scale, but also within the context of the histories of specific families. Fewkes's and Brown's discussion of kin relations among colonizers and colonized alike also draw attention to how, while kinship was classically studied among so-called "native" peoples, the same anthropological gaze has rarely been applied to the European colonial administrators, bringing us back to the WEIRD (Western, Educated, Industrialized, Rich, Democratic) bias in academia that Church alludes to in the introduction.

Friendship is another type of "intimate" relation depicted in this book that is analyzed in relation to these histories of domination. Fewkes notes colonial conceptions of friendship that exist within unequal power structures of domination, as in the letters from a British officer to Bahauddin Khan, which simultaneously questions the trader's actions officially, and speaks about family matters. These uneven power relations embedded in friendships between individuals are echoed in other chapters in this book, reminding us that intimate relationships are not necessarily equal. In the colonial setting of the

Gambia, Hultin addresses a coercive version of "friendship," showing how the concept of such a relationship was manipulated, through an information campaign, in the attempt to create a particular type of public sphere in the Gambia. This aspect of domination is important to understand the complexity of real human relationships within exploitative systems. Historian Bianca Premo explores the concept of *familiaridad* as "nonbiological relations across class and caste divisions and down through generations within shared households" in colonial Latin America (2013, 298) and cautions that we "should be wary of labeling any emotion or statement of emotion false simply because the affiliation on which the emotion was based had a material or labor component," as "the economic functioned as the cradle for the emotional" (2013, 311). In the Iberian American colonies, as well as the U.S. south (Genovese 1976), relations of servitude involved intimate practices of wet-nursing, childrearing, care, and childhood friendships that produced bonds of affection between individuals from powerful and powerless groups. As children grew, however, the unequal power differences manifested in vastly different rights and opportunities based on the relative status of each. In chapter 2 Audrey Horning examines other friendships, suggesting unexpected forms of social relations between English and Irish neighbors in seventeenth-century Ireland, and asking what we can understand about the society of the time period based on accounts of these neighbors drinking together in familiarity, destroyed by the unwelcome intrusion of rebels. Horning too demonstrates that actual human relationships do not obey the rules of the official proclamations on the books, for Irish Catholics and Protestant planters engaged in convivial activities, and some planters even allowed banned religious practices to continue.

The concept of intimacy as relations associated with private, domestic spaces swirls through many of these chapters as well, and in doing so reveals the crucial, but often muted, role of women in history. Brown shows the role of women in developing a cosmopolitan society, and Fewkes as relationship brokers between South and Central Asian and European colonial families. In chapter 4 Rachel Corr demonstrates a similar idea by highlighting women's "food work" in the history of the colonial textile economy. Corr's work on the enslavement of indigenous communities during the Ecuadorian colonial period demonstrates that the domestic hearth played a significant role in colonial social relations, allowing indigenous men working in mills to maintain both social relationships and a sense of self in the face of dehumanizing conditions. Corr thus recenters narratives to highlight women's work and understand the value of that labor, just as Brown's chapter shines light on women's labor that has been commonly dismissed as "helping." In contrast, Anna S. Agbe-Davies's chapter 3 shows that African American women's contributions *were* considered work in the narratives of *The Chicago Defender* newspaper. Agbe-Davies analyzes *The Chicago Defender* as an artifact (informed by her work as an archaeologist with material culture), focusing on advertised products, photos, institutions, and instructions regarding bodily comportment. She points out that some stories in *The Chicago Defender* actually sought to make private, family life public. For example, news of trips to visit friends and relatives in other regions—where families had dispersed during the Great Migration—were made public and created the sense of an African American community linked to a larger collective identity with a historical experience of migration in the United States.

Intimacy in these senses of the term—the interior, personal, interpersonal, and/or exclusive—thus ties together a number of issues central to the study of anthropology—gender, kinship, relationships, power, agency, reciprocity, and race to name just a few—allowing us to consider their relationships to each other in the specific locales studied by the authors of chapters in this book. Such conceptualizations of intimacy allow us to contemplate how these issues overlapped in daily lives, interrogating how these aspects of the human experience were mutually constitutive and enriching our understanding of aspects of the past that are typically rendered invisible by authoritative voices in historical records.

THE METHODS OF ETHNOHISTORY, AND WAYS OF KNOWING THE PAST

The intimate, of course, has other connotations as well. In verb form the term is derived from the Latin *intimare* (to impress upon or make known), an etymology that suggests attention to methodological considerations. As one of the distinctive features of this book is the combination of methods used to explore the relationship between the public/private in historical contexts, this sense of the term is worth exploring further.

All contributors in this volume are anthropologists with extensive experience doing ethnographic or archaeological fieldwork, and therefore have a unique insight to reading the past for the everyday, hidden, and private lives of people, even as these are linked to public spaces and institutions. In each of the chapters, the authors have turned their anthropologically trained gaze to new sources of information: comment books, receipts, old newspaper articles, maps, and material remains. Through their textual, ethnographic, and material analysis of these sources the authors suggest a new perspective on the ways in which the subfields of American anthropology—in this case the cultural and archaeological—are linked beyond oft-discussed and long-standing theoretical entanglements (see for example discussion in Longacre

2010), as a relationship between fieldwork and document/archival histories. Horning, Agbe-Davies, and Church have all begun their work with material culture as archaeologists, and linked that work to other bodies of evidence to expand their understandings of past social settings. Church's introduction to the volume is enriched through her experience as a historical archaeologist (e.g., Church 2002), demonstrated, for example, in her focus on the role of particular commodities such as sugar and tea. Horning's earlier work with Ulster Plantation sites (e.g., Horning 2013) is expanded through the inclusion of port documents, court records, and maps, while Agbe-Davies's long-standing archaeological research for several years at the site of the former Phyllis Wheatley Home for Girls (e.g., Agbe-Davies 2011) focused her initial interest in the topics analyzed in *The Chicago Defender* articles. Similarly, Rahier, Corr, Fewkes, Brown, and Hultin all bring their ethnographic backgrounds and previous field studies (see for example Rahier 2014, Corr 2010, Fewkes 2008, Brown 2004, and Hultin 2015) to bear on their research, as contemporary issues in the communities that they work with have prompted them to work with archival materials. The chapters share sources such as court documents (Horning and Corr) that contain hints about the past that are not only enriched but actually decoded in relation to the authors' fieldwork experiences; without Corr's understanding of women's labor at the hearth, for example, we would have little conception of the labor (and personal investment) represented by testimonies that the wives of carders would bring seasoned guinea pig meat to their spouses at the mills. Rahier's attention to the role of affect in how people view themselves and others weaves together ethnographic observation and textual analysis to illuminate a sense of African diasporic solidarity that is not manifest in other contexts. The product of this engagement between cultural and archaeological anthropological inquiry demonstrates a way of knowing the past that is central to the work of ethnohistory.

Ethnohistory of course has been a part of American anthropology from the beginning of the discipline, and nineteenth-century attempts to record Native American histories incorporating archaeological and ethnographic evidence (Chaves 2008, 487–89) mirror twentieth-century discussions of ethnohistory as a convergence point for these two subdisciplines (see for example Trigger 1982). The conceptual goal of this methodological confluence has been, curiously, one of cultivating a more intimate understanding of the past. Ethnohistorians have been tasked with developing emic understandings of histories that "take into account the people's own sense of how events are constituted, and their ways of culturally constructing the past" (Gewertz and Schieffelin 1985, 3). In our own work we have expressed the desire to produce histories that are "grounded in a specific locale and peopled by individuals with experiences rather than historical outcomes" (Fewkes 2008, 12–13), linking methodology to some of the senses of the term intimacy as discussed earlier in this chapter. The "ways of knowing" the past in this book are intimate not only in reference to interpersonal relationships between people, but also in reference to a deliberate engagement with methods that will engender a way of understanding how people have felt and interacted in the past. In this sense, we are applying Lila Abu-Lughod's concept of "ethnographies of the particular" to historical contexts. Abu-Lughod advocates the methodology of writing narrative ethnographies of the particular as a way to counteract "othering" in anthropology and to understand how lives are lived in everyday structures, writing, "the effects of extralocal and long-term processes are only manifested locally and specifically, produced in the actions of individuals living their particular lives, inscribed in their bodies and in their words" (Abu-Lughod 1991, 50). Similarly, the contributors to this volume are dedicated to employing methodologies that enable them to "know" people of the past through their relationships, experiences, and personal feelings.

The "intimate past" in this context is based on our understandings of the past itself, as suggested by Rahier's chapter in the form of the responses of many visitors to the West African slave memorial sites of Elmina and Cape Coast in Ghana; here we are given a view of the ways in which the past is intensely personal to contemporary communities. The intimate past here is also the one that is held close for examination so that in Corr's chapter a "little shirt" becomes a detail that plunges us into an understanding of the testifier in a seventeenth-century legal deposition.

Furthermore, it enables us to better understand, as Church has outlined in the introduction to this volume, how the division between the public and private is not simply porous, but deeply suspect as a conceptual construct. While this is patently clear in chapters such as Brown's where a focus on intimate relationships demonstrates how colonial economics and politics are shaped by marriages, even careful attention to the construction of the public—commonly thought of as the opposite of the intimate—makes known details of intimate subjects as well. Thus both Horning and Hultin demonstrate forms of public projects that were meant ultimately to shape intimate details of individual consciousness and interactions, a way of dealing with subordinates who were thought to need "civilizing." Horning notes this when commenting that "[p]lantation was supposed to be about identity transformation, but only the unidirectional sort, with the Irish becoming 'civilized' through adopting and internalizing English ways of being"; Hultin shows the same when discussing how colonial institutions supported the "civilizing mission" of promoting European literary culture among African elites.

SPACES OF THE PUBLIC/PRIVATE PAST

The contents of the volume also suggest that while there is no one past that we can embrace (in an intimate fashion or otherwise), certain sites are fruitful touchpoints for historical inquiry. The concept of space is a central feature of many of the works in this volume, whether a particular space such as Horning's seventeenth-century English-style timber-framed houses in Newtown Limavady, or a more abstract space such as Hultin's Gambian public sphere. We find Henri Lefebvre's work in *The Production of Space* helpful for deconstructing these approaches, to think critically about the role of space in human experience, and (consequently) in historical processes (2009). Lefebvre writes that while spaces are not agents, they are also not merely "container[s] waiting to be filled by content" as they play an active role in shaping social practices (Lefebvre 2009, 170). He passionately argues to readers, "could space be nothing more than the passive locus of social relations, the milieu in which their combination takes on body, or the aggregate of the procedures employed in their removal? The answer must be no" (Lefebvre 2009, 11), and later suggests instead that space can play various roles in human interactions, for example as a medium, instrument, or goal (Lefebvre 2009, 411). Each of these roles of space appears in chapters of this book: for example, in Horning's work illicit alehouses functioned as a medium for Irish and English neighborly interactions, the workspaces for nineteenth-century tea processing in Brown's chapter were instrumental in recognizing women's labor, and certain types of homes were lauded as goals of the social project outlined in Agbe-Davies's discussion of *The Chicago Defender* articles. The active and multi-dimensional roles of space in turn point to its diachronic nature. Lefebvre argues to his readers,

> Is it true, or sufficient, to say that a temple in Kyoto has a public part, a part set aside for rites, and a part reserved for priests and meditators? I grant that your scheme explains something very important: difference within a framework of repetition. Considered in its various contexts, for example, the Japanese garden remains the same yet is never the same: it may be an imperial park, an inaccessible holy place, the accessible annex of a sanctuary, a site of public festivity, a place of "private" solitude and contemplation, or merely a way from one place to another. This remarkable institution of the garden is always a microcosm, a symbolic work of art, an object as well as a place, and it has diverse "functions" which are never merely functions. (Lefebvre 2009, 157)

This discussion highlights the dialectical nature of the production of space, drawing our attention to the ways in which time constructs—and is constructed by—the social uses of space, demonstrated amply throughout this book in sites such as public squares, castle/dungeons, mills, townships, trading posts, boarding houses, domestic hearths, and workspaces.

As Lefebrve points out in the above example, a focus on space is helpful for demonstrating the porosity of the public/private dichotomy, as attention to a space reveals that while there are frequently patterns of usage, the varied uses, users, and meanings of a particular site may not always conform to that divide. In the cases presented in this volume we are therefore prompted to contemplate the sites of inquiry as multivocal. This is clearly expressed in Rahier's chapter in this book, where memorial sites of the trans-Atlantic slave trade become the focus of varied contemporary engagements, and there are multiple versions of historical sites due to visitors' heterogenous experiences of the locations.

The dialogical nature of spatial production demonstrates the need for attention to interactions between space, time, and agents in order to understand history, as also established by anthropologist Michel-Rolph Trouillot in *Silencing the Past: Power and the Production of History* (Trouillot 1995). In this book Trouillot's attention to the construction of histories of the Haitian Revolution is fundamentally spatial, focused on particular sites and objects within those sites (demonstrating a tendency toward some of the methodological overlaps discussed above). He documents a visit to the site Sans Souci—a palace in Haiti built by the early nineteenth-century Haitian revolutionary Henry Christophe—and recounts the site's history not as a definitive historical narrative, but rather as points that a particular individual might—or might not—tell you (the visitor to Sans Souci) while visiting the remains of the palace. Trouillot later reveals that there are actually three Sans Soucis, as it is the name of: 1) the Haitian site that he visits, 2) a rebel commander killed by Christophe a decade before the palace was built, and 3) another palace located just outside of Berlin (Trouillot 1995, 33–45). Considering the relationships between the three Sans Soucis, Trouillot notes that no one version is a complete history as "[s]ilences are inherent in history because any single event enters history with some of its constituting parts missing. Something is always left out while something else is recorded. There is no perfect closure of any event, however one chooses to define the boundaries of that event" (Trouillot 1995, 49). The Sans Souci site therefore acts as a meeting point for the fragments of histories.

Trouillot's work may first seem to most clearly parallel Rahier's engagement with multiple perspectives on West African sites, where the spatial layout of slave castles interacts with narratives of the sites as spaces of historic brutality that affected individuals' lives. It is also echoed, however, in Fewkes's analysis of how the use of household spaces for business activities made the intimate world of family and kinship intertwined with the public worlds of business and trade, and Agbe-Davies's discussion of how racial segregation led people to open their homes to host travelers. Corr's discussion of indigenous homes in relation to colonial mill labor, which "re-centers" narratives of the textile economy to better focus on indigenous women's labor, demonstrates even further the ways in which attention to particular spaces allows us to gather together pieces of multiple historical narratives.

Indeed, many of the works in this book lead to the same conclusions: spaces are not merely containers of neatly bounded narratives about the past but rather symbolic touchpoints for varied meanings that bespeak of the myriad of complex and even messy versions of the past that continue to be reinterpreted today. Spaces are sites of the investigation of history not simply because they offer hints of what else might be known, but because, as Corr demonstrates with her focus on the relationship between mill and home sites to better understand the anguish in the *testimonios*, they render the unknown (and perhaps even unknowable) more thinkable. This brings us in full circle back to the earliest senses of the term "intimate" mentioned in this chapter.

CONCLUSIONS

The titular invocation of the intimate for this volume was therefore initially intended to develop a view of the past that sought to draw attention to small moments, interpersonal interactions, emotional/sentimental engagements, and individually lived experiences, with the goal of understanding both the distinctions and porosity between these private moments and that which is conceived of as the public. In doing so we have depended upon an interdisciplinary methodology that makes this past known, drawing from a combination of ethnographic experiences/understandings, archival materials, and material culture.

Quite separately from this endeavor, we recently discovered a body of literature on what is called, by Alisse Waterston and Barbara Rylko-Bauer, "intimate ethnography" (2006). Waterston and Rylko-Bauer intended the phrase to focus their ethnographic work on the roles of emotion, subjectivity, and positionality, while engaging in dialectical work that linked these more private aspects of human experience to larger publics (Waterston and Rylko-Bauer 2006; Waterston 2019). Waterston notes that

> [i]n its dialecticism, intimate ethnography follows in the intellectual tradition of Marxist anthropology, historical materialism, and political economy, a tradition that emphasizes change and contradiction over stasis and equilibrium, and historical analysis of social relations over positivism, universalism, and synchronism. In that tradition, social life and cultural ideas are understood

dialectically as produced and reproduced in the process of dynamic, contingent, and contradictory relationships. (Waterston 2019, 8)

While not sharing in this same exact project—a particular form of ethnographic inquiry—the works in this book have engaged the public/private in a similar way through ethnohistorical inquiry. Each chapter does indeed emphasize change and contradiction, and social relations are necessarily historically contextualized in order to understand how the dichotomies that reinforce public and private, as well as resistance to these dichotomies, are dynamically constructed through contradictory and contingent relationships between the private and public realms. Furthermore, our use of varied sources—public records, films, personal journals, letters, newspapers, guest books, material culture, maps, public performances, etc.—has revealed the dialectical nature of the past, an interplay between private sentiments and public culture/society that challenges the notion of any divide between the public and private at all. Each chapter has explored linkages between private lives and public settings, adding to our understanding of how people continue to exist within, adapt to, and/or resist dominant cultural narratives in communities around the world and through time. Perhaps most importantly, by focusing on changing spaces and social relations over time, the authors in this book have made the invisible (e.g., work, kinship relations, feelings of solidary, sentiments that connect individuals) visible, rendering previously unknown histories into understandings of the past that challenge notions of the existence of public/private dichotomies as a lived reality.

REFERENCES

Abu-Lughod, Lila. 1991. "Writing against Culture." In *Recapturing Anthropology: Working in the Present*, edited by Richard G. Fox, 137–62. Santa Fe: School of American Research Press.

Agbe-Davies, Anna S. 2011. "Reaching for Freedom, Seizing Responsibility: Archaeology at the Phyllis Wheatley Home for Girls, Chicago." In *The Materiality of Freedom: Archaeologies of Postemancipation Life*, edited by J. A. Barnes. Columbia: University of South Carolina Press.

Ahmed, Sara. 2004. "Affective Economies." *Social Text, 79. 22*(2): 117–39.

Brown, Melissa J. 2004. *Is Taiwan Chinese? The Impact of Culture, Power, and Migration on Changing Identities*. Berkeley: University of California Press.

Chaves, Kelly K. 2008. "Ethnohistory: From Inception to Postmodernism and Beyond." *The Historian 70*(3): 486–513.

Church, Minette. 2002. "The Grant and the Grid: Homestead Landscapes in the Late Nineteenth Century Borderlands of Southeastern Colorado." *Journal of Social Archaeology 2*(2): 220–44.

Corr, Rachel. 2010. *Ritual and Remembrance in the Ecuadorian Andes.* Tuscon, AZ: University of Arizona Press.

Das, Veena. 2010. "Engaging the Life of the Other: Love and Everyday Life." In *Ordinary Ethics: Anthropology, Language, and Action,* edited by Michael Lambek, 376–99. New York: Fordham University Press.

Fewkes, Jacqueline H. 2008. *Trade and Contemporary Society Along the Silk Route: An Ethnohistory of Ladakh.* London: Routledge.

Genovese, Eugene D. 1976. *Roll, Jordan, Roll: The World the Slaves Made.* New York: Vintage Books.

Gewertz, Deborah, and Edward L. Schieffelin, eds. 1985. *History and Ethnohistory in Papua New Guinea.* Sydney: University of Sydney.

Horning, Audrey. 2013. *Ireland in the Virginian Sea: Colonialism in the British Atlantic.* Chapel Hill: University of North Carolina Press.

Hultin, Niklas. 2015. "Leaky Humanitarianism: The Anthropology of Small Arms Control in the Gambia." *American Ethnologist* 42(1): 68–80.

Lefebvre, Henri. 2009. *The Production of Space.* Translated by D. Nicholson. Malden, MA: Oxford Blackwell.

Longacre, William A. 2010. "Archaeology as Anthropology Revisited." *Journal of Archaeological Method and Theory* 17(2): 81–100.

Ortner, Sherry. 2016. "Dark Anthropology and Its Others: Theory Since the Eighties." *Hau: Journal of Ethnographic Theory* 6(1): 47–73.

Premo, Bianca. 2013. "Familiar: Thinking beyond Lineage and across Race in Spanish Atlantic Family History." *The William and Mary Quarterly* 70(2) [Special Issue, Centering Families in Atlantic Histories]: 295–316.

Rahier, Jean Muteba. 2014. *Blackness in the Andes: Ethnographic Vignettes of Cultural Politics in the Time of Multiculturalism and State Corporatism.* New York: Palgrave Macmillan.

Trigger, Bruce. 1982. "Ethnohistory: Problems and Prospects." *Ethnohistory* 29(1): 1–19.

Trouillot, Michel-Rolph. 1995. *Silencing the Past: Power and the Production of History.* Boston, MA: Beacon Press.

Waterston, Alisse. 2019. "Intimate Ethnography and the Anthropological Imagination." *American Ethnologist* 46(1): 7–19.

Waterston, Alisse, and Barbara Rylko-Bauer. 2006. "Out of the Shadows of History and Memory: Personal Family Narratives in Ethnographies of Rediscovery." *American Ethnologist* 33(3): 397–412.

Index

Page references for figures are italicized

About the Editors

Rachel Corr is a professor of anthropology at the Harriet L. Wilkes Honors College of Florida Atlantic University. She received her BA in anthropology from Ithaca College and her PhD in anthropology from the University of Illinois at Urbana-Champaign. She has done extensive ethnographic fieldwork and archival research in Ecuador. Her interests include ritual, shamanism, history, and ethnogenesis. She is author of *Ritual and Remembrance in the Ecuadorian Andes* (2010) and *Interwoven: Andean Lives in Colonial Ecuador's Textile Economy* (2018), which was awarded the Judy Ewell Award by the Rocky Mountain Council for Latin American Studies. Her research has also been published in *Ethnology*, *Food and Foodways*, the *Journal of Latin American and Caribbean Anthropology*, *Latin American Research Review*, and *Procesos: revista ecuatoriana de historia*.

Jacqueline H. Fewkes is a professor of anthropology at the Harriet L. Wilkes Honors College of Florida Atlantic University. She received her BA in anthropology from Johns Hopkins University and her PhD in anthropology from the University of Pennsylvania. Fewkes has conducted research in many different parts of the world, including India, Indonesia, the Maldives, Saudi Arabia, and the United States. In addition to several articles and chapters, Fewkes is the author of the books *Locating Maldivian Women's Mosques in Global Discourses* (2019) and *Trade and Contemporary Society along the Silk Road: An Ethno-history of Ladakh* (2008), as well as editor of *Anthropological Perspectives on the Religious Uses of Mobile Apps* (2019) and co-author of *Our Voices, Are You Listening? Children's Committees for Village Development* (2001).

About the Contributors

Anna S. Agbe-Davies is an associate professor of anthropology at the University of North Carolina at Chapel Hill. She is the author of *Tobacco, Pipes, and Race in Colonial Virginia: Little Tubes of Mighty Power* (2015) and co-editor with Alexander Bauer of *Social Archaeologies of Trade and Exchange: Exploring Relationships among People, Places, and Things* (2010). She is currently working on a book about women's civic activism through the lens of archaeological investigations at the Phyllis Wheatley Home for Girls and at the childhood home of human rights leader Pauli Murray.

Melissa J. Brown is managing editor of the *Harvard Journal of Asiatic Studies*. She received her BA and MA degrees from Stanford University and her PhD in anthropology from the University of Washington-Seattle. She was on the faculty at the University of Cincinnati and Stanford University before moving to the Radcliffe Institute for Advanced Studies at Harvard in 2011 and joining the *HJAS* staff in 2014. Brown's publications include *Is Taiwan Chinese? The Impact of Culture, Power, and Migration on Changing Identities* (2004), *Explaining Culture Scientifically* (2008), "Marriage Mobility and Footbinding in Pre-1949 Rural China" (*Journal of Asian Studies* 71.4, 2012), "Dutiful Help: Masking Rural Women's Economic Contributions" (in *Transforming Patriarchy*, 2016), and "Economic Correlates of Footbinding: Implications for the Importance of Chinese Daughters' Labor" (*PLOS ONE*, 2018, e0201337).

Minette C. Church is a professor of anthropology at University of Colorado, Colorado Springs. In 2016 and 2017, she was visiting research fellow in the Department of Anthropology and Palaeoecology in the School of Natural and Built Environment at Queen's University, Belfast, United Kingdom. She has a certificate in museum curatorship (1991) and a PhD in American civilization/historical archaeology (2001), both from the University of Pennsylvania. Her areas of geographic interest are Belize, Central America, and the United States-Mexico borderlands. In both regions she focuses on landscape archaeology, decolonization of anthropology and of borderland regions, archaeology of parenting and childhood, and colonial/postcolonial identities.

Audrey Horning is Forrest D. Murden Professor of Anthropology at William & Mary and professor of archaeology at Queen's University Belfast. Her research interests include comparative colonialism, archaeological ethics, and the integration of archaeology with conflict transformation. She is author of *Ireland in the Virginian Sea: Colonialism in the British Atlantic* (University of North Carolina Press, 2013), which was awarded the CHOICE Outstanding Academic Title of the Year and the James Mooney book award, and of *In the Shadow of Ragged Mountain: Historical Archaeology of Corbin, Nicholson, and Weakley Hollows* (Shenandoah Natural History Association, 2004) which won second place book, US National Interpretive Media Awards. She has also edited five books within the discipline of historical archaeology.

Niklas Hultin is an assistant professor in the Global Affairs Program at George Mason University. He has a PhD in anthropology from the University of Pennsylvania and an LLM from Queen's University Belfast. He has done extensive research in the Gambia with the support of the National Science Foundation and the Isaac Newton Trust at Cambridge University. His research has appeared in journals such as *American Ethnologist, Social Anthropology, African Affairs*, and *Critical African Studies*.

Jean Muteba Rahier is a professor of anthropology and African and African diaspora studies at Florida International University (FIU). He is the author of *La Décima: Poesía Oral Negra del Ecuador* (Quito, Ecuador: Abya-Yala, 1987), *Kings for Three Days: The Play of Race and Gender in an Afro-Ecuadorian Festival* (The University of Illinois Press, 2013), and *Blackness in the Andes: Ethnographic Vignettes of Cultural Politics in the Time of Multiculturalism* (Palgrave-Macmillan, 2014), and the editor or co-editor of four books: *Representations of Blackness and the Performance of Identities* (Westport: Bergin & Garvey, 1999), *Problematizing Blackness: Self-Ethnographies by Black Immigrants to the United States* (Routledge, 2003), *Global Circuits of Blackness: Interrogating the African Diaspora* (The University of Illinois Press, 2010), and *Black Social Movements in Latin America: From Monocultural Mestizaje to Multiculturalism* (Palgrave-Macmillan, 2012). He has authored numerous articles and book chapters.

www.ingramcontent.com/pod-product-compliance
Lightning Source LLC
Chambersburg PA
CBHW050653280326
41932CB00015B/2892